The Good Retirement Guide 2019

D0150279

33rd Edition

The Good Retirement Guide 2019

Everything you need to know about health, property, investment, leisure, work, pensions and tax

Edited by
Allan Esler Smith

Publisher's note

Every possible effort has been made to ensure that the information contained in this book is accurate at the time of going to press, and the publishers and authors cannot accept responsibility for any errors or omissions, however caused. No responsibility for loss or damage occasioned to any person acting, or refraining from action, as a result of the material in this publication can be accepted by the editor, the publisher or the author.

Thirty-third edition published in Great Britain and the United States in 2019 by Kogan Page Limited

2nd Floor, 45 Gee Street	c/o Martin P Hill Consulting	4737/23 Ansari Road
London	122 W 27th St, 10th Floor	Daryaganj
EC1V 3RS	New York NY, 10001	New Delhi 110002
United Kingdom	USA	India

www.koganpage.com

© Kogan Page, 2013, 2014, 2015, 2016, 2017, 2018, 2019

ISBNs

Hardback	978 0 7494 9763 7
Paperback	978 0 7494 8397 5
eBook	978 0 7494 8398 2
ISSN	2397-1967

British Library Cataloguing-in-Publication Data

A CIP record for this book is available from the British Library.

Typeset by Integra Software Services, Pondicherry
Print production managed by Jellyfish
Printed and bound by CPI Group (UK) Ltd, Croydon, CR0 4YY

Cover endorsements were provided for previous editions of this book.

CONTENTS

PART TWO Save More and Earn Better 119

07 Cutting costs and getting better at complaining 121

08 Avoid being scammed 133

ACKNOWLEDGEMENTS

I am indebted to Frances Kay for guiding me as co-editor in the 2013 to 2017 editions. Frances, and her encouragement, wit and wisdom, was fantastic to work with and I wish her a continuing 'good retirement' and a wealth of happiness. I am also grateful to my father, Stanley Smith, a retired senior civil servant, and my wife, Karen, whose assistance and guidance were invaluable. I also value incisive professional input; in this regard, Martin Gorvett, a Chartered Financial Planner of Lavender Financial Planners Ltd, cuts an effective knife through the complexities and language of investments and pensions. On tax and weighing up the world's largest tax book, I am indebted to Graham Boar, a tax partner of UHY Hacker Young. Graham boils down complex issues into straightforward planning tips and guidance. On legal matters, wills and powers of attorney, I thank the father-and-son team of Mike and Tom Bottomley of Ewart Price Solicitors. Legal issues are so vitally important to smoothing the path of an estate and their 40 years of combined experience and resulting contribution and advice are appreciated. Keeping safe and on top of the scammers continues to keep us on our toes and I thank the Metropolitan Police Organized Crime Command (FALCON) for continuing to support this book. The Financial Ombudsman knows a thing or two about navigating the world of finances, insurances and pensions, and we continue to go to the top of the tree with David Cresswell, Director of Strategy, for help, hints and tips – thank you, David, for your support. Thank you to Kogan Page for the encouragement, patience and belief in this title – the teamwork has been outstanding.

Introduction

This book will help you develop your retirement planning so that you can understand where you are now, where you want to get to and how you can achieve your retirement objectives. I am passionate about helping you achieve just one thing – a better retirement.

The longer you have until retirement, the more you can do to improve your prospects, as so much flows from increasing your knowledge around pensions and investments, and how they interlink with tax. This throws up an immediate challenge because the UK has the most complex tax regime in the world. There are hundreds of opportunities to improve your retirement by saving more, earning that little bit extra and making the most of your life, from a great home focusing on personal relationships and, if you have the time, getting into hobbies and volunteering.

In this book I first tackle the three stages of retirement and how your finances can change radically as you progress through each stage. Next, I look at how to plan more. The five chapters in Part One will help you do this. I want to help you with the often-complex financial decisions you will encounter and doing the retirement sums, and show you how these fit into the three phases of retirement. There is a key chapter on the difficulties faced by the so-called sandwich generation (those with dependent young adults and dependent elderly relatives requiring care). I then shift the focus towards demystifying financial speak. The way that pensions, savings and tax are presented can sometimes be hard to understand. I try to cut through the waffle and get you focused on what really matters – such as grabbing as much free money as you can from employers on pensions, ramping up your pension's tax efficiency and working the tax bands so you have more money in retirement. I also look at investments that can save you tax. There is important advice on avoiding predators and dealing only with FCA-registered advisers on pensions and investments, and staying within the UK regulatory system, which provides a good safety net.

Part Two focuses on how to achieve a good retirement by saving more and earning better. The impact could be amazing. Complacency is costing us too much money, but it can be solved by the forces of competition and getting better at complaining when things go wrong. Help is provided on knowing your rights and upping the ante if you get fobbed off. I also look at avoiding scams, which can be devastating if you get caught out – our hints and tips will help keep you safer. The other side of the economic equation is earning better, and that may mean finding a better job in order to ease your path to retirement. There is a chapter on career transitions and other paid work that will prepare you for change. However, your retirement plans could call for something more radical. The chapter on starting your own business could open the door to a new career or just help you to earn more money for extra holidays or leisure activities.

Part Three shines a spotlight on the retirement years and the key building blocks of living better. This section is all about getting the home right, retuning your personal relationships, staying healthy, volunteering, and leisure and holidays. Perhaps you wish to expand your home to cope with boomerang children, or downsize, or relocate to free up capital to fund the retirement you aspire to. Or perhaps it is time to rethink those important relationships. I explore how to stay healthy. Then there is the wonderful world of volunteering, which really can bring you so much in so many ways. The final chapter in this section is all about holidays and leisure. Let's not kid ourselves here – this is often the turn-to chapter when opening the guide. Yes, it is what you have been looking forward to, and, yes, if you can get this right you might just have found your perfect retirement.

The final two chapters, in Part Four, cover taking care of elderly relatives, wills and final plans. There will be bumps and bruises and some difficult, challenging or sad times, but we are a resilient bunch and we can gear up to help make sure we take care of elderly relatives in the best way we can. The challenges, as well as the impact of care costs, are significant to say the least. Guidance is provided to give you that little bit more knowledge to ease you across the waves that you may be about to navigate. We then hit the end of life. It is so very difficult to bring ourselves to turn the page to this concluding chapter, but tough discussions and decisions are often not so difficult once the subject is broached. There is information on wills, power of attorney, executors (a more vital role than even a best man or chief brides-maid) and help on funerals. The last section is mainly about worries and how to minimize them.

I close the book by providing two helpful tables, which will help you plan your own good retirement. The only accompanying advice I can give, at this stage, is limited to two words: your choice. 'Choice not chance determines your destiny' (Aristotle). Plan more, save more, live better and be happier with *The Good Retirement Guide*.

CHAPTER ONE

The three phases of retirement and doing the sums

When I was young I thought that money was the most important thing in life; now that I am old, I know it is.

OSCAR WILDE

Welcome to 2019. Could this be the year of making changes to your retirement planning that will combine together and help you plan more, save more, live better and, ultimately, be happier? Before we get into your 'good retirement' take a glance at some of the anniversaries that will be remembered during 2019, including:

- The 60th anniversary of: postcodes being introduced in the UK (first in the city of Norwich); the first Mini going on sale and the births of Ben Elton, Sheena Easton and Morrissey.

- The 50th anniversary of: the first maiden flight of the Boeing 747; the lunar module Eagle/Apollo 11 landing and Neil Armstrong takes the first historic steps on the moon surface; *Scooby Doo* airs its first episode in the United States and the UK provides the first airing of *Monty Python's Flying Circus*.

- The 40th anniversary of: Trevor Francis signing for Nottingham Forest in the first £1 million deal and the Thorpe Park theme park opens; there were tens of thousands of public workers striking in the 'Winter of Discontent' and the James Callaghan Labour government fell; Margaret Thatcher became the first female prime minister; the Vauxhall Astra replaces the Viva and the sports stars Jonny Wilkinson and Michael Owen are born.

- The 30th anniversary of: Sky Television broadcasting as the first satellite TV service in the UK and of the Hillsborough football stadium and Marchioness riverboat disasters. Recession fears see the stock market fall and house prices also fall rapidly, leading to years of negative equity for some. Negative equity – now there's a word we have not heard in UK economic circles for a while and this may remind us of how the timing of economic events can impact even the best retirement planning.

This chapter at a glance

- Understand the three phases of retirement (active, passive and with care) and, ultimately, the life you wish to lead in each of these retirement phases.

- Use our simple approach to doing the sums. The word 'budget' can send most sane folk running to the hills. But let's face facts from the start of this book. The life you wish to lead in each phase of retirement will come at a cost, and the simple fact is that people struggle to estimate the reality of the cost of this and also struggle to determine what funds they may have in retirement. This chapter therefore sets out an approach to help put you in a better position and provides signposts to further help.

Pre-retirement planning

The important thing to remember is that it is never too soon to do your pre-retirement planning. Things to consider include: what standard of living you want, how much money you will need in order to achieve it and what sort of social life you wish to enjoy. *The Good Retirement Guide* covers all these matters and buying this book is an excellent first step.

A pre-retirement course could be helpful – does your employer offer some kind of course or guidance? If not, ask friends who have already retired for their advice – what did they do? They may come up with useful recommendations or have information that their employer provided – some retirement courses are extensive, informative and provide invaluable assistance. Can you access or borrow some of the help they received?

Typically, the information will cover finances, health, housing, leisure, and the adjustments that need to be made before or when you retire. Your research may also unearth residential courses on retirement planning where discussions will take place with your partner and others in similar situations, designed to stimulate your planning efforts around the following areas:

- reviewing your current and future expenditure;
- making a list of all your financial assets;
- whether or not to consider deferring retirement;
- making sufficient provision for living longer;
- helping you to assess whether your plans are practical.

Unfortunately, however, these courses and the thinking that needs to be done usually come far too late – at a point where there is little or no time to do anything significant about your retirement finances. The thinking really needs to be done in your forties or fifties, so if you are in that age bracket give yourself a slap on the back – this book has just become even more valuable. The other pressure point that has sharpened the need for pre-retirement planning over the last decade is the 'sandwich generation': people who are looking after young adults and elderly relatives requiring care. We devote Chapter 2 to that very issue. However, if you are in your late sixties or beyond, there are still lots of actions you can take, so let's get started.

The three stages of retirement

Active retirement

Your active retirement years start when you leave your regular full-time work or you sell your business and will usually begin anywhere between your fifties and late sixties. The 10–15 years after this commencement point are your 'active retirement years'. You may also downsize your regular job to a less stressful position with perhaps fewer hours, so that you maintain a very active life and enjoy a decent income to supplement your pension and savings. You are still 'buzzing' and enjoying a great social life with maybe more holidays and more hobbies, and may even relocate within the UK or abroad. It will be an expensive time and you will probably eat into your savings so that you can enjoy these years to the full.

Passive retirement

Your passive retirement years are generally in your late seventies and eighties. Work income may have largely dried up and you are now largely reliant on pension income and savings that are left after the active retirement years. Any part-time job or business you run may provide some extra money for holidays or buying that new car. Finances will be tighter and you will probably have to accept there will inevitably be changes in what you can and cannot do as medical issues arise (as they are prone to do in these years with increasing frequency). Associated with this will be questions about your location and proximity to social and medical facilities and, overall, you will be reassessing if your home remains manageable and in the right location.

Retirement with care

As you reach your late eighties and your nineties your income may rely solely on state and occupational pensions, so your spending will need to be cut to meet your income. Medical and other care needs may dictate what you do and where you live. Your home may need to be used to underwrite care-home fees, which can average about £30,000 per year without medical care and £40,000 per year upwards with medical care. For these figures there can be huge variations from the averages, depending on location and the lifestyle choices and amenities provided.

Top tip

Grasp and understand the three stages of retirement and how your income, savings and expenditure patterns will change over the three periods. The earlier you 'do the sums' for your three phases of retirement the better chance you have of reaching and exceeding your ambitions. Too many people leave this too late and by the time they are approaching retirement there is little they can do about it to make significant impacts.

Doing the sums

You will have to accept that once you retire there will inevitably be changes in your financial affairs over three distinct phases. Your income will change but so, too, will your pattern of expenditure. Many people worry about this, but the good news is that provided you are prepared to do a little planning things will work out better. The earlier you do this the better as you will have more time to plan how you can influence the key numbers either by saving more, increasing your tax planning, earning more or cutting costs.

The starting point, not least for your peace of mind, is to spend time putting together an annual budget and assessing your present pension and savings plans. If you are someone who has always had a personal budget when you were working then things should be fairly straightforward and you simply need to take a hard look at your changed income and expenditure once you retire and over the three phases of retirement. However, some people operate on a sort of auto budget during their working life. They get used to an income level and then in the light of experience know more or less what they can afford to do on that budget, without thinking about it a great deal. But even they must understand that things will change on retirement. Very few 40- and 50-year-olds grasp the reality of their pension and savings plans and what that will mean in reality for their retirement years.

If you are not used to personal budgeting it may seem a bit daunting. But in fact, unless your financial affairs are extremely complex, budgeting is no more than simple addition and subtraction. You simply add together all your likely actual income and subtract from that all your estimated expenditure, and if the two balance then you can rest easy. It may take a little time when you first do it but it will be time well spent. It becomes much easier once you have the basic figures in place for the first time.

Estimating income

Let's start with your income calculations, which should be relatively straightforward. You first need to get an estimate of any pension entitlements, as described in Chapter 4 (pensions). Those entitlements might come from your previous employment or from any private pension provision you might have made. Such pensions are, however, taxable. In your calculations you would need to make an allowance for any tax due on them, less tax allowances such as the Personal Allowance (more on this in Chapter 6 on tax). If you are of pensionable age you then include any State Pension due to you, as per Chapter 4. State Pensions are not taxable at source. However, the tax authorities will usually adjust your Personal Allowance to take account of what you receive in State Pension and use that to set an appropriate tax code for your employment or private pensions, which usually means those pensions are paid net of basic-rate tax.

An additional point about a State Pension is that some people retire before pensionable age. In those circumstances they may have to use any savings and investments (Chapter 5) to balance the books until such time as they become eligible for their State Pension. One positive thing about this is that when the State Pension does eventually arrive they may well feel better off.

You then need to add any income you expect from investments or savings – again taking account of any tax that may be due, albeit there are beneficial new tax breaks that allow you £1,000 of interest tax free if you are a basic-rate taxpayer and £500 for higher-rate tax payers (£0 for additional-rate taxpayers) (more on this and this terminology in Chapter 5). Finally, you may have prospects of some paid work (employed or from your own new small business) or perhaps you may plan to serve as a non-executive director on some advisory body or quango. Any income from such sources should be included – again allowing for Income Tax and National Insurance (the latter continues until you reach state-retirement age).

Estimating expenditure

Estimating expenditure, while perhaps slightly more complex and less precise than income, is also relatively straightforward. The first thing is to identify those areas of expenditure for which you are responsible, and this can vary between individuals and within families. If expenditure on certain areas is shared with others you need to check that their circumstances are unchanged – if that is not the case you need to take account of this in your planning.

Broadly speaking, expenditure is likely to fall within the following areas:

- food and drink;
- household and property;
- travel (including cars);
- leisure (especially holidays);
- sundry expenditure.

Food and drink

What is purchased and what it costs can vary greatly from family to family. Your eating and drinking habits may increase in the active retirement years, reducing in the passive years and then again reducing further in the retirement with care years. Check through everything you spend on food and drink over, say, a two-month period and use that figure in your estimates as a starting point. Remember to include eating out. If you have not done this before, then the total will surprise you, so don't put off this task.

Household and property

The obvious items are utilities, rent, Council Tax/rates, water rates and insurance. Factor in any outstanding mortgage, although many plan to end their mortgage payments around the time they are due to retire – so this might represent a major saving in retirement. There are other major items such as telephone – don't overlook the cost of mobiles and TV-package payments. You also need an amount to cover upkeep such as window cleaning and decorating. Don't forget that if you are a keen gardener these costs can mount up and as you reach passive retirement you may need some part-time help with the heavier tasks, especially if you have a large garden. Household repair and maintenance costs tend to trip up any budget. Rather than not making any provision you would be best advised to set something aside for this when doing the sums.

Travel

If your employment involved extensive travelling this is another area where you might find there are savings but, in all probability, you will still retain one or more cars. If you were provided with a company car while working then this could involve quite significant additional expenditure. You need to include fuel, tax, insurance, servicing, replacement parts (eg tyres) and any subscriptions to motoring organizations. Also, don't forget that cars do not keep going forever, so you may need to think about setting something aside for an eventual replacement. The good news is that many new cars come with exceptionally good three-, five- or even seven-year warranty provision, so do shop around and look for value here – even if you do have to give up that cherished 'brand' that you have always bought. Another option that can work if you prefer a monthly budget is to use a 'personal contract purchase' ('PCP'), which is a loan to help you buy the car but after 24 or 36 months you can pay a one-off fee (called the final balloon payment) to take ownership of the car or hand it back and your obligations end. There are too many pros and cons of PCPs to go into here but you can start to explore the option via guidance on www.moneysavingexpert.com (search for 'personal contract purchase'.)

Leisure

The whole idea of retirement is that you should have more time to enjoy yourself. While some of the most enjoyable things in life are free others do require some expenditure. If you are a golfer, for example, you will still have to pay your club fees, plus those for any other social clubs you are involved with or want to join to broaden your horizons. But probably the main item of expenditure could be holidays and short trips – you will almost certainly have more time for these and this cost may rise significantly in the active retirement years. This is a difficult area to estimate but you should not ignore it and should make your best guess. If you are overly ambitious you can cut back, and conversely if you are overly careful you may find you can afford to do more than you anticipated. Don't forget holiday insurance and the fact that premiums tend to increase as you get older. It would be impossible to list all leisure pursuits – each person needs to look at what interests them and make an appropriate allowance.

Sundry expenditure

You will need to set aside something to cover sundry expenditure. These are relatively small amounts that, taken individually, you may scarcely notice but which can mount up. For example, if you buy a newspaper every day this could amount to around £500 over the whole year. Similar comments apply to occasional morning coffee outings. You will also need to allow for entertaining at home, nights out and other entertainment. You will want new clothes from time to time and you will need to purchase a range of small items regularly such as toiletries. If you have a pet, their food and insurance can be increasingly expensive. There is also the occasional gift. The list could go on and on as, by their nature, sundries are virtually impossible to define. You need to look at your own lifestyle and set aside a reasonable amount each month to cover this type of expenditure. This could be one area where there is an element of trial and error, and it may just take a little time to get the full measure of what you might need. But it would be unwise to ignore it, as it will mount up over the year.

The big one-offs

The life stages of family members and their needs will need thinking through. Millennials (those born roughly between 1981 and 2000) face the prospect of high debt and not being able to own their own house and you may want to help. Do you wish to help with wedding costs (the average cost of a wedding is now £27,000), university costs (fees, accommodation and maintenance costs of about £50,000 over three years) or a house deposit (£20,000)? Have you earmarked some of your savings and investments for such events and if so how much and when? You will need to attach your plans to your budget. It is especially tough for those under 25 years old as they are dealing with significant university loans (following the changes introduced in 2012). Older generations are, therefore, looking at ways they may be able to help and, at the same time, often look into gifting away inheritances at a much earlier stage than may have happened in previous generations. This is done as part of their estate and tax planning (see Chapter 6, Tax, for more information).

Balancing the books

Having set everything out, the next step is to see if it all balances. If at the first count your income balances with expenditure and your savings and investments look like covering any big one-off payments then you are either very lucky or a financial genius. If your income exceeds expenditure then you have no problems, and after checking that there are no errors in your figures you can go and book an extra holiday! The likelihood is, however, that you will find that expenditure exceeds income.

In these circumstances you might find you still have time to increase your pension income (see Chapter 6 on tax and deferring income from higher-rate tax to basic-rate tax for some potentially significant tax savings that emerge later as improved income). You should, however, check that you have included everything in the income column – for example, have you missed a pension entitlement or an investment? You might also look at the possibility of further paid work (part-time) in your active retirement years. Or, if radical rebalancing is required, you may need to look at releasing capital in your home by downsizing, relocating, selling off part of your garden for a house to be built on (if you are lucky enough to have a big garden with access) or via some form of equity release (see Chapter 5).

It will probably be necessary to review your expenditure. There are certain areas where you cannot do much – you will still need to eat, most household and property-related expenditure cannot be avoided and if you keep a car the running costs will be largely unchanged – although if you are a two-car family you may need to review this now that you are retired. The likelihood is that you will need to look at your leisure/holiday expectations and cut back a bit – at least until you see how things pan out after a year. You may also need to look at your sundry expenditure and ensure you are not overly indulgent. The opportunities to save more can be significant and more on this is set out in Chapter 7.

How to go about it

You cannot keep all of these figures in your head; as a minimum you need a yearly budget to look at your life now, using the evidence you have in the form of bank statements and credit card bills, etc. Table 1.1 (at the end of this chapter) gives an outline of how you might do this. At this stage, just look at the general headings and ignore the months. The headings are not set in stone as people have differing patterns of income and expenditure and you need to tailor it to your own personal needs and circumstances. The intention of the table is to give you a broad framework within which you might operate.

While you may be able to get by with a yearly budget, it is probably worthwhile to take a little more time and set everything out on a monthly basis along the lines of Table 1.1. Many payments, and probably some income, do not occur on a regular monthly basis – many bills come in quarterly, insurance policies are often paid annually, and holidays and other breaks tend to be irregular. It is therefore much easier to keep track of things if you operate on a monthly basis. This also has the advantage that you can see if things are not quite working out as you go along, rather than being surprised at the end of the year. In this respect it is very unlikely that in practice everything will work out as you plan. There can be unforeseen expenditure; some things may cost more than you have estimated, or you may even find your income increases. All of this is easier to deal with if you can adjust things on a monthly basis to compensate for what will probably be inevitable changes.

Next, specifically track how your savings and investments become diluted (if expenditure exceeds income) and what happens as you progress through the active years into the passive years (perhaps less expenditure) to then the retirement with care years (when your home may be used to finance care-home fees).

One final suggestion is to put it all on a spreadsheet. If you have been used to dealing with spreadsheets in your working life this will not be difficult – indeed it would probably come naturally to do so. If you are not familiar with them, the sort of very simple spreadsheet suggested in Table 1.1 is very easy to set up and run. If you are stuck, ask a younger member of your family circle to help you. It would certainly be worthwhile as it enables you to update things virtually automatically, and an additional advantage is that when it comes to the next year all you need to do is slot in updated figures and the spreadsheet does the sums automatically.

A final word on doing the sums

Don't be put off by all of this – you do not need to follow the suggestions slavishly. The intention is to start you thinking about the way your financial affairs might change when you retire and then pass through the three phases of retirement. Everyone has different circumstances and you need to pause and think about your own situation. If you follow the suggestions in this chapter, adjusted as necessary to your own personal needs, then you should have better control over your affairs. But don't forget that personal budgeting is not a precise science; you have to be flexible and prepared to make adjustments as you go along. If things seem too complex then you may need to engage the services of a good financial adviser (see Chapter 3) who will be used to shaping these sorts of projections and can also adapt quite easily for 'what if' scenarios.

The most important message of this chapter is that the earlier in life you do this exercise the better chance you have of achieving the retirement you aspire to.

Top tip

The earlier you 'do the sums' and estimate the finances you will have in the three phases of retirement the better chance you have of reaching and exceeding your ambitions. Too many people leave this too late and lose out as there is insufficient time to plan and take correcting action. The key to unlocking it all lies in the four sections of this book: plan more, save more, live better and be happier. Your own 'Plan for a good retirement', found at the end of the book for you to fill in, is possibly the most important section. Turn to this now – is it time to make your first entry?

A final throw of the dice on increasing your retirement income

There is one other possibility that might yield results if you have not already tried it – tracking down lost insurance policies, pensions or shareholdings, which can be done quite easily via Experian's Unclaimed Assets Register (www.uar.co.uk). There is a £25 charge to run a search but it trawls 4.5 million records from about 80 different companies, saving you the trouble of calling firms directly. Alternatively, try the government's pension-tracing service, which will trace any missing work pensions for you free of charge (www.gov.uk/find-lost-pension). For lost or dormant bank accounts, try www.mylostaccount.org.uk.

Inspired? Remember to fill in your plan for a good retirement at the end of the book.

Table 1.1 Example budget for the year

	January	February	Repeat monthly (March–December)	Annual total
INCOME				
Private/work pension received (after tax)				
State Pension (less any tax due)				
Any other pension (after tax)				
Interest on savings (after tax)				
Dividends from investments (after tax)				
Paid work (after tax)				
Boards, trusts, etc				
Any other sundry income				
Total income (A)	January (A)	February (A)		(A) total for year
EXPENDITURE				
Food and drink				
Food and drink (eating in)				
Meals out				
Household/property				
Mortgage				
Rent				
Council Tax				
Water rates				
Insurance				
Electricity				
Gas				
Oil				
Telephone				
Mobile				
General upkeep				
Garden				
Repairs and maintenance				
Any other				
Total household/property				
Transport/car				
Petrol				
Tax				
Insurance				
Service				
Motoring organizations				
Replacement tyres, etc				
Any other regular transport costs				
Total transport/car				
Leisure				
Subscriptions to clubs, etc				
Short trips				
Major holidays				
Anything else				
Total leisure				
Sundries				
Overall monthly estimate of incidental expenditure				
Total expenditure (B)	January (B)	February (B)		(B) total for year
Surplus/deficit to carry forward each month (A–B)				(A–B) total for year

PART ONE

Plan More

CHAPTER TWO

The sandwich generation

Never give in. Never give in. Never, never, never, never – in nothing, great or small, large or petty – never give in, except to convictions of honour and good sense.

WINSTON CHURCHILL

The sandwich generation is the shorthand being adopted to describe the people who are looking after both dependent young adults and dependent elderly relatives. It is a growing issue in terms of the number of people affected and the finances and emotions involved. It is challenging because many in the sandwich generation who are in their fifties have lost out on those gold-plated final pension schemes that may have promised fixed amounts in retirement for as long as they lived, and this may exacerbate the financial pressures both now and in the future.

One main driver is a debt-laden younger generation, with university leavers from the 2012 entrance year and beyond racking up £50,000 in student loans that (at the time of writing in 2018) have onerous interest rates. Buying a first house will be challenging for them and many sandwich-generation parents may feel that their children still need a helping hand in the near future, even though they are well into their twenties. The prospect of helping to shield them from some or all of the student loan impact may create financial (and emotional) stress that increases if you have two, three or more children entering this phase of their lives.

Those same children may go on to get married, with the sandwich-generation parents looking to follow in their parents' footsteps and foot the bill or part of it. With the average price of a wedding running at £27,000, multiplied by the number of your children, it is fingers crossed that you can go halves with the other parents.

The other pressure point on our younger people is unaffordable housing, which has led to home ownership halving and, instead, our young people paying out 'dead money' in rent and not acquiring an asset base early enough. The size of a mortgage deposit is too much and the lending deal may simply be unaffordable, irrespective of help-to-buy schemes, especially if you live in south-east England or other property 'hot spots'.

Looking up a generation to the parents of the sandwich generation, the pressures are both emotional and financial and both are interlinked as quality care has a significant cost (or, put another way, 'you pay your money and make your choice'). With care costs running at £30,000 to £60,000 per year, depending on location and the extent of medical assistance needed, the sandwich generation may find the financial pressures of their children are compounded by the financial pressures of elderly relatives, where the state funding or the relative's assets are insufficient.

Things may look difficult but, in the words of Winston Churchill, 'Never give in. Never give in. Never, never, never...' Read on to learn more, plan more and help create a better overall outcome.

This chapter at a glance

- Some facts about the retirement prospects of our younger people.
- Boomerang children returning home after university/college and the need for space.
- Helping millennials on the way with pensions planning and funding.
- Planning for the big events that may be just around the corner: university fees, weddings, house deposits and grandchildren.
- Planning for care-home fees.
- A reminder about the happiest people.

The big picture: the Resolution Foundation and changes in intergenerational outcomes – some facts

Millennials refers to those born between 1981 and 2000 (although this range does vary depending on who you ask) and thus a very relevant age group to 'sandwich generation' parents. The retirement outcomes of the millennials put many of our own concerns into sharp focus and are worth thinking through as the sandwich generation (and their parents) may need to rethink priorities and retirement planning.

The Resolution Foundation undertakes research on living standards in the UK. Their report 'A New Generational Contract' published on 8 May 2018 highlighted issues relevant to the sandwich generation, which included the following key findings:

- Their research showed that millennial families are only half as likely to own their home by age 30 as baby boomers were by the same age, and four times more likely to rent privately (baby boomers are those born between 1946 and 1965).

- Earnings progress has stalled for young adults today. Millennials are earning the same as those born 15 years before them were at the same age.

- There is pessimism about young adults' chances of improving on their parents' lives – pessimists outnumbered optimists by two to one. This marks a dramatic and very rapid turnaround in outlook. As recently as 2003, optimists outnumbered pessimists by nearly four to one.

- Health care is the most pressing area of worry for British adults: 42 per cent place it in their top three concerns for the country, whereas internationally it ranks in fifth place. These concerns may partly be anchored in the increasingly parlous state of adult social care services, with the number of people in England who do not get the care they need having doubled since 2010 to 1.2 million. Baby boomers feel they are at risk of not getting the health and care they need in later life.

Boomerang children and adapting the home

The term 'boomerang children' describes those who go to university or college and then return 'home' after completing their course or graduating.

They may be saddled with debt, and the employment opportunities in terms of income, security, pension and other benefits are eroding in real terms. Many cannot afford to rent and cannot afford to buy a house, so the benefits of several years living back with parents may assist. This allows them to save a deposit for a house or progress in their career to earn enough to rent.

The issue for the sandwich generation of homeowners may be to have sufficient space for each other under one roof; sandwich-generation parents may therefore be interested in home adaptions or home expansion as a way to a solution (see Chapter 11, Home). In addition, contributions by parents, grandparents or a close relative into a help-to-buy ISA or a LISA will be boosted by 'free money' from the government (more in Chapter 5, Savings). Could some sort of matched funding be agreed with the young person to help them on their way in the future?

Pensions for the millennials

Pensions knowledge and retirement planning are poor amongst millennials and disposable cash is limited. Government initiatives around automatic enrolment are finally starting to lead to decent amounts being saved into pensions as the employer is compelled to contribute as well as the employee. The amount of employer contribution has increased, so it is a form of deferred pay rise. But it remains short of ideal levels and only impacts the employed – therefore, the self-employed or unemployed millennials are still left struggling on pension funding. Could this be where grandparents, parents and close relatives help millennials with contributions into a pension? This is either to top up the employer/employee contributions or to kick-start pensions for other millennials. This has half an eye on inheritance tax planning, as gifting and surviving seven years can reduce inheritance tax: the question is whether those with large estates should be gifting earlier. More on this in Chapter 4 (Pensions) and Chapter 6 (Tax) and, as tax planning can be complex, professional advice should be sought (Chapter 3).

Planning for big events: university fees, weddings, house deposits and grandchildren

Let's take these one by one against the backdrop of millennials and, as shown above, their stagnating earnings. How can sandwich-generation parents help (and, indeed, cope)? The first thing that will hit parents of younger millennials is the sharp increases in university fees from 2012. University fees soared more or less overnight from around £3,500 to around £9,000 a year. Add on top of this about £5,000 a year for accommodation and about £3,500 for maintenance (basically food, drink, entertainment, travel and, hopefully, some books). This equates to around £50,000 over three years but less if you stay at home. At the same time the interest rate applied to the loans changed significantly and now sees a two-tier system of interest. If your children started university after 2012 the interest on their loans will be charged at about 6.3 per cent (as of summer 2018). The basic theory goes like this: if your children don't earn enough the loan will eventually be written off and the interest charged on the remainder partly reflects this 'bad debt' provision. But if it is likely that your children are going to pay off their loans then should you look around at alternative forms of finance for part or all of the loan, especially if you have the money or can access low-interest-rate finance of around 3 per cent in alternative ways, such as the equity in your home via a remortgage?

Then we have the wedding. *The Sunday Times* (Jessica Brown) on 6 May 2018 wrote an article about couples who 'face pressure to splash out even more cash on their weddings' and 'how to cut the cost without spoiling the big day'. The article reported the wedding website Hitched.co.uk; their survey showed that the average bill for wedding arrangements had risen to £27,161 and offered a range of cost-cutting ideas to reduce costs without spoiling the big-day 'feel'. Picking a cheaper month, hiring a marquee and selecting your own caterers all nibbled away at the headline cost. Alternatively, could there be another way with the sandwich-generation parents looking to help things out with clever use of pension tax-free lump-sum planning and playing the tax-rate bands to ultimately provide more money at the right time? Or maybe grandparents could think about anti-inheritance-tax gifting into ISAs for the lucky couple. Chapters 5 and 6 show how these could work.

Still struggling on limited earnings and having moved out of the family home the millennials will come to the need to find a deposit for their first home as they become fed up with the dead money of renting. By dead money it means it is not part of their asset wealth that will, eventually, help finance their own retirement or their own children's 'big events' or their own nice care home. Again the sandwich generation parents could look to help things out with clever use of pension tax-free lump-sum planning, with maybe grandparents thinking about anti-inheritance-tax gifting into help-to-buy ISAs or, even better, LISAs for the lucky couple. Chapters 5 and 6 show how these can work together.

Related to purchasing a home the sandwich-generation parents could consider lending their names to the new home mortgage. These are called 'Joint Borrower, Sole Proprietor' mortgages, which take into account the income of two borrowers (parent and child) but only put the child's name on the deeds. This should avoid the extra 3 per cent stamp duty that a property-owning parent would incur if their name was on the deeds but the maximum age (maybe 70 to 75?) at the end of the mortgage term may limit the availability of this solution. A solicitor should be consulted to review what happens if the relationship does not work out and how everyone's interests can be protected.

The next big event will be grandchildren. *The Times* (Mark Atherton) reported on 28 April 2018 about getting to grips with the big financial events of your life and that 'A newborn baby will cost £229,251 to raise to the age of 21, according to the Centre for Economic and Business Research. This includes child care and education-related costs but not private school… add £141,863 for a day pupil and £260,927 for a boarder.' Sandwich-generation parents may still be able to help at this stage but, if not, some of the best advice you can give is about having an emergency fund and to review their life cover.

Planning for care-home fees

In managing potential care-home planning for elderly relatives the potential positive is that there is likely to be some capital (in the form of a house) to fall back on and there may also be state help available. If you are in the position of caring for an elderly person, be that a parent, relative or loved one, you will contribute to make their remaining years happy, comfortable and meaningful. Chapter 10 will help you grasp the issues, help and options available. As the 'meat' in the sandwich between younger and older generations you can be that little bit more effective with some improved knowledge.

Age UK (www.ageuk.org.uk), the national charity that campaigns for making life better for elderly people, has 'five key ambitions', where everyone in later life:

1 has the opportunity to enjoy life and feel well;
2 feels safe, comfortable and secure at home;
3 has enough money to live on;
4 can participate in society and be valued for their contribution;
5 has access to quality health and care services.

Use the information in Chapter 16 and the resources available from Age UK to help you. In terms of the main 'elephant in the room' issue it will be down to you, your relatives, close family and the family solicitor to determine policy and planning around the care-home fees. As a reminder from Chapter 6 (Tax), tread carefully if someone offers you a magic wand to 'protect your assets from the tax office' or schemes to shelter assets from 'claims for care-home fees' based loosely on schemes involving trusts. The ideal scenario is that you would want to be dealing with the trusted family solicitor regulated by the Law Society in your jurisdiction (for instance in England and Wales at www.lawsociety.org.uk) and you would want a solicitor accredited on their Wills and Inheritance Quality Scheme (WIQS). If you depart from this route there are some questions set out in Chapter 6 that may help you steer a safer course.

The happiest people

We mentioned above an article featured in *The Times* on 26 April 2018. Turn the page and we move from news that could be worrying to news that is happy – saving the best of all to the end *The Times* reported that 'older people are the happiest' (Philip Aldwick, Economics Editor). This arose from an Office of National Statistics survey on 'annual wellbeing', which reported that 20 per cent of people aged between 16 and 34 exhibited signs of depression, anxiety or other signs of mental ill health, compared to 12.5 per cent of those aged 65 to 74. So follow the moral of this book and you can help reduce the latter band even more by planning more, saving more and living better. Lastly, those over 75 who are still working report the greatest level of job satisfaction – at 87 per cent. Continue reading through the next chapters on 'plan more' and you will be working your way to a better retirement.

Inspired? Remember to fill in your plan for a good retirement at the end of the book.

CHAPTER THREE

Professional advisers

*The stock market is filled with individuals who know
the price of everything, but the value of nothing.*

PHILIP FISHER

It is amazing how many people cut corners to save on professional adviser fees but then end up in a complete pickle. This chapter, part of the 'plan more' section of this book, aims to guide those who need help with their understanding of the issues and decisions that lie ahead. The journey involves knowledge, research and an improved understanding to assist your pension, savings and investment decisions. You may be able to do it yourself but two factors will drive you to taking professional advice – either a difficulty with numbers and finances or the significance of those numbers and, therefore, the risk of getting things wrong. This chapter will steer you through the professional advisers you may encounter in the UK on retirement-related issues and planning and the protection you get from operating in this framework. Armed with this help and planning you will then be able to move more easily through the remaining sections of this book and start saving more, living better and you will be happier.

> ## This chapter at a glance
>
> - An outline of the professional advisers you may encounter in the UK.
> - Explaining how you can check that a financial adviser is regulated – and how this simple check gives you vital protection if things go wrong.
> - Outlining the UK's regulatory system and how this provides you with vital help and protection. If you work outside the 'safety net' you may be on your own and lose out.
> - Other vital advisers in the world of retirement planning are solicitors and accountants – what to look out for and where to go for help if things don't work out.
> - The Financial Ombudsman's top tip for staying safe.

Choosing a financial adviser

The role of financial adviser has become more important since the number of investment, mortgage, pension protection and insurance products has multiplied and financial decision making has become increasingly complicated. Common areas where you might want expert help include:

- life protection and income protection;
- annuities;
- financial planning and structuring to assist with the three phases of retirement;
- investments and linking this to your tax planning;
- mortgages;
- pensions and pension transfers and linking this to your tax planning.

Advisers are divided into two types:

- *Independent financial advisers*: IFAs are unbiased and can advise on, and sell, products from any provider across the market.
- *Restricted advisers*: these advisers specialize in particular providers' products or specific areas of advice. Their 'restricted' status means they can only sell and advise on a limited range of products, or from a limited number of firms.

Since 31 December 2012, independent and restricted advisers have to charge a fee for investment and pension advice rather than accepting commission. You can pay upfront for the adviser's time, rather like an accountant or solicitor, or you can agree a commission-like fee that is deducted from the money you invest in a product purchased through them. Ask upfront what the cost will be – it is vital so that you can compare different financial advisers.

When choosing a financial adviser, ask for and consider their qualifications, Financial Conduct Authority (FCA) registration, fee structure, how long they have been in business (and with whom), and the convenience and accessibility they provide. Understand any 'hidden charges and fees' such as charges that will apply each year and if you decide to change advisers (exit fees). Ask family or friends who they would recommend, or try talking to some of an adviser's existing clients and don't be afraid to ask for references. Most reputable professionals will be delighted to assist, as it means that the relationship will be founded on a basis of greater trust and confidence. Most importantly (and this is worth repeating), check whether your adviser is registered on the FCA's Central Register website, www.fca.org.uk (go to 'register') or phone 0800 111 6768.

Also remember you will then receive their advice and recommendations in writing. Read it carefully and if you don't understand, ask. Everything should be clear as to what is being recommended and why, and it should set out any risk and any tax impact. Fees and charges must be clearly set out.

Regulation and protection are via the FCA, the Financial Ombudsman Service (FOS) and the Financial Services Compensation Scheme (FSCS), as outlined below.

Top tip

Never do business with a financial adviser without checking they are regulated (thus giving you some protection). Check this on the FCA's Central Register (www.fca.org.uk) and go to 'register', or phone 0800 111 6768. Perhaps this is a point to note on your own plan for a good retirement, which can be found at the end of the book. If you have not turned to it yet, have a glance now.

Banks

Banks can provide comprehensive services in addition to the normal account facilities. These include investment, insurance and tax-planning services, as well as advice on how to draw up a will. Regulation and protection are via the FCA, FOS and FSCS.

Insurance brokers

The insurance business covers a very wide area, from straightforward policies – such as motor or household insurance – to rather more complex areas, including life assurance and income protection. Whereas IFAs specialize in advising on products and policies with some investment content, insurance brokers primarily deal with the more straightforward type of insurance such as motor, medical, household and holiday insurance. Some brokers are also authorized to give investment advice. A broker will help you choose the policies best suited to you, assist with any claims, remind you when renewals are due and advise you on keeping your cover up to date.

Regulation and protection are via the FCA, FOS and FSCS.

Stockbrokers

A stockbroker is a regulated professional broker who buys and sells shares and other securities through market makers or agency-only firms on behalf of investors.

The three main types of stockbroking service are:

- *Execution only*: this means the broker will carry out only the client's instructions to buy or sell.
- *Advisory dealing*: where the broker advises the client on which shares to buy and sell, but leaves the financial decision to the investor.
- *Discretionary dealing*: where the stockbroker ascertains the client's investment objectives and then makes all the dealing decisions on the client's behalf.

While some stockbrokers now charge fees in the same way as a solicitor, generally stockbrokers make their living by charging commission on every transaction. You will need to establish the terms and conditions before committing yourself as these vary between one firm and another.

To find a stockbroker you can approach an individual through a recom-mendation or visit the London Stock Exchange website (www.london stockexchange.com) or the Wealth Management Association (formerly the Association of Private Client Investment Managers and Stockbrokers) website (www.thewma.co.uk). A broker may be employed by a brokerage firm and many investors now transact their share dealings with online firms that have reduced transaction fees.

Regulation and protection are via the FCA, FOS and FSCS.

For your protection

Most financial transactions involving banks, investments, pensions and insurance take place without any problems but sometimes things go wrong. This is where the UK's regulatory regime steps in.

The **Financial Conduct Authority (FCA)** is accountable to the Treasury and aims to make sure the UK financial markets work well so that consumers get a fair deal. It registers individuals and companies that are suitable to work in the industry, checks that they are doing their job properly and fines them if they do a bad job. The FCA has a range of helpful guides and factsheets to help consumers understand the UK's financial markets and the role of the FCA (more at www.fca.org.uk).

The **Financial Ombudsman Service (FOS)** is a free service set up by law with the power to sort out problems between consumers and registered financial businesses. It is an impartial service and will investigate your complaint if you have been unable to resolve matters with the registered individual or company (ie registered with the FCA, as above). If the FOS considers the complaint justified it can award compensation (more at www.financial-ombudsman.org.uk).

The **Financial Services Compensation Scheme (FSCS)** is the body that can pay you compensation if your financial services provider goes bust. The FSCS is independent and free to access. The financial services industry funds the FSCS and the compensation it pays. There are limits on how much compensation it pays and these are different for different types of financial products. To be eligible for compensation the person or company must have been registered by the FCA (more at www.fscs.org.uk).

Other types of advisers

Accountants

Accountants are specialists in matters concerning taxation. Many accountants can also help with raising finance and offering support with the preparation of business plans. Additionally, they may be able to advise on the tax implications of your pensions and investments but are unable to advise on the products themselves unless they are registered with the FCA.

When choosing an accountant, ask for and consider their qualifications, registration with one of the relevant professional bodies (see below – anyone can set themselves up as an accountant without holding any qualifications so this check can be important), fee structure and hourly rate, how long they have been in business (and with whom) and convenience. Check they hold professional indemnity insurance. If you need help in locating a suitable accountant the following will have registers of their members:

Association of Chartered Certified Accountants (ACCA): www.accaglobal.com

Institute of Chartered Accountants in England and Wales (ICAEW): www.icaew.co.uk

Chartered Accountants Ireland (for both Northern Ireland and the Republic of Ireland): www.charteredaccountants.ie

Institute of Chartered Accountants of Scotland (ICAS): www.icas.com

Anyone with a complaint against an accountancy firm should first try to resolve the matter with the firm through its complaints-handling process and if they remain dissatisfied then contact the company's relevant professional body (from the list above) for advice and assistance.

Solicitors

Solicitors are professional advisers on subjects to do with the law or on matters that could have legal implications. Their advice can be invaluable in vetting any important document before you sign it. Often, the best way to find a suitable solicitor (if you do not already have one) is through the recommendation of a friend or other professional adviser such as an accountant. If you need a solicitor specifically for a business or professional matter, organizations such as your local Chambers of Commerce, small business associations, your professional institute or trade union may be able to put you in touch with someone in your area who has relevant experience.

Two organizations to contact for help are the Law Society (www. lawsociety.org.uk) and Solicitors for Independent Financial Advice (SIFA), which is the trade body for solicitor financial advisers (www.sifa.co.uk).

Unlike accountancy, where literally anyone can set themselves up (hence the importance of the check points outlined above), only solicitors regulated by the Solicitors Regulatory Authority can describe themselves as a solicitor and trade as such. You may find that others may seek to skirt around this with such terms as 'legal services' and the like. If you are unhappy about the service you have received from your solicitor, you should first try to resolve the matter with the firm through its complaints-handling partner. If you still feel aggrieved you can approach the Solicitors Regulation Authority (www. sra.org.uk).

For practical assistance if you are having problems with your solicitor, you can approach the Legal Services Ombudsman (www.legalombudsman.org.uk).

For queries of a more general nature you should approach the Law Society (www.lawsociety.org.uk). For those living in Scotland or Northern Ireland, see the Law Society of Scotland (www.lawscot.org.uk) or the Law Society of Northern Ireland (www.lawsoc-ni.org) respectively.

The Financial Ombudsman's tip

David Cresswell is Director of Strategy at the Financial Ombudsman Service and wants to help keep investors safe. His top tip for choosing a financial adviser or stock broker is a simple question: '*Are they regulated?*' David explains why:

> The Financial Ombudsman Service and Financial Services Compensation Scheme are there to help if the person or company you are dealing with is on the official Financial Conduct Authority register and things go wrong. Because of this added protection you should always check, if you are offered investments or pension products or advice, whether the company is on the register: go to www.fca.org.uk and go to 'register' or phone 0800 111 6768. If they are not on the FCA register it is unlikely that either the FOS or FSCS will be able to help if things go wrong.

More tips from the FOS about staying safe from scammers can be found in Chapter 8.

Inspired? Remember to fill in your plan for a good retirement at the end of the book.

Useful help

Financial Conduct Authority (FCA) FCA's Central Register: www.fca.org.uk and go to 'register' or phone 0800 111 6768

Financial Ombudsman Service (FOS): www.financial-ombudsman.org.uk

Financial Services Compensation Scheme (FSCS): www.fscs.org.uk

Accountants

Association of Chartered Certified Accountants (ACCA): www.accaglobal.com

Institute of Chartered Accountants in England and Wales (ICAEW): www.icaew.co.uk

Chartered Accountants Ireland (for both Northern Ireland and the Republic of Ireland): www.charteredaccountants.ie

Institute of Chartered Accountants of Scotland (ICAS): www.icas.com

Solicitors

Law Society: www.lawsociety.org.uk

Law Society of Scotland: www.lawscot.org.uk

Law Society of Northern Ireland: www.lawsoc-ni.org

CHAPTER FOUR

Pensions

The question is not at what age I want to retire. It is at what income.
GEORGE FOREMAN

Pensions provide the main income in retirement so the above quote by George Foreman seems to be spot on in today's flexible pensions environment. It is all about the income we want to have in retirement, and in 2019 we have more control over both the age when we retire and how we turn on/ turn off pension income. This is because our pensions world has changed radically in recent years, which is due to two main drivers. The first is the flexibility in careers with extended and flexible working being possible beyond the state retirement age, if that is what you want. This includes the potential to take a top-up or part-time job that can allow you to reach the income you need depending on the phase of retirement you are in and your needs at that time. The second is the most radical change in living memory in the pensions world: it came with pension changes introduced in 2015 that created a more flexible pension environment, which potentially allows you to turn off/turn on your pension income and bring in more tax planning to work with your pension planning.

The downside, however, is that this chapter could be like wading through treacle, but dip in and it may leave a sweet taste. The treacle factor comes from the simple fact that the biggest financial decision you will make (probably even bigger than a mortgage) gets little attention, is poorly understood and is surrounded in baffling 'finance speak'. For that reason, financing your retirement through pensions is put on the back burner and too many people get a nasty shock when reality strikes. A common theme is that pensioners are 'disappointed' that they hadn't grasped the issues and opportunities earlier. By retirement day, or when sitting in a retirement planning course paid for by your employer, it is really too late to do anything meaningful and make a significant impact to increase your income in retirement. At that 'too late' stage there are some other options in order to work around the harsh reality of a modest pension and higher living aspirations. The first option is to work longer or start your own small business to ramp up your income; another option could include raiding your savings and investments. A third option is perhaps downsizing your house, relocating to a cheaper area or using an equity release scheme to release capital in your home to give you more money to spend. The other option is to cut your costs and learn to live on less money. All these options and more are outlined in this book to help give you some ideas to put in your plan at the end of this book. Best of all, however, could be to wade through the treacle and start making some changes now so you have a more tax-efficient income. So read on and get your head around pensions planning and how it interweaves with tax and your investments. You should build better pension plans, save more, live better and be happier.

Importantly, this chapter is only a guide and it is neither legal nor financial advice; it is no substitute for taking professional advice from a financial adviser or other professional adviser (see Chapter 3). Any potential tax advantages (as of summer 2018) may be subject to change and will depend on your individual circumstances, so individual professional advice should be obtained.

This chapter at a glance

- Mind the gap – what pensions you may receive and when and recognizing the gap with your retirement income aspirations.

- Information to help you understand your State Pension entitlement and any company and private pension entitlement. You should get a State Pension forecast and ask your current and former employers for a pension forecast and if they have free help available.

- Guidance about defined pensions options and important new pension drawdown facilities that provide flexibility on planning your retirement income. Drawdown, tax-free amounts and other tax opportunities and pitfalls.

- Pointers to free guidance offered by the government's impartial service about your defined contribution pension options. This will help provide clarity on your pension pot and how much money you will have in retirement. Book in your appointment (via www.pensionwise.gov.uk).

- Reminders about the importance of getting proper financial advice. If the sums involved are significant, the benefits should outweigh fees that you may have to pay. Ask friends and work colleagues if they can recommend a financial adviser and always ensure your adviser is on the FCA's Central Register (www.fca.org.uk).

- Beware of 'pensions predators'. There are unauthorized advisers out there trying to help you get your hands on part of your pension before the age of 55 or, worse, crooks looking to defraud you of your pension pots. Beware and take care. Accessing pensions before 55 is almost impossible and you will probably get stung, irrespective of how impressive they may seem if you try to unlock your pension pot before 55 (crooks in suits are clever!). This is so important that it is worth saying twice – you must always ensure your adviser is on the FCA's Central Register (www.fca.org.uk).

- Combine your pensions planning with your savings plan to finance your retirement. But also keep half an eye on the tax implications (which can change) of both, as therein lie both opportunities and pitfalls.

How long have I got?

The Office of National Statistics (ONS) estimates that a male aged 65 in 2018 has a life expectancy of 86 (and a 4.7 per cent chance of reaching 100). A female of the same age has a life expectancy of 88 (and a 7.4 per cent chance of reaching 100) (according to ONS data released in November 2017 based on 2016 data). But note that there are big variations in how long you may live depending on location, wealth, health and your lifestyle choices – sometimes by five years or more.

Average pension income

The Prudential estimated that the average income for those retiring in 2018 was expected to be about £19,900 a year, including the State Pension. The Prudential research also found that nearly half (46 per cent, a 1 per cent rise on 2017) of people planning to retire in 2018 feel they are not financially well prepared for retirement or are unsure about their preparations. Is this you? If so, keep reading.

Access ages and 25 per cent tax free

The minimum age you can take money from a pension is currently 55 (it rises to 57 in 2028) but employer pension schemes are able to set their own rules on accessing pensions so the access age could be higher. Generally speaking most defined contribution schemes (explained below) let you access the money at 55 and employer schemes have a higher age.

You can withdraw up to 25 per cent of your pension tax free. This is fairly simple for defined contribution schemes but final salary schemes (again explained below) are a little more complicated and a calculation involving a 'commutation' works out a reduced final salary in lieu of taking 25 per cent of your pension tax free.

Playing the tax bands

One good way to increase your income in retirement is by playing the tax bands in the years when you are earning. This has particularly good impact if you are earning above the higher-rate tax band (£46,350 in 2018/19) and even bigger impact if your earnings are in the tax 'kill zone' of £100,000 to £123,700. The tax 'kill zone' is described further in Chapter 6 (Tax). Pension planning can shift income from being taxed at 40 per cent to being taxed at 20 per cent (and then it gets even better as one-quarter of the amount is tax free). It can even, potentially, shift tax from being taxed at 60 per cent in the 'kill zone' to 20 per cent (and again a quarter of the money shifted will be tax free). It seems amazing that prospective pensioners just don't seem to 'get this' and seek to shift more of their earnings into their pension funds at a much earlier age.

Top tip

Get to a better understanding of your income now and what it will be in retirement and look at ways of shifting income from being taxed at a higher rate now to a lower rate later when you draw your pension (subject to reliefs and allowances outlined below). This could increase your retirement funds by at least 20 per cent of any additional funds contributed.

The pensions expectation and 'mind the gap'

The ONS measure the average weekly pay (including bonuses) and in February 2018 this was £513 per week so about £26,700 per annum. As a very rough rule of thumb a reasonable goal is to expect an income in retirement of 40–75 per cent of your employed earnings. Some examples detailed below will help you see how much you need to bridge the gap between State Pension and your retirement income ambitions. All four examples assume that no significant savings or investments have been built up and that retirement income is being financed only by pension income.

Theresa is aged 65 and is on average earnings of about £26,700; her pension aspiration is to have an income in retirement commencing in 2019 at about £20,000 before tax (75 per cent of earnings). This is very close to the average pension income of £19,900 for those retiring in 2018. Theresa has no final salary pension so the numbers will work like this (the term 'final salary' pension is explained later in this chapter but for now it means a great form of salary as it pays a percentage of your final salary and keeps on paying year after year no matter how long you live):

Theresa can probably expect to get a State Pension of about £8,500. This means she would need a pension pot of £306,000 to generate a 25 per cent lump sum of about £76,000 and then further pension income of about £11,500 rising by the Retail Prices Index (RPI) each year. This gives Theresa a total income in retirement before tax of about £20,000 (then increasing by RPI) for an estimated 20 years. The tax-free lump sum is assumed to be allocated to 'one-off' expenditure – perhaps a new car, kitchen and a holiday fund for the next 10 years whilst she enjoys her active retirement phase. She can then expect to gear down her spending as she moves into passive retirement when her pension pot runs out at about the age of 85 and then live on just her State Pension, with equity in any home or state benefits paying any subsequent care-home fees. If she wants more income in the 85+ years then she needs to reduce the £11,500 drawn from her pension pot over 20 years.

Let's next look at David, a high earner aged 65 with his own business that brings in around £100,000 per annum (from salary and dividend income). He also has a previous employer final salary scheme from the 1980s, which will pay about £12,000 per annum from the age of 65. His goal from 2019 is an income in retirement commencing at about £43,000 before tax. His numbers will work like this:

David can probably expect to get a State Pension of about £8,500 and will also receive £12,000 per annum from his final salary pension scheme (after commutation and taking a 25 per cent tax-free lump sum). He will have needed to build up a further pension pot of around £600,000 to generate a further 25 per cent tax-free lump sum of about £150,000 (which he may have earmarked for a holiday home abroad) and the pension pot will then pay further pension income of around £22,500 per annum, rising by RPI for an estimated 20 years to reach the £43,000 income-before-tax goal. To achieve this he would have been paying in about 25 per cent of his £40,000 income in 1990 and consistently paying in about 25 per cent each year up to the £100,000 income level in 2018 when he retires (this assumes income increasing at a steady rate between 1990 and 2018). By about 85 his pension pot will be exhausted under these assumptions and it will be 2039 and David can expect to then live on just his State Pension and final salary pension. Originally in 2019 these were about £8,500 and £12,000 but by 2039 both will have risen by RPI to protect their equivalent purchasing power. This should still allow David some nice extras in his passive/care-home years.

Next is Gordon, aged 65, who has substantial public service and a 'good' final salary pension of about £25,000 per annum before tax and after commutation, which could have provided him a tax-free lump sum of approximately £75,000 (the 'before-commutation' amount may have equated to about two-thirds of his final salary as he had always served in the public service) and a State Pension of about £8,500. Again the lump sum is assumed to be allocated to 'one-off' expenditure – this time being set aside to help with the children's future university fees and anticipated future weddings. Gordon's income in retirement of about £33,500 before tax will run for as long as he lives (increasing by the RPI to protect him against inflation).

A final illustration could be useful. Tony is aged 65 in 2019 and hoping for an income in retirement at about the average annual earnings level of £26,700 and has no final salary pension. His income will be a State Pension of about £8,500 and a pension income of about £18,200 per annum rising by RPI for an estimated 20 years. He wants to withdraw his 25 per cent tax-free lump sum over six years and places this in ISAs over these years (contributing in £20,000 a year from age 65). He then plans to draw on these tax-free ISA funds to finance extra holidays over the next decade of active retirement. Tony would need to build up a pension pot of about £485,000 to achieve this and have £121,000 as his tax-free lump sum. He then lives off his remaining £364,000 pension pot and state pension. Then, when aged 85, he would live on just his State Pension in his passive/care-home years, as per the first example, Theresa.

Bridging the pensions gap

The above examples are at a high level and serve to illustrate some of the numbers and how this could, in turn, relate to you and perhaps help you identify potential gaps in pension expectations. The key next step for you is to do some preparation work to get to grips with your own pension position and then consider options if you find a gap. Martin Gorvett, a Chartered Financial Planner, of Lavender Financial Planners Ltd, has helped hundreds of individuals understand and bridge the gap. Martin advises:

> For many the kick-starter for funding a pension comes from our first job. In our early years we may accumulate several small pension pots as our career progresses. It is important to keep track of what you have and ensure that inertia does not creep in. Whilst in the early years you may only be able to contribute a little towards your pension, every pound is important. The more you can fund in the early years the longer it has to grow (the effect known as 'pound cost averaging'). Those starting later in life face a daunting reality. The rule of thumb is that you should take your age, halve it and that is the percentage of earnings that you should contribute. For example, someone who is 50 should contribute 25 per cent of their earnings to a pension in order to have any chance of a decent retirement, whereas someone who starts at 20 should contribute 10 per cent.

Preparation part 1: understand your State Pension entitlement

The State Pension is a regular, weekly payment from the government and is funded by national insurance contributions and based on the amount you have contributed. Because people are living longer the state could not afford to fund the State Pension for the previous retirement ages of 65 (male) and 60 (female). Therefore, since 2010 we have seen the retirement age for women increasing and other previously laid-out plans on pension age increases being accelerated. Put simply, the funding solution was met by equalizing the retirement ages of men and women and then making people wait longer to receive it. The State Pension will be paid at age 66 for both sexes by 2020, then at 67 by 2027, increasing to age 68 in 2037 to 2039. The www.gov.uk website and a search for 'State Pension calculator' will give the age at which you will receive yours.

The State Pension and related additional elements to it have changed over the years and this has led to further confusion. The latest change took place in April

2016 when a new flat-rate pension structure was brought in for those retiring after 6 April 2016. Those who retired before then remain on their old scheme.

To qualify for the old State Pension scheme and receive a full basic State Pension you required 30 years' full National Insurance (NI) contributions. For 2018/19 the full single-person basic state retirement pension is £125.95 per week). If you are married and both you and your partner have built up a State Pension, you will get double this amount.

Some people also receive an additional State Pension (also called the State Second Pension or, before 2002, it was called SERPS), which is the government's earnings-related additional pension. How much additional State Pension you get is complicated and depends on your NI contributions and whether or not you 'contracted out'. You will have been contracted out if you opted for NI contributions to be diverted to a work or personal pension. There is then a range of further options including: deferring your pension (by deferring it you can have a bigger pension when it starts); adult dependency increases (for a husband, wife or someone who is looking after your children); Pension Credit (an income-related benefit); payments to an overseas address; provisions for married women and widows; divorce, death and disputes; and the Christmas bonus. More detailed information can be found at www.gov.uk and at www.pensionsadvisoryservice.org.uk – whose help is always free.

Then we have the new 'simpler' regime for those retiring after 6 April 2016, which pays £164.35 for 2018/19 (about £8,500 per annum) if you have the 'full' 35 years of service. You will get a reduced amount providing you have at least 10 qualifying years on your NI record. You will receive a proportionate amount if you have between 10 and 34 qualifying years and you may receive more if you have accrued SERPS or State Second Pension. You can estimate what you will receive by dividing your years by 35 and multiplying the resultant fraction by £164.35. For example, 20 years will grant you a State Pension of $(20/35) \times £164.35 = £93.91$ per week. Whatever figure you are due to receive no one will receive an amount under the new scheme that is less than they would have done under the old scheme. But don't worry too much as the simple and easy step is to get a State Pension forecast, as shown below.

Early retirement and your State Pension

Because some people retire early they can mistakenly assume it is possible to get an early State Pension. While the information may be correct for some employers' schemes it does not apply to the basic State Pension.

Next steps – getting a State Pension forecast

You can request a pension statement estimating your State Pension based on your current NI record. You can apply online at www.gov.uk/check-state-pension, by telephone on 0345 3000 168, by text phone on 0345 3000 169 or by post to:

The Pension Service 9
Mail Handling Site A
Wolverhampton
WV98 1LU

Top tip

Nearly half the population is not prepared for retirement. Spend 10 minutes getting your State Pension forecast and you are starting to get back some control.

If you don't have full NI records don't worry. You can buy missing years from the HM Revenue and Customs (HMRC). This is usually a sensible option to explore, especially if you are in good health and expect a long life.

Top tip

Get an estimate for buying missing years from The Pension Service – do the numbers and make a choice.

Sources of further free help or advice on the State Pension

The Pensions Advisory Service: www.pensionsadvisoryservice.org.uk

www.pensionwise.gov.uk

The Service Personnel and Veterans Agency: www.gov.uk/government/organisations/veterans-uk

Citizens Advice: www.citizensadvice.org.uk

Preparation part 2: understand your other pension income

Private (or personal) defined contribution pensions and 'drawdown'

Private (or personal) defined contribution pension schemes are a pension 'pot' from which future pension income payable to you will depend on the investment growth of your contributions. These contrast massively with defined benefit schemes, which are often known as 'final salary' pension schemes and were the norm until the late 1980s (more below). Defined contribution pensions are now the norm.

The 2014 Budget brought in 'pensions liberation' in April 2015. In the 'old world' most people bought an annuity with their defined contribution pension pot on retirement. The annuity then provided a fixed income for life. The 'old world' system attracted criticism as it was perceived as representing poor value and some annuities were mis-sold to those in ill health or were unsuitable as they may have resulted in no or limited financial protection for dependants on the death of the annuity holder.

The 'new world' of pensions liberalization resulted in a dramatic change and since April 2015 everyone now has a right to access their defined contribution pension pots from age 55 and no one is forced to buy an annuity. Instead we have the new concept of 'drawdown', which is financial speak for taking money out of your pension as an income. You will pay income tax depending on your tax band. The risk, however, is that you may outlive your pension pot and exhaust your funds as there is not the same certainty that annuities provided. The other risk is the fact that financial markets fluctuate. So what happens if the markets collapse just as you are about to start drawing on your funds? Some readers may remember the Japanese asset price bubble of the early 1990s (Nikkei 225 at 13,000 in December 1985, rising to 39,000 four years later in December 1989 before crashing to 14,400 in August 1992) and a decade of despair that followed for investors. Or others will remember the US bear market of 2007 to 2008 (between October 2007 and June 2009 the Dow Jones Industrial Average, Nasdaq Composite and S&P 500 all fell 20 per cent from their peaks in 2007). Fluctuations vary according to the risk that you have selected for your funds. The bigger the risk the bigger the potential fluctuation and this can, of course, create big winners as well as big losers. If you have significant funds in defined contribution funds you must, therefore, understand and accept your risk levels. Related to this is another risk and that is one of complacency. Most people just accept the drawdown scheme offered by their existing pension company and do not shop around. However, plans are hard to compare in terms of risk, reward, fees and other charges.

Martin Gorvett, a Chartered Financial Planner of Lavender Financial Planners Ltd, explains the fee structure on advice and what to look out for in fees, charges and costs when considering defined contributions and 'drawdown':

> More often than not people are tempted to avoid professional fees in favour of directly accessing retirement products. If you have the knowledge, all well and good. Just look out for the 'unknown unknowns'. Professional fees do vary and have historically been hidden. However, the modern financial-planning advice market is designed to provide a service based on value, not a toll gate to products. Regulated financial planners will charge a fee relevant to the work expected of them. This will either be a fixed fee or percentage based. Average costs in the industry have dropped from 5 per cent to around 3 per cent over recent years. Some advisers will take 1–2 per cent. Don't be afraid to challenge the fee being charged. A good financial planner will be able to justify their fee. Thankfully the modern pension market is designed to be portable. Very few modern financial contracts harbour surrender penalties. If there are they will be disclosed at the outset. Again, don't be afraid to ask for clarification. Typically you would expect to pay fees as a percentage of your fund. There are three layers of cost to an advised product:
>
> - Advice – typically between 0.5 per cent and 1 per cent.
> - Product – typically between 0.25 per cent and 0.35 per cent.
> - Investment – typically between 0.2 per cent (for a passive solution) and 1.8 per cent (for an actively managed solution).
>
> As with other industries, going direct to a provider could end up costing you more, as the retail price of direct offerings may be higher.

You can take as little or as much drawdown as you need and therefore income levels can be varied to take advantage of other income you may be earning (perhaps from a new part-time job, or having started a small business) or whilst waiting for the State Pension to kick in. This might make your tax affairs more efficient and could save you money. The point is that you can manage your income more easily to take advantage of the zero-rate and basic-rate tax bands more efficiently and this may save you tax and provide more of an income (as flagged up earlier in a top tip). Importantly, the new regime ensures you can now pass on your pension on death to a loved one more tax efficiently up to the age of 75, because up to that age defined contribution pension pots do not form part of someone's estate for Inheritance Tax purposes. Under previous rules there used to be a 55 per cent Pensions Death Tax. Now, if you die before 75 there is no tax to pay on funds passing from defined contribution schemes. A death after the 75th birthday will be subject to your pension beneficiaries' marginal rate of Income Tax. Most pension experts agree that pensions liberation is a good thing but also add a note of caution. Martin Gorvett, Chartered Financial Planner, advises:

> The rule changes have helped enormously in making my clients' retirement strategies more efficient. For those with other savings, pensions have become an efficient way of handing on your wealth to those whom you leave behind. But the new freedom brings temptation and a lot of new responsibility. At the other end of the spectrum, there is a danger that some pension savers will draw their pension savings and fritter it all away without any constraints to hold them back. Most pension providers are acting as a second line of defence for savers looking to draw pension benefits under flexi-access. They will ensure that professional advice has been considered and that savers are not being scammed.

Top tip

Plan carefully when first drawing down pension benefits under 'flexi-access' as emergency HMRC tax codings can cause havoc. The HMRC may assume that your income will continue each month for the remainder of the tax year at the level you first draw down on the pension pot. If you draw a significant amount of income early in the tax year as a 'one-off' you may invoke 40 or 45 per cent tax on some of your pension income, as HMRC may assume this will continue and will sign a tax code accordingly. You can always sort out any overpaid tax with HMRC and get it back later but, alternatively, drawing a notional amount (£100) first, or by drawing later in the tax year, may avoid this.

Annuities

Since April 2015 and pensions flexibility you are no longer compelled to buy an annuity if you have a defined contribution pension to fund your pension.

The concept of annuities needs some explanation as the option of purchasing an annuity still remains. When you buy an annuity you hand over a lump sum (your pension fund after taking out 25 per cent of it as a tax-free lump sum) to an insurance company in return for a regular, guaranteed income for the rest of your life, called an 'annuity', and the income is subject to Income Tax. Under the current rules the earliest age you can do this is 55 (this increases to 57 in 2028). Once you have bought your annuity, the income you receive is effectively free of investment risk. The risk has been transferred to your provider. There is little danger of running out of money, as your provider has to pay you for as long as you live.

When you approach retirement your pension company will contact you about purchasing an annuity and provide you with a quotation, which will tell you the amount of money you have in your 'pension pot', the amount of tax-free lump sum you are entitled to take and the level of income you will receive each month (should you convert your pension fund to an annuity with them) and will explain the options available to you, including flexible drawdown.

Types of annuities

There are several different kinds of annuity. The most basic is a *level annuity*. This pays you a fixed income for the rest of your life. If you die, the income usually stops. Crucially, it will not change if prices rise. So in an inflationary world, your annuity will lose real value every year. For example, if inflation averages 4 per cent per year, the purchasing power of your annuity income will halve in 18 years.

To avoid this you could buy an *increasing annuity*. Here, the amount of income you receive will rise in line with inflation each year, or by a set percentage. If you are worried about your insurance company keeping a large chunk of your pension fund should you die after only a few years of retirement, you could buy a *guaranteed annuity*. So if you bought a five-year guarantee, and you died after two years, your nominated beneficiary (your spouse perhaps) would receive annuity income for another three years.

Another option is a *joint-life annuity* where your partner can receive some or all of your pension income if you die before them. If you want to take a bit more of a risk, you could choose an *investment-linked annuity*. Here you start with an initial level of income while your fund is invested in an insurance company's with-profits fund. If the fund makes a profit, your income goes up. If it loses money, however, your income goes down.

Your health can also have a significant impact. If you are a smoker or have an illness, you may be eligible for an *enhanced annuity* or *impaired-life annuity*. These pay a higher annual income than a standard annuity. In short, the annuity provider is betting that you won't live as long as you might otherwise have done, so it can afford to pay you more.

Other annuity options

If you don't want to buy an annuity because of low rates, there are a number of strategies you can use. One is known as *phased retirement*. This is where you set up a series of annuities and drawdowns with 25 per cent tax-free lump sums. You will get a lower starting income but if you think annuity rates are going to rise it might be worth considering.

Another possible option is *fixed-term annuities*. Here you set up an annuity for a fixed period (say 5 or 10 years). You get paid an income for the fixed term but at the end of the period you have a guaranteed pot of money to reinvest again. As with phased retirement, your income will be lower than from a standard annuity.

Finally, remember that due to pensions flexibility you can now avoid buying an annuity and, instead, manage your own defined contribution pension under flexible drawdown, as outlined above.

Self-invested personal pensions (SIPPs)

If you want to use a pension to save for your retirement, you don't have to give your money to a fund manager in a personal pension provider. Instead you can manage your own retirement fund with a self-invested personal pension (SIPP). You can buy a range of asset classes, from stocks to bonds to gold bullion (though you cannot buy fine wines or residential property). Monthly contributions can be as low as £50 or as much as 100 per cent of your annual salary (subject to the tax restrictions set out further below). These were designed for people who wanted to play a more active part in their investment strategy. The investments that can be held in the SIPP are quite wide and can even include commercial property, and for this reason some owners of small businesses may look at holding their commercial property within their SIPP to good end effect. A specialist pension adviser should be able to assist further. Martin Gorvett, Chartered Financial Planner, advises:

> Specialist pension products, SIPPs, are becoming a lot more mainstream. If you are venturing away from the more traditional investment routes, especially

buying commercial property, it is important to ensure that a 'pure' SIPP is used where you are a co-trustee of the SIPP and hence a co-landlord of the property. Just be careful that if you don't need a 'pure' SIPP, you are not inadvertently paying for one. 'SIPPs' have become somewhat of a buzz word for pension wrappers. Ensure that the functionality of the product meets your needs (and nothing else). A SIPP can be anything from a drawdown providing an open-architecture personal pension to a full-blooded personalized pension trust that has the capacity for esoteric investments. Just check the label first.

If you are someone who finds the idea of investing your own money daunting, a SIPP may not be for you.

How much should you pay in?

So how much should you put away if you are now 45 and have done nothing much for the last 20 years on pensions? Well, it is going to come as a bit of a shock but Money Savings Expert has a basic rule of thumb that we will share – and then let's do the numbers. They say: 'Take the age you start your pension and halve it. Put this percentage of your pre-tax profits (or before-tax salary) aside each year until you retire.' So that would be 22.5 per cent of your profits for the next 22 years (until aged 67) and you may then attain a reasonable retirement pension income.

Restricting tax relief on pensions

You can save as much as you like towards your pension but (and it is a big but) there is a limit on the amount of tax relief you can get. For that reason, linking savings together with pensions can be wise for your retirement planning and especially for high earners. The rules on how much you can contribute and still receive relief have been tightened over recent years and it is currently £40,000 per year. There are provisions to use three previous years' unused allowance and if this becomes a potential issue the sums involved would usually justify specific professional advice. Another restriction, called the 'tapered reduction', hits big earners as it reduces the amount of tax relief that can be obtained on pension contributions for taxpayers with 'adjusted income' in excess of £150,000. Where an individual is subject to the taper, their annual allowance will be reduced by £1 for every £2 by which their income exceeds £150,000, subject to a maximum reduction of £30,000. The annual allowance of £10,000 will, therefore, apply to taxpayers with adjusted income of £210,000 or more.

The other big restriction on the tax relief available on pension contributions is the 'lifetime allowance', which limits the maximum amount that can be paid into pension savings tax efficiently to £1,030,000. The 'cap' has been slashed significantly since 2011/12 when it had stood at £1,800,000 and there are HMRC protection schemes that preserve, for instance, £1,250,000 of lifetime allowances existing at 5 April 2016 – more at www. gov.uk (search for 'pension schemes protect your lifetime allowance').

Timing of withdrawals – don't shoot yourself in the foot

Receiving tax relief on £40,000 of contributions and the backdating provisions of unused relief are valuable planning tools for tax efficiency, especially for the small business owner who may face volatile income streams and variable spending patterns, or those facing redundancy (for any payments beyond the initial £30,000 relief from income tax). Once you start withdrawing funds from your defined contribution pension pot a barrier comes down. After that date, tax relief on contributions into a pension will be limited to £4,000 per year. This is to prevent the 'relaundering' of pension income back into pensions to try and get double tax relief on the tax-free element of a withdrawal. There are some exemptions to this rule for small pension pots, where withdrawals can be taken without being subject to the reduced allowance. If in any doubt check it out with a financial adviser and carefully consider your future income and anticipated pension contributions before starting to draw down on your pension, as this action could restrict the future tax efficiency of contributions.

> **Top tip**
>
> Tax rules and tax reliefs can and do change and their exact value depends on each individual's circumstances; however, pension savings are still one of the most tax-effective investments. If in doubt check it out with a financial adviser.

Employer pension schemes

Types of employer pension schemes

The pension that your employer offers may be 'contributory' (you and your employer pay into it) or 'non-contributory', which means that only your employer does. There are four main types of employer pension:

- a final salary pension scheme (a defined benefit scheme and often considered to be the 'king' of pensions for those lucky enough to have one and who had promotions late in their careers);
- another defined benefit pension scheme called a 'career average' pension scheme;
- a defined contribution money purchase pension scheme;
- a defined contribution group or personal pension scheme.

Final salary pension scheme Final salary pension schemes are known as a type of defined benefit scheme. You build up a pension at a certain rate – one-sixtieth is quite common – so for each year you have been a scheme member you receive one-sixtieth of your final salary as a pension. The pension benefit keeps paying for as long as you live and, therefore, the cost and risk of funding the pension sit with the employer. This is, potentially, a very big win for employees given extending life expectancy rates. This is probably the main reason why many private-sector employers have exited this sort of arrangement as the cost of funding them has become just too onerous. The biggest winners of all are those employees who secure big salary increases towards the end of their employment.

If you work for one of the few remaining employers with a final salary scheme you would need a compelling reason not to join it. Again you would probably need a compelling reason to shift the benefits to another scheme after you leave the employer. Whilst this holds true some large employers have been offering increasingly large sums to buy leavers out of their scheme. Some considerations may make this a worthwhile option to review with a financial adviser. Perhaps the prompt could be that the amount offered seems 'too good to be true'. On review, factors such as health concerns of the future pensioner and/or the spouse pension being low may make the option more viable. One other factor could be the inheritance tax breaks that apply to defined pension contribution pots, as these do not apply to final salary scheme payments on the death of the pensioner. Once in a defined contribution pot and under 75 the inheritance tax breaks may apply, which could be tax-free money for the recipient. It is vital to remember that any such review would need to be undertaken by an independent financial adviser, regulated by the FCA. Martin Gorvett, Chartered Financial Planner, provides some guidance on this:

> Final salary pension schemes are usually the 'golden goose' of the pensions world as these schemes just keep paying, which will be a nice win if you live to over 100. Only in the rarest of exceptions would there ever be a

need to shift out of a final salary pension scheme – if you are unmarried or fear decreased mortality due to health concerns you may wish to seek advice on this topic. If you are tempted to move your final salary benefit to a defined contribution scheme just make sure that the temptation is not driven by the ability to invest into an unregulated investment vehicle that promises the earth, as happened with some British Steel workers. Also, there is only modest risk, as if a salary-related occupational scheme or the sponsoring employer gets into financial trouble, the Pension Protection Fund can provide some protection. You can normally get a pension of up to 90 per cent of your expected pension, subject to a cap (more at www. pensionprotectionfund.org.uk).

Career average pension scheme This is another type of defined benefit scheme and differs from the final salary pension scheme outlined above as the benefit (your pension) is worked out using an average of your earnings in the time that you are a member of the scheme, rather than the final salary.

Money purchase pension scheme These are defined contribution schemes, as described earlier, and therefore provide additional benefits through flexible access options and inheritance tax breaks (up to age 75). The money paid in by you and your employer is invested and builds up a fund that buys you an income when you retire; significantly, the funding risk sits with the employee (in contrast to the defined benefit alternatives above, where the funding risk sits with the employer). The fund is invested, usually in stocks and shares and other investments, with the aim of growing it over the years before you retire.

You can usually choose from a range of funds to invest in. The Pensions Advisory Service has an online investment choices planner to help you decide how to invest your contributions (see www.pensionsadvisoryservice. org.uk and go to 'choosing investment funds').

Group/personal pension scheme These are also money purchase schemes and a defined contribution scheme so, again, the funding risk sits with the employee but there are additional benefits through flexible access options and inheritance tax breaks (up to age 75). Typically, your employer offers access to a personal pension plan, which you own, and can take with you if you get a new job. Your employer will choose the scheme provider, deduct the contributions you make from your salary and pay these to the provider, along with their employer contributions.

Automatic enrolment

This was introduced in 2012 because people in the UK were living longer but were not saving enough to finance their increasing retirement. Auto-enrolment (as it is called) was designed to help shift the responsibility away from the state and towards the individual and their employer. It commenced in October 2012 and now covers all employees.

To be eligible an individual must live in the UK, be between 22 and state pensionable age and earn more than £10,000 a year. Some employers may offer schemes that better the auto-enrolment rates but for all other employers each individual will pay 2.4 per cent of their qualifying earnings, rising to 4 per cent in April 2019. Their employers will pay a minimum of 2 per cent rising to 3 per cent in April 2019. The government makes a contribution through tax relief of 0.6 per cent rising to 1 per cent from April 2019. So by April 2019 UK employees will be paying in at least 8 per cent of their earnings into a pension. Many employers use the National Employment Savings Trust ('NEST') as their pension scheme for auto-enrolment purposes. This is a national defined-contribution workplace pension scheme established by the government to support auto-enrolment. It is transportable between employers and has relatively low charges (more at www.nestpensions.org.uk). Other auto-enrolment schemes are available.

Whilst auto-enrolment is starting to help address the pensions gap it still seems to be modest provision in the context of the pension aspirations of many. Will we see bigger percentage increases in years to come? For instance, the Australian model is employer contributions of 9 per cent and employees are free to add money to the pension pot.

Questions on your employer pension scheme

If you have a query about your company pension they (or their delegated representative) should be able to assist with the usual questions that arise such as: could you have a refund of contributions if you were to leave shortly after joining? What happens if you become ill or die before pension age? What are the arrangements if you want to retire early? What will your pension be on your present salary? What spouse's pension will be paid on the death of the pensioner? Can a pension be paid to other dependants? What happens if you continue working with the organization after retirement age?

> **Top tip**
>
> With all forms of employer pension scheme check the answer to this question: 'What is the maximum amount or percentage the employer will match or contribute?' Then review if you are missing out on free money to help boost your retirement.

Lifetime Individual Savings Account (LISA) – a different pension?

The new Lifetime ISA has been available since April 2017 for adults provided they were aged under 40 when they opened the account. There is an annual contribution limit of £4,000 and savers will receive a 25 per cent government bonus. The intention is to encourage individuals to save towards their first home or for retirement. More on LISAs in Chapter 5 (Savings) but, for now, they could be an early step in a new approach to pension funding where taxed money goes in and is tax free on the way out (with the 25 per cent government bonus being a welcome addition). This switches the traditional pensions world on its head. The difficulty for many imminent retirees is that it is currently only available to the under-40s – and lack of availability as not many of the traditional ISA providers have introduced the product. In addition, better tax relief can currently be obtained by higher- and additional-rate taxpayers using traditional pensions.

Individual Savings Account – for a top-up 'income' or 'rainy day' planning

Individual Savings Accounts (ISAs) provide significant tax breaks as you do not pay any tax on the interest or the income (dividends) you make and there is no Capital Gains Tax if shares in your ISA soar. They are not, however, tax free on death and could be subject to the 40 per cent Inheritance Tax if the estate is above tax-exempt levels.

You can currently (2018/19) put up to £20,000 into an ISA so that is £40,000 between yourself and your partner. There is no age restriction, as found with the Lifetime ISA outlined above. Whilst pensions win for overall tax efficiency ISAs are a great second option for any savings or investments that are not tax sheltered already and for any free money that you receive (lottery, gaming or inheritance) or excess income received that you wish to 'put away' if you have used up your pension lifetime allowance or are beyond the pension annual allowance (£40,000 per year subject to restrictions for big earners and a three-year claw back of unused allowances, as outlined earlier). More on this in Chapter 5 (Savings).

Minimum retirement age

The minimum age at which you are allowed to take early retirement and draw your pension is 55 and rises to 57 in 2028, maintaining a 10-year gap from the State Pension age. It may be possible to draw retirement benefits earlier if you are in poor health and unable to work.

Beware of predators stalking your pension

Beware of anyone claiming that they can help to cash in a pension early and before you are 55. Whilst initially attractive, the sting in the tail is that you could face a tax bill of more than half your pension savings. The Pensions Advisory Service call it 'pensions liberation fraud' and warn that it is on the increase in the UK. The main warning signs are unsolicited text messages and phone calls, a transfer overseas and seeking to access a pension fund before the age of 55; the crooks also try to create some false urgency.

To counter this you must always check that any financial adviser is registered with the FCA (see Chapter 3, Professional Advisers); always obtain a written statement about any tax charges; never allow yourself to be rushed into agreeing to a pension transfer; and create a 'time out' to check things out. The benefit of dealing with a financial adviser who is registered with the FCA is the safety net if things go wrong – in the form of the Financial Ombudsman Service – and, if the firm fails and is insolvent, the Financial Services Compensation Scheme (more on this in Chapter 3, Professional Advisers).

Six must-do steps

Martin Gorvett, Chartered Financial Planner of Lavender Financial Planners Ltd, helps you get to grips with financing your retirement with his six 'must-do' steps to help you firm up on your preparations. Perhaps some of these should feature in your own plan for a good retirement guide at the end of the book:

1 *Keeping track of your retirement goals.* Retirement is not uniform. Everyone has different expectations. Start by understanding your likely expenditure by splitting your spending into three categories:
   - *must-have*: day-to-day living costs such as food and heating etc (see the budget planner set out in Chapter 1);

- *like-to-have*: a holiday twice a year;
- *nice-to-have*: a new car, a new kitchen or a legacy for the children.

Consider how these categories will change during the phases of retirement. Then you can start to consider the income you need in order to meet your personal retirement goals.

2 *Don't rely on the state.* The State Pension is certainly no substitute for private pension provision and other savings but it does provide a secure guaranteed baseline income on which to build. Ensure you understand what you will be entitled to and when from the State Pension.

3 *Retirement isn't just a pension.* You may need professional help to think differently about your goals for later life and how you want to finance them. The traditional view is that your pension provides income, and other investments are viewed as 'rainy day' funds.

4 *Understand just how long retirement could last and the effect of inflation.* A 65-year-old can now typically expect to live for another 22 years, and in all likelihood may well live a lot longer. Any income that will finance your retirement that is not inflation proofed will reduce in value over time. Getting the investment strategy right may sustain the funds for longer and may provide the desired investment returns while also limiting volatility.

5 *Pensions are still the most tax-privileged savings.* Pensions still offer the best tax breaks for mainstream savings. Where else can you get tax relief on contributions, tax-free investment returns and take 25 per cent out tax free? Treat the pension annual allowance of £40,000 like your ISA allowance of £20,000 and save, save, save.

6 *Martin's top tip. Your pension is now perhaps the most efficient device for sheltering part of your wealth (the pension fund) from Inheritance Tax if you are under 75.* Look upon this as part of your savings armoury and, potentially, save 40 per cent for those you leave behind – by carefully planning how you create your savings and pensions and which you draw from first.

Martin also explains that modern pensions allow much more flexibility than ever before. 'Flexi-access' – modern pension freedoms – can allow you to 'mould' your pension income (and tax-free cash) into any shape you wish:

With expenditure typically higher in the early years, planning can ensure value if extracted from your pension savings when you need it most. Retirement income doesn't have to come from the pension alone. Having a variety of savings and investments can achieve the optimum tax-efficient income. Do take professional advice – the benefits arising usually justify any cost.

Other help and advice

Previous schemes

In addition to understanding your current pension scheme, you may also need to chase up any previous schemes that you cannot seem to track down due to takeovers and mergers. For free help tracking down a pension go to www.gov.uk and then to 'Pension Tracing Service'.

Trustees or managers of your pension scheme

These are the first people to contact if you do not properly understand your benefit entitlements or if you are unhappy about some point to do with your pension.

The Pensions Advisory Service

The Pensions Advisory Service provides general information and guidance on pension matters and assists individuals with disputes with personal and company pensions. It can also help you find missing pensions schemes (more at pensionsadvisoryservice.org.uk).

Protection from the Pensions Ombudsman

You would normally approach the ombudsman if the pension scheme manager (or trustees) and the Pensions Advisory Service are unable to help. The ombudsman can investigate complaints of maladministration by the trustees, managers or administrators of a pension scheme or by an employer. The ombudsman will assist with disputes of fact or law with the trustees, managers or an employer. The ombudsman does not, however, investigate complaints about mis-selling of pension schemes, a complaint that is already subject to court proceedings, or those that are about a state social security benefit. The Pensions Ombudsman has also taken on the role of Pension Protection Fund Ombudsman, which helps final salary pension scheme members who are at risk of losing their pension benefits owing to their employer's insolvency. Members below the scheme's normal retirement age will receive 90 per cent of the pension protection fund level of compensation plus annual increases, subject to a cap and the standard fund rules (more at www.pensions-ombudsman.org.uk).

Some aspects of complaints about pensions can be investigated by the Financial Ombudsman Service (FOS) such as complaints about the suitability of advice to start a personal pension arrangement (perhaps they would have been better off being advised to join, remain or top up their employer's company pension scheme) (more at www.financial-ombudsman.org.uk). The interaction between the FOS and the Pensions Ombudsman can seem confusing but don't worry too much as they have good arrangements to point you in the right direction if you end up with the wrong ombudsman.

Other help in retirement – benefits

Pension Credit is an income-related benefit. It is an extra payment that guarantees most people over 65 a minimum income, and many people fail to claim it. For single pensioners with weekly income (including pension) below £163, Pension Credit will top you up to £163. If you have a partner and your joint weekly income is below £248.80 it will top you up to that amount. You might get more if you are a carer or disabled. You must live in England, Wales or Scotland (there are separate rules for Northern Ireland and you will not get pension credit if you move abroad permanently). When you apply, the government looks at all of your income. This includes both your basic and additional State Pension, any income from other pensions, income from any jobs you have and any savings above £10,000. For more information visit www.gov.uk and go to 'Pension Credit' or call 0800 99 1234.

Useful help

As well as the Pension Advisory Service (pensionsadvisoryservice.org.uk) outlined above there is further free and impartial government help and guidance available. This can help you understand your pension pot, your options and what to look out for on taxes and fees, and how to avoid pension scams. The service is at www.pensionwise.gov.uk and it can help you make sure your money lasts as long as you do.

Inspired? Remember to fill in your plan for a good retirement at the end of the book.

CHAPTER FIVE

Savings, investments and protection

An investment in knowledge pays the best interest.

BENJAMIN FRANKLIN

This chapter follows close on the heels of the chapter on pensions as the two subjects are interlinked. They often work well together in the active years of retirement when expenditure tends to be much higher than the subsequent phases of retirement in the passive years and then when care is necessary. The phases of retirement are important and were outlined in Chapter 1. The active retirement phase is when you may be spending more of your retirement fund reserves that are held in your savings and investments. In the active retirement years you still have the appetite and energy to devour all those things we set out in Part Three (Live better) of this book and many of the activities come at a financial cost. Just like pensions, the world of savings and investments is poorly understood and filled with 'financial jargon'. This chapter will help you start investing in knowledge. With improved understanding and knowledge you can hopefully make better plans and save more, live better and be happier.

This chapter at a glance

- One of your biggest investments is your home, which in raw financial terms is a property asset and part of your wealth, savings and investments. Releasing funds for your retirement by equity release is increasing in popularity. Some pros and cons are outlined together with alternative routes to releasing significant funds to help with your retirement.

- Reminders about the importance of getting proper financial advice. The benefits obtained from good financial advice should more than outweigh the fees that you may have to pay. Ask friends and work colleagues if they can recommend a financial adviser and always ensure your adviser is on the FCA's Central Register (www.fca.org.uk).

- The strength of the UK regulatory system – *staying within the safety net.* Split up your savings so that no more than £85,000 is held per bank or building society and check the institution is covered by the Financial Services Compensation Scheme (FSCS). Cover after certain life events that result in you holding up to £1 million for up to six months is also covered. The best example is selling a house and holding the funds for a few months whilst you rent and find a new house. You get £1 million coverage for a short period of time, as clearly £85,000 is insufficient and it saves you the trouble of opening up lots of £85,000 accounts with separate banks for a short time.

- Combine your pensions planning with your savings plan to finance your retirement. But keep half an eye on the tax implications (which can change) of both, as therein lie both opportunities and pitfalls.

- Tax-efficient savings and investment products. ISAs, LISAs, some National Savings products and some higher-risk alternatives can shelter savings and investments from tax or reduce the tax.

Importantly, this chapter is only a guide and it is neither legal nor financial advice; it is no substitute for taking professional advice from a financial adviser or other professional adviser (see Chapter 3). Any potential tax advantages (as at the time of writing) may be subject to change and will depend upon your individual circumstances, and individual professional advice should be obtained.

How do I find a good financial adviser and why should I have one?

Two easy questions to ask but not so easy to answer. Your starting point is to revisit the hints and tips in Chapter 3 (Professional advisers), which is then supplemented below with a focus on savings and investments.

You are free to manage your own savings and investments and this may interest you, especially if you have a good knowledge of the financial markets. Financial advisers offer an alternative, for a fee, and their knowledge and skills may remove the work from you and, potentially, improve returns over the long term. Another alternative is a financial services company that sells funds and shares and related products, and provides you with information through its website to assist you in making decisions. They then make money from dealing and transaction fees, which will usually be less than a financial adviser's fees.

The following mantra from Nobel prize-winner Paul Samuelson may assist your understanding of a good financial adviser:

> Investing should be more like watching paint dry or watching grass grow. If you want excitement, take $800 and go to Las Vegas.

Samuelson is basically saying that if you think investing is gambling then you are doing it wrong:

- Always ensure your adviser is on the Financial Conduct Authority register at www.fca.org.uk – if not, you are left outside the impressive UK regulatory safety net if things go wrong.

- Trust your instincts – if in doubt walk away and find another adviser.

- Look for recommendations from trusted family, friends or other professional advisers and then talk to at least two before deciding. Charges vary widely and should be set out clearly on any proposal letter provided to you before you decide. Check that everything fee and charge wise is understood before you sign up, including adviser fees, product provider fees, hourly rates, annual management fees and any fee charged if you move advisers (exit fees). Over 20 years the difference between 1 per cent and 3 per cent in annual fees can mount up. But also remember that quality comes at a price.

- The adviser's assessment of your appetite for risk should help the adviser to recommend more suitable products. The higher your appetite for risk the higher the variation in returns. For instance, a high-risk investor may expect returns that could either rise by 15 per cent per annum or fall by 15 per cent per annum. A no-risk investor will expect no downside risk and may accept returns of 2–3 per cent per annum. An investor's appetite for risk can change over time and it is not uncommon to see risk reduce as the retirement years approach, as individuals may not wish to see their funds erode by the highs and lows of the stock market. Remember to then deduct all relevant costs from the returns so that you can understand the actual net return over a year. The financial adviser's costs are either paid by fees from the return they make for you (perhaps an hourly rate) or they may charge a percentage of the funds they manage. In addition there may be charges levied by the fund management company itself.

- A financial adviser will gain a good understanding of you and your partner's wealth and in the event that one of you dies the financial adviser's knowledge and advice will be invaluable to the person remaining (especially if they were not the one used to doing the finances).

- If a financial adviser gets things wrong you will usually have a remedy against them and their professional indemnity insurance or through the Financial Ombudsman and FSCS (more below – see section on 'Investor protection'). For instance, a decent example of a potential claim is if you only want to invest in no-risk or low-risk funds but they invest your money in high-risk funds and you lose out.

- A good financial adviser will usually work with your other professional advisers, including solicitors and any accountant/tax adviser, to assist your overall tax efficiency.

Releasing funds for your retirement by equity release, downsizing or relocating

If there is a significant gap between the retirement lifestyle you desire and the reality of your pension income and your investment income there are a few options that can make a significant impact on the numbers. The first is earning more by taking a job, starting a business or perhaps letting out a room and this is covered in Chapters 9, 10 and 11 respectively. The alternative approach is accessing the equity stored in your property by either: 1) borrowing money against your property through an equity release scheme to help provide additional income; or 2) freeing up wealth by downsizing or relocating. Essentially you are converting wealth that is stored up in a property into income to spend, but each route comes at a price and with pros and cons.

Equity release

The process of equity release works by you taking out a mortgage on your property whilst continuing to live there and then receiving a lump sum or drawing down funds against that mortgage. Interest then rolls up on the mortgage debt, which will be repaid when you sell the house and downsize or move into alternative accommodation. The interest on the mortgage may be slightly more than on other commercial mortgages.

The industry was subject to significant mis-selling in the late 1980s and early 1990s when some financial advisers persuaded elderly homeowners to remortgage their houses and then gamble on the stock market to try and achieve returns to beat the mortgage interest. It went spectacularly wrong for many with the intervention of some poor selling techniques and rogue advisers, the recession, stock market turmoil and high interest rates.

However, if arranged properly, equity release mortgages may provide a possible solution but these things still carry an instinctive risk as the interest just rolls up in the background. So it is vital to get trusted relatives on board to help you fully appraise any scheme and look at it from all angles. A good financial adviser who is independent of the scheme should be able to help you understand the financial implications and help you consider other property-related options. For the equity release perspective the Equity Release Council is the industry body and it aims to facilitate the safe growth of the equity release market (www.equityreleasecouncil.com).

Some negatives to consider about equity release:

- Your family will receive a smaller inheritance as some of the value in your home, maybe all of it, will go to the mortgage provider.

- The fees to arrange the release. Ensure you understand all fees involved including any adviser's fee, valuation fee, mortgage fee and solicitor's fees.

- The money released may affect your state benefits. Borrowing may be limited to about 35 per cent of the value of your home.

- The compounding effect of interest at 4 or 5 per cent should not be underestimated as interest builds on interest. Ensure you understand how this adds up over 5 years, 10 years and 15 years (on top of the actual mortgage that was obtained).

- If you wish to downsize in the future the equity remaining after repaying the mortgage and interest may limit your choice and options (could this point to downsizing or 'rightsizing' now – more below).

- You retain responsibility for maintaining the property and paying the bills.

Some positives about equity release:

- You can stay in your home.
- In terms of long-term care planning equity release can be useful if you are looking to fund care and stay in your own home.
- All Equity Release Council members offer a 'no negative equity guarantee', which means that, no matter what happens to the housing market, customers will never owe more than the value of their home.

If you do go ahead with equity release, think carefully about whether you need all the funds in one go or if you can draw it down in tranches. The latter is called a 'drawdown lifetime mortgage' and is usually cheaper on interest costs as you don't draw the money until you need it and, therefore, save on the interest costs on the amount deferred. This could be useful if your needs were, say, £10,000 now in year one for a holiday of a lifetime, £25,000 between years three and five to help with a child/grandchild's three years of university accommodation and subsistence costs, and £25,000 at some future point to help with a house deposit, wedding or such like for a child/grandchild.

Downsizing or relocating – an alternative worth exploring

You should also consider if there is a better way – for instance is downsizing a better option? See Chapter 11 (Your home) for some of the benefits of, potentially, a brand new home, new view, the right size, lower property running and maintenance costs, lower Council Tax/rates, manageable garden and proximity to the shops, facilities and services, which you assess that you need for the next phase in retirement. Against this, issues such as a smaller space and new neighbourhood can be considered together with the costs of buying and selling (which may include expensive stamp duty). Again, the money released may affect your state benefits.

Another factor to consider is whether it is better to downsize/rightsize at the present time rather than in the future and before you get too set in your ways. Perhaps the younger the better, as it may help with developing new social circles.

Alternatively you could look at relocating to a new area where property prices are cheaper and you can still have a similar size house, if 'size' is important to you but you still want to free up significant equity. The regional variations in house prices can be significant, especially if you are moving out of a sought-after area or high-price region.

> **Top tip**
>
> Why equity release when you can downsize/relocate and get a super new all-mod-cons living space with a nice new view and retain a big surplus to have fun with or pass on?

Property investments

With the advantage of more time available and perhaps some maintenance skills you can understand why property investment is on the radar in retirement planning. Plan it right and you may even have a bolt hole to go off to in the sun. But then key discussion points arise and the decision is not so clear. Things like minimizing your property tax bill in an era when the government has made successive attacks on the buy to let, deciding whether to use a letting agent or not, complying with all the red tape and avoiding 'tenants from hell'.

Remember that there are many players in this market – including mortgage lenders, mortgage brokers, developers, property syndicates and letting agents – and that most will know more than you at the start and all will want some of your money. Some even pay for your flights and travel expenses to visit property abroad, but be wary if they play on this in a subsequent high-pressure sales environment. Be careful – there is usually another day, another deal. For anyone thinking about property investment abroad, turn to the information in Chapter 11 (Home – see section 'Moving abroad: full-time or part-time') and cost out the full budget of running a second home abroad. For those looking to invest in the UK the must-have guide is David Lawrenson's best-selling property book *Successful Property Letting: How to make money in buy-to-let* (also view his website: www.lettingfocus.com). This will open your eyes to some of the issues touched upon here and will give you straight-forward and clear advice and information on this market. Armed with this and advice from friends and relatives who have invested in property, you might then be ready to put your toe in the water and start to explore this area.

Buy to let

Buy-to-let properties have become an increasingly challenging investment. The recent 'hits' taken by this sector include increased stamp duty on second homes and restrictions on the amount of mortgage interest that you can deduct if you are a higher-rate taxpayer. The other wider economic challenge is over the affordability of housing and whether this may prompt more/other action to supress house price increases. Up to 2018 the prospect of a capital gain has been one of the factors that property investors hoped for and, indeed, probably attained. Will this continue? Time will tell. After that it comes down to the numbers and factoring in the cost of finding tenants and managing the property if you decide to outsource these tasks to an agent. Then factor in your time in 'managing' the activity. Finally factor in the risk of you ending up with a 'tenant from hell' and being left with unpaid rent, damaged property and lots of stress. At the end of the day one of the key issues is the bottom-line 'yield' (income less costs as a percentage of the amount you invested in the property). How does this compare to investment returns that you can earn for little or no effort?

Furnished holiday lettings

Furnished holiday lettings at home or abroad – these still benefit from ample tax breaks and the stamp duty and interest caps do not presently apply. To get the tax breaks there are strict rules over the number of days that the property must be available for short-term lettings – the number of days actually let and restrictions to stop lettings of more than a month to one person counting towards short-term lettings. The invisible benefits are the availability of a holiday home for you to use when it is not let out and this can provide a lovely retirement lifestyle if you find the right property. Remember the golden rule of property: 'location, location, location'.

The total cost of maintaining and managing a property income can mount up and the budget planner in Chapter 11 (Homes) should be worked through if you are a first-time property investor.

Commercial property and a SIPP

Commercial property is another option and there is the bonus of a big tax break as it can be held as part of a self-invested personal pension (SIPP – see Chapter 4, Pensions) with the property, in turn, providing an investment and then income in retirement planning. This is significant as residential property cannot be held in a SIPP. Commercial property can, therefore, feature in the retirement and tax planning of individuals with sufficient SIPP funds and a knowledge or connection with business.

Property investment funds

Finally there are also property investment funds. When the economy is doing well there are more business tenants seeking space for their offices, shops and warehouses. If there is high demand then landlords can charge higher rents and investment funds that specialize in property tend to do well. If there is a recession the opposite happens. Investment funds are covered further below, but are mentioned here so you have an appreciation that there is another route into property where the charges are lower and the risk is spread.

Top tip

Fewer houses are being bought for buy to let due to a more challenging tax environment. The tax burdens on furnished holiday lettings are much less onerous (at the time of writing). Therefore, if you can achieve the conditions to qualify for the tax breaks on a furnished holiday letting this may give you a better investment yield and better retirement as it also gives you a holiday home.

Savings as part of your retirement planning

Money in savings and deposit accounts at banks has been earning minimal interest in recent years (maybe 1 per cent) and the value of funds held in banks is being eroded by inflation, which has been hovering around 2 per cent to 3 per cent. This has caused real pain to many who have led thrifty lives and saved for old age in traditional bank accounts. Savings play a critical role in the way that the whole economy works so we have seen positive government intervention in the increase in the Individual Savings Account (ISA) annual limit to £20,000. This allows savers to protect part of their wealth from Income Tax and Capital Gains Tax. Between a couple and over several years that can equate to a powerful tax-free fund that can help in retirement. The first £1,000 (£500 for higher-rate taxpayers) of interest and the first £2,000 in dividends (2018/19) will not be subject to Income Tax on your self-assessment return – another useful tax-planning tool.

Successful investing has never been easy, but for those who are interested in saving and investing for retirement, and for the long term, the principles remain the same. Martin Gorvett, Chartered Financial Planner of Lavender Financial Planners Ltd, explains the golden rules:

> Keep the costs down; shelter as much money from the tax office as you can; buy assets when they are cheap and sell when they are expensive (albeit that few people have the financial knowledge or crystal ball to really make a success of this but the motto, generally, is worth remembering). To be a successful investor

you have to be disciplined. You need to decide on a strategy, allocate your money to your investment accordingly, then stick with that through the ups and downs that the markets will inevitably bring. Remember, once a market has fallen, the stock it contains is 'on sale'. Equally when markets are at an all-time high, it could be overpriced (although markets will always continue to increase in value over the long term).

But there is a big difference between 'saving' and 'investing'. Investing is for the long term. It is money you can put away for your retirement, and in the long run it should grow more rapidly than in a savings account. If you are saving for a shorter-term goal, perhaps in less than five years, then you are looking to get the most interest paid on your money. Martin Gorvett provides more valuable insights and tips:

1 *Buy what is right for you and don't believe everything you read or hear.* Just because an investment works well for someone else doesn't necessarily mean it will be right for you. Social media promotions can be misleading. Ensure that the investment provider is regulated by the FCA; you don't have to wander off the beaten track just to avoid the herd.

2 *Diversify and don't put all your eggs in one basket.* Consider spreading your risk by diversifying across a mixture of asset classes, industry sectors and geographical areas. When the value of one asset is falling, another might be rising so could help to compensate.

3 *Invest for the long term.* Adopt a strategy and stick with it. Investing is not a matter of 'timing the market', it is about 'time in the market'. Similarly, try not to get emotionally attached to your investments. Review and rebalance your portfolio regularly to ensure you have not strayed from the original strategy.

4 *Take professional advice.* Investing is not free. Every avenue to market has a cost. Professional advisers will have a tried-and-tested process, often accessing institutional prices, rather than retail classes available to direct investors.

5 Lastly, *don't risk investing money that you cannot afford to lose.* Investments carry a huge caveat – you may get out less than you put in. So don't overstretch, stick within your means and know when to walk away.

Since everyone has different financial aims, there is no 'one-size-fits-all' approach to investing. In very simple terms, there are four different types of investment you could consider:

1 *Cash investments.* Made into a bank account or cash ISA. These are generally short term and offer easy access to your money and lower risk,

so the potential returns are much less than other types of investment. Your money is secure up to £85,000 (covered under the FSCS limits) but it could lose value due to tax on interest and if inflation rates exceed interest rates.

2 *Bonds and gilts*. Effectively, an IOU from the government or big companies. When you buy one you are lending money that earns an agreed fixed rate of interest. Government bonds (called gilts) are backed by the state and hopefully are as good as guaranteed. Corporate bonds carry greater risk in the event that the issuing company goes bust or cannot afford to repay you, but because of this element of risk they offer the possibility of improved returns.

3 *Investing in property*. Directly as a buy-to-let investor or as a furnished holiday-let investor or indirectly through certain investment funds. Property prices go down as well as up, and it can take time to sell property and get your cash back. Don't do anything without reading *Successful Property Letting: How to make money in buy-to-let*, by David Lawrenson (2017).

4 *Shares*. Sometimes referred to as 'equities', this basically means putting money on the stock market. You can do this by buying shares in individual companies or by investing through a professionally managed investment fund, such as a unit trust.

As a rule of thumb, some investors keep an emergency fund equal to at least three months' living costs. Once this sum is set aside you could consider investing for higher-potential returns.

Sources of investable funds

These are the sorts of places you usually find funds to invest:

- *Long-term savings* built up out of excess income over expenditure.
- *Commuted lump sum/25 per cent tax free from your pension*: one-quarter of your pension can be taken as a tax-free lump sum. The remainder will then be paid out subject to the ordinary rates of Income Tax.
- *Insurance policies (such as endowment policies)*: designed to mature on or near your date of retirement. These are normally tax free.
- *Profits on your home*: if you sell it and downsize or relocate to less expensive accommodation. Provided this is your main home, there is no Capital Gains Tax to pay.
- *Redundancy money, golden handshake or other farewell gift from your employer*: currently you are allowed £30,000 redundancy money free of tax.

- *Sale of SAYE and other share option schemes*: the tax rules vary according to the type of scheme and the rules are liable to change with each Budget statement.

- *Inheritance or a big lottery/premium bond win*: self-explanatory!

General investment strategy

Investments differ in their aims, their tax treatment and your tax objectives and the amount of risk involved. Your investments should be tailored to provide either income to supplement your pension or capital appreciation to build up over time for the longer term, or a mix of both depending on your needs and the products you are likely to encounter, as outlined below.

National Savings and Investments (NS&I)

The main reason for saving with National Savings and Investments is that they are secure as they are backed by HM Treasury and if that institution goes bust we may as well all pack up.

NS&I investments include:

- *Investment accounts*. This is an easy way to build up your savings, with instant access to your money (up to £1 million per person) and the option to save regularly by standing order.

- *Guaranteed income bonds and guaranteed growth bonds*. Useful if you can leave your money invested for a year or longer in return for a higher rate of interest. The maximum is £1 million per issue, per person.

- *Direct ISA*. Interest is tax free.

- *Premium bonds*. The maximum amount that can be saved into premium bonds is £50,000. Prizes range from £25 per month to £1 million. Prizes are paid out tax free every month. The rate used to calculate the prize fund is currently (as of summer 2018) 1.4 per cent. The 'fun' of investing up to £50,000 per person in premium bonds provides a tax-free 'average' return that beats many routine savings accounts (but you may do better in ISAs and if you shop around); you can get a return of the capital within days (so it is easy to access, if need be) and you may even win £1 million – but the odds are 36 billion to 1 (and 24,500 to 1 for the smallest prize of £25) for winning in one month.

See www.nsandi.com for more on this.

Top tip

For those with very large savings who don't wish to carve up their funds into **£85,000** blocks for FSCS protection NS&I is attractive as it is backed by HM Treasury.

Variable interest accounts

The accounts include instant access accounts, high-interest accounts and fixed-term savings accounts. Should the bank or building society get into serious financial difficulty up to £85,000 (double that if in joint names) of your money will be 100 per cent protected under the FSCS and the cover can increase for up to six months to £1 million to cover certain life events (for instance moving home). Visit www.fscs.org.uk for more information.

For 2018/19 the first £1,000 of interest earned is tax free, reducing to £500 for higher-rate taxpayers and £0 for additional-rate taxpayers. If you only have State Pension income and bank interest in 2018/19 remember you don't pay Income Tax in 2018/19 until you have more than about £9,350 in savings interest. This is estimated by adding the personal allowance at £11,850, the £5,000 starting savings allowance and the personal savings allowance at £1,000 to give a total of £17,850. Then deduct the State Pension of about £8,500 (it could be more, so adapt to your own figure), which gives £9,350. If you largely rely on your savings income and believe you are or have been paying excess tax you can reclaim this from HMRC using form R40 or reclaim it through self-assessment.

Top tip

If your funds are not with NS&I (see above) and you have more than **£85,000** you should split your savings across different banks for **100** per cent safety of your funds via the FSCS. Remember the limit can increase for up to six months to **£1** million to cover certain life events. Find out more at www.fscs.org.uk, where you can also check out banks and their different brands.

Fixed-interest securities

Gilt-edged securities

Gilts, or gilt-edged securities, are bonds issued by the UK government that offer the investor a fixed interest rate for a predetermined set time, rather than a rate that goes up or down with inflation. You can either retain them until their maturity date, in which case the government will return the capital in full, or sell them on the London Stock Exchange at market value. Index-linked gilts are government-issued bonds – glorified IOUs – that you can buy to obtain a guaranteed rate of return over inflation. Gilt interest is paid gross (before tax). No Capital Gains Tax is charged on any profit you may have made, but equally no relief is allowed for any loss. The government guarantees the payment of interest and the repayment of the capital sum.

Permanent interest-bearing shares (PIBSs)

These are a form of investment offered by some building societies to financial institutions and private investors as a means of raising share capital. They have several features in common with gilts, including a fixed rate of interest that is set at the date of issue. The interest is usually paid twice yearly; there is no Stamp Duty to pay or Capital Gains Tax on profits. Despite the fact that PIBSs are issued by building societies, they are very different from normal building society investments. In the event of any losses PIBSs are not covered by the FSCS.

Equities and some other investments

These are mainly stocks and shares, purchased in different ways and involving varying degrees of risk. They can achieve capital appreciation as well as give you some regular income. Equities include unit trusts, open-ended investment companies (OEICs), ordinary shares, investment trusts and real estate investment trusts (REITs).

Unit trusts and OEICs

Unit trusts and OEICs are forms of shared investments, or funds, which allow you to pool your money with thousands of other people and invest in world stock markets. They are simple to understand, you get professional management, there are no day-to-day decisions to make and they invest in a broader spread of shares so that your risk is reduced. The minimum investment in some of the more popular funds can be as little as £25 per month or a £500 lump sum. Investors' contributions to the fund are divided into 'units' (and the term is changed to 'shares' in OEICs) in proportion to the amount invested. As with ordinary shares, you can sell all or some of your investment. The key differences between the two are:

1 *Pricing*: when investing in unit trusts, you buy units at the 'offer price' and sell at the lower 'bid price'. The difference in the two prices is known as the spread. An OEIC fund, contrastingly, has a single price, directly linked to the value of the fund's underlying investments. All shares are bought and sold at this single price.

2 *Flexibility*: an OEIC fund offers different types of share or sub-fund to suit different types of investor. The expertise of different fund management teams can be combined to benefit both large and small investors. There is less paperwork as each OEIC will produce one report and accounts for all sub-funds.

3 *Complexity*: unit trusts are, legally, more complex, which is one of the reasons for their rapid conversion to OEICs. Unit trusts allow an investor to participate in the assets of the trust without actually owning any. Investors in an OEIC buy shares in that investment company.

4 *Management*: with unit trusts, the fund's assets are protected by an independent trustee and managed by a fund manager. OEICs are protected by an independent depository and managed by an authorized corporate director.

5 *Charges*: unit trusts and OEICs usually have an upfront buying charge, typically 3–5 per cent, and an annual management fee of between 0.5 and 1.5 per cent. It is possible to reduce these charges by investing through a discount broker or fund supermarket, but this means acting without financial advice. Charges on OEICs are relatively transparent, shown as a separate item on your transaction statement

Investment trusts

One of the biggest benefits that investment trusts offer is to income investors. While open-ended funds must pay out all the income they receive, investment trusts can hold some back in reserve. This allows them to offer a smoother and more certain return. There are four major advantages that an investment trust has over a unit trust or OEIC:

- *Cost*: the initial charges on unit trusts typically range from 4 to 6 per cent but there is also the annual fee costing in the region of 1.5 to 2 per cent. An investment trust also levies annual fees, but on average they are lower because most investment trusts do not pay commission to financial advisers.

- *Gearing*: like other companies, investment trusts are fairly free to borrow for investment purposes. Unit trusts, however, are usually restricted by regulation. But when markets are rising and the trust is run well, gearing will deliver superior returns.

- *Size*: investment trusts tend to be smaller than unit trusts on average, and so are less unwieldy and more focused on their investment objectives. To grow beyond their initial remit, they need permission from shareholders. Many also have a fixed life expectancy. Conversely, unit trusts are called 'open ended' because they can expand and contract to meet demand – 'big' is not always beautiful.

- *Discounts*: because their shares are listed and traded freely (unlike a unit trust), investment trusts can end up with a market capitalization that is greater than (at a 'premium') or lower than (at a 'discount') its assets under management (the 'net asset value', or NAV).

Ordinary shares listed on the London Stock Exchange

Public companies issue shares as a way of raising money. When you buy shares and become a shareholder in a company, you own a small part of the business and are entitled to participate in its profits through a dividend, which is paid annually or a few times a year. It is possible that in a bad year no dividends at all will be paid. The money you invest is unsecured. This is vital and means that, quite apart from any dividends, your capital could be reduced in value – or if the company goes bust you could lose the lot. The value of a company's shares is decided by the stock market. The price of a share fluctuates daily. Stockbrokers will buy or sell the shares on your behalf and you will be charged both commission (which can be as low as £15 a trade) and Stamp Duty (the latter is currently 0.5 per cent).

Currently in 2018/19 an individual can receive £2,000 of dividend income tax free. A special Income Tax rate of 7.5 per cent is payable through your self-assessment if further dividend income takes you beyond £13,850 of income (personal allowance of £11,850 and dividend allowance of £2,000).

This increases to 32.5 per cent if it falls in the higher-rate tax band and then increases further to 38.1 per cent if it falls in the additional-rate tax band.

Top tip

An important wealth warning on shares – the financial pages of the Sunday newspapers carry regular stories about investors who have been scammed into buying worthless shares traded on some obscure stock exchange. Don't be caught out by the scammers – read Chapter 8.

Individual Savings Account (ISA)

An Individual Savings Accounts ('ISA') is a 'tax wrapper' that holds cash or investments and the effect of the 'wrapper' is to provide significant tax breaks. It shields the cash and investments so you do not pay any Income Tax on the interest or Capital Gains Tax on the profits you make. They are not, however, tax free on death and could be subject to the 40 per cent Inheritance Tax charge if the estate is above tax-exempt levels.

Shop around for the best rates and take full advantage of your annual allowance. You can currently (2018/19) put up to £20,000 into an ISA. Some ISAs are 'flexible', which allow you to replace money that you take out of your ISA, without eroding your £20,000 allowance – only if you do so within the same tax year.

On death your spouse will inherit an Additional Permitted Subscription (APS) allowance equal to the value of your ISA. This may help your tax-free funds remain so for your spouse. The APS does not apply to ISAs passed to children on death.

Top tip

It is usually easier to protect your pension from Inheritance Tax on any wealth being passed down to children. Therefore, if you expect Inheritance Tax on your estate, it may be better to live off your ISAs than pensions so that more is left in a pension to pass on tax efficiently. Some pensions may not have been set up in a manner that allows this so professional advice is usually recommended to help understand and leverage this tax-planning opportunity.

> **Top tip**
>
> If IHT planning is driving your ISA investment decisions you may be able to avoid your ISA savings being subject to IHT on your death by investing in Alternative Investment Market ('AIM') shares within your ISA that specifically meet a niche tax exemption called Business Property Relief (BPR). This is about as complex as this chapter gets but it illustrates a point as shares that qualify for BPR fall outside of the scope of Inheritance Tax as long as the shares have been held for at least two years, and are still held at the time of death. This is a bit niche and is a higher-risk investment but it offers a window to leave ISA funds to beneficiaries free from IHT (albeit remember that funds passing on death to a spouse are exempt from IHT – more on this in Chapter 6 (Tax)).

Help-to-buy ISA

These accounts are available from banks and building societies and can be opened by individuals who are at least 16 years old and, generally, they offer decent rates of interest that are in a 'tax wrapper' so the interest is tax free. Help-to-buy ISAs are available to prospective first-time buyers purchasing properties in the United Kingdom and are only paid when purchasing the first home (on purchases up to £250,000 outside London and £450,000 in London). Deposits can then be made of up to £1,200 when the account is opened followed by deposits up to £200 each month and can continue saving until December 2029. The big benefit of help-to-buy ISAs is that the government boosts the young person's savings by 25 per cent, ie £50 for every £200 saved. So free cash, which always gets the attention. The maximum free cash bonus is £3,000 on £12,000 of savings. You can transfer from the help-to-buy ISA to the LISA providing you meet the LISA conditions (aged 18 to 40) and you are also free to transfer it to another provider.

Lifetime Individual Savings Account (LISA)

A new Lifetime ISA (LISA) is another 'tax wrapper' that became available from April 2017 and offers those under 40 a savings device where interest is tax free and there is no Capital Gains Tax on the growth of investments. Provided you start a LISA before 40 years old you can then keep saving into it until you hit 50. The big reason to take out a LISA is the government will give you up to £1,000 of free cash every year, but there are significant restrictions on what you can spend the LISA funds on. Here is how it works. You can save up to £4,000 a year either by a lump sum or saving regular amounts and the government will then add 25 per cent as free cash into the fund. The restrictions are fairly simple as the LISA can only be used for either a pension after age 60 or savings towards a first home. Significantly the property can cost up to £450,000 across the UK so there is no outside London cap of £250,000 as found in the help-to-buy ISA.

If one of the two events does not happen and you draw out the funds you will lose the free cash and may receive less than you initially invested, although there are allowances to retain the bonus if you die or are terminally ill. You are free to transfer it to another provider and you are allowed to split the overall ISA limit of £20,000 for 2018/19 between an ISA and a LISA (LISA up to £4,000). You can have a LISA and a help-to-buy ISA but you cannot get the first-time-buyer's bonus on both, although you could, for instance, use the help-to-buy ISA on a home and then retain the LISA for retirement. As outlined in Chapter 4 (Pensions), a downside on pensions planning through a LISA is that better tax relief can currently be obtained by higher- and additional-rate tax payers using traditional pensions. But the biggest challenge is finding a financial company or bank that actually sells these products.

Top tip

LISAs seem attractive at first glance for the under 40s looking to plan their retirement but better tax relief can currently be obtained by higher- and additional-rate taxpayers using traditional pensions. The LISA is better than a help-to-buy ISA for properties between £250,000 and £450,000 outside London.

Enterprise Investment Scheme, Seed Enterprise Investment Scheme, venture capital trusts and social investment

Unquoted companies (ie those whose shares are not traded on a recognized stock exchange) can face problems when trying to raise finance. The Enterprise Investment Scheme (EIS) and Seed Enterprise Investment Scheme (SEIS) offer tax relief at 30 per cent and 50 per cent respectively, and for amounts up to £1 million and £100,000 respectively if the shares are held for three years. The risk level of such investments is high and specialist advice and recommendations should be secured before venturing down this path, albeit the tax breaks prove enticing to some with the appropriate risk attitude and, perhaps, with specialist knowledge of the business concerned (perhaps through family or other connections).

Another variant is venture capital trusts (VCTs), where tax relief can be secured at 30 per cent on new shares up to £200,000 in any tax year providing the shares are held for five years.

A final variant is social investment tax relief, which helps social enterprises raise finance by offering tax relief to investors. These can be set up by community interest companies and charities and offer investors 30 per cent tax relief and Capital Gains Tax breaks.

Martin Gorvett, Chartered Financial Planner, explains more:

With restrictions on the amount of tax relief available to investors through pensions (£40,000 per annum) and ISAs (£20,000), the use of EISs/VCTs/SEISs has become more mainstream for higher-rate and additional-rate taxpayers. These products should be approached with your eyes wide open. You are getting tax relief for a reason. They are high-risk investments by their very nature and should be approached on their risk merits, rather than the tax relief available.

SEISs carry the highest of risk. That is why you get 50 per cent tax relief. Next EISs, with 30 per cent after three years. Finally, VCTs offer 30 per cent relief but over five years, taking more time to achieve profit status. Once the tax-relief period has expired, ditch them or reinvest for more relief. Don't let inertia sink in. Some products reduce risk by the investment choices they make, such as solar power, renewable energy and 'peer to peer' lending. They are worth researching.

How do you tell which will succeed and which will fail? In short you can't. Expect one-third of your investment to fail, one-third to do nothing and one-third to do well. It is the latter third that makes up the return you achieve. Alternatively, seek the use of EIS/VCT/SEIS platforms where significant due diligence has already been completed. Don't be tempted by online crowdfunding-type operations, these 'opportunities' tend to be the ones that the professionals have already discounted. Tread carefully, take advice and invest within your means.

Top tip

Are EISs, SEISs and VCTs 'dodgy' and a sort of tax avoidance? No. Chapter 6 (Tax) defines tax 'evasion' and tax 'avoidance' but here we have an example of 'tax planning'. Put simply, the government has designed the tax-break structure of these schemes to incentivize investors to take a punt on more speculative investments. Some may come off and some will fail and you may lose everything. Each will set out the risks and, if in doubt, stay out and always take professional advice. The FSCS does not cover losses due to financial performance.

Entrepreneurs relief

Further tax breaks are also available under entrepreneurs relief, which enables a low 10 per cent Capital Gains Tax rate on selling shares in, for instance, a family company. These were previously only available to employees and officers of a company who held more than 5 per cent of shares for more than three years before selling them for a gain. The relief has now been extended to include external investors. Martin Gorvett also has some thoughts on entrepreneurs relief:

As a business owner entrepreneurs relief is your new best friend. It allows you to sell a trading business and avoid high taxes on the value you extract. Just don't leave the decision too late. Shares in an unlisted business are also inheritance efficient if held for more than two years. Make sure you remember to at least consider re-entering the arena in later life.

Investing for your child/grandchild

Children without any other form of income don't pay Income Tax in 2018/19 until they earn more than £17,850 in savings interest. This is the personal allowance at £11,850, the £5,000 starting savings allowance and the personal savings allowance at £1,000 all added together.

To deter parents from giving away cash to children to reduce the parent's Income Tax on savings there is a basic tax rule where money given by a parent or step-parent that generates more than £100 per year in interest is taxed at the parent's tax rate. The interest on money deposited by grandparents is not caught by this rule and parents saving into a Junior ISA avoid this potential tax trap as it is tax free.

Children's savings account

All you need to set this up is the child's birth certificate. Interest rates are currently as high as 4 to 6 per cent if you shop around, as the banks are keen to sign up new potential customers as early as possible.

Junior ISA (JISA)

You can currently save up to £4,260 a year into a JISA (2018/19). The child can take control of the account at 16 but cannot access the fund until 18 when it is usually converted to an adult ISA. There is both a cash variant and a stocks and shares variant of the JISA and both can share the one annual limit. The interest is tax free so the £100 parent's tax-rate rule does not apply.

Child trust funds (CTFs)

All babies born between September 2002 and 2 January 2011 got £500 or more free from the government to save in a CTF. Children born after December 2010 are not eligible for a CTF. However, accounts set up for eligible children will continue to benefit from tax-free investment growth and you can still add £4,260 a year tax free. Withdrawals will not be possible until the child reaches 18. These are now a defunct product and with less competition the interest rates tend not to be as good as a JISA (which you can switch to).

Pension

For really long-term saving, pay into a pension. Your grandchild takes control at 18, but can only access the money aged 55. Tax relief currently applies so the government will top up a payment of £2,880 to the limit of £3,600.

Martin Gorvett says:

> What better way to teach your child about the value of long-term savings. If you start a pension for them early enough, the effect of compound growth will give them a huge step up the retirement savings ladder when they themselves begin to focus on their own financial future.

Help-to-buy ISA

Once they are 16, set up a help-to-buy ISA to access the generous bonus paid, which can be put towards a first house (see above for more on help-to-buy ISAs).

LISA

Once they are 18 think about setting up a Lifetime Individual Savings Account instead of or together with a help-to-buy ISA to access the generous bonus paid, which can be put towards a first house or retirement (see above for more on LISAs).

Long-term lock-ups

Certain types of investment, mostly offered by insurance companies, provide fairly high guaranteed growth in exchange for your undertaking to leave a lump sum with them or to pay regular premiums for a fixed period, usually five years or longer.

Bonds

The London Stock Exchange operates a retail bond platform designed to make trading corporate bonds as easy as trading listed shares. Bonds generally offer less opportunity for capital growth but they tend to be lower risk as they are less exposed to stock-market volatility, and they have the advantage of producing a regular guaranteed income. The two main types of bonds are:

Gilts These are government bonds, and were explained earlier in this chapter. They are the least risky. They are secured by the government, which guarantees both the interest payable and the return of your capital in full if you hold the stocks until their maturity.

Corporate bonds These are fairly similar to gilts except that you are lending to a large company rather than owning a piece of it, as you do with an equity. The company has to repay the loan at some point, known as the bond's redemption date. It will pay out the 'face value' of the bond and the company also has to pay interest on the loan, known as the 'coupon' – generally the coupon rates are far superior to bank interest but you are running a much higher risk. After they are issued, bonds trade in the secondary market, just like shares. Most bonds have a fixed income; the longer the time to maturity, the more sensitive the bond is to changes in interest rates. One reason to hold bonds is for a good rate of income. The main risks arise from increases in UK interest rates (leaving you behind on a fixed but low rate of interest), as well as credit risk, which means if the company goes bust you may lose the lot.

Investment bonds

Not to be confused with debt-based investments, investment bonds are tax wrappers rather than specific investment instruments. They are a method of investing a lump sum with an insurance company over the long term.

Available in both onshore and offshore variants, both offer life assurance cover as part of the deal, although this is usually only 101 per cent of the fund value at time of death.

The underlying investment of any type of investment bond will be retail unit trusts and OEICs – similar to those available under ISA or SIPP wrappers. The manager/adviser will be able to tailor the investment strategy to meet your risk/reward requirements. They are generally used to produce long-term capital growth and can generate regular (tax deferred) income.

The tax position of an investment bond depends on whether it is onshore or offshore. Whilst both types can offer the investor withdrawals of up to 5 per cent of the initial investment each year, without creating a liability to tax, the amount drawn does remain restricted to the value of the original investment and can therefore be deemed to reduce in line with inflation each year.

Onshore investment bonds are subject to a special rate of Corporation Tax on any growth or income within the bond so basic-rate taxpayers are deemed to have no further liability on surrender or encashment (known as a chargeable event).

Any further tax liability for higher- and top-rate taxpayers is calculated using complicated 'top slicing' rules – where, in short, the overall growth is annualized and then assessed alongside the recipient's other income for the tax year in question. If this pushes the recipient into the higher-rate threshold or top rate of tax threshold, further tax will be due.

Offshore investment bonds, on the other hand, are only subject to a nominal withholding tax, so all investors will be subject to tax at their marginal rate on any growth achieved on repatriation of the funds to the United Kingdom – including the value of the permitted 5 per cent withdrawals drawn, which are added back in.

Any increase on an investment bond is subject to Income Tax and therefore your Personal Allowance can be used to reduce any tax payable but your Capital Gains Allowance cannot be used to offset tax.

There has been much interest in offshore bonds from high earners looking for an alternative to pensions for their retirement savings. These can provide significant tax savings because of the 5 per cent withdrawals, with no immediate tax to pay. Ongoing charges for offshore bonds are high – typically an extra 0.4 per cent per annum in addition to usual investment costs. Professional adviser charges on top mean that bonds are generally best for investments greater than £100,000.

It should also be noted that any ongoing professional adviser charges deducted from the bond will either create a chargeable event each year, or reduce your 5 per cent withdrawals. So a bond with a 1 per cent annual fee will only provide net 4 per cent withdrawals.

Martin Gorvett says:

> Investment bonds may seem friendly on the outside but they can pack a tax punch if not regularly reviewed by a professional adviser. Don't let investment inertia settle in. They are not tax free (but are often promoted as such), they are tax deferred. Returns in your hands are net of special rate of Corporation Tax. It may be that when other income ceases, freeing up your personal and basic rate allowances, investment returns 'live' to tax may offer greater 'net' returns.

Professional advice will pay dividends here. Reviewing your investment bonds can be like wading through a tar pit. Warning: drawing more than the 5 per cent per annum may cause the relevant year's part of the 'top slice' calculation to be reset to zero, causing otherwise unnecessary tax to be levied. Also, if the total gain in any one tax year pushes the investor's income from other sources above £100,000 the tax consequences could be significant once the loss of the Personal Allowance is factored in if your income falls in the tax 'kill zone', which is mentioned in Chapter 6.

Structured products

A structured product is a fixed-term investment where the payout depends on the performance of something else, typically a stock-market index (eg FTSE 100 or S&P 500). They are complex and can carry hidden risk because they can appear on the surface to be an alternative to cash.

There are two main types of structured product – structured deposit and structured investments:

- *Structured deposits* are savings accounts but they are not cash based. The rate of interest (or rate of annual return) provided depends on how the underlying stock-market index performs. So if the stock-market index rises you receive a predetermined rate of interest; if it falls you get nothing.

- *Structured investments* offer either an annual rate of return or a return over a fixed term. They are typically comprised of two underlying investments, one designed to protect your capital and another to provide the bonus/'kicker'. The return you get will be stated at the outset and will depend on how the underlying stock-market index performs. If it performs badly, or the counterparty (the company providing the stated return) fails, you may lose some or all of your original investment.

Be careful to peel back the label on these investments. The use of the word 'guaranteed' in the literature does not mean what you may first think! It means you are 'guaranteed' to get the returns stated *only* if the stock-market index performs as required in the product's terms and conditions – noting that fees and charges may ultimately mean you get back less than you put in. Professional advice would be recommended for anyone seeking to make this type of investment.

Protection products

Protection products in financial services have been designed to pay out in the event of death, serious illness or accident. Different products have different names, costs and eligibility criteria, and a knowledge of the main ones may help you shore up your protection.

Life assurance policies and endowments

Life assurance can provide you with one of two main benefits: it can either provide your successors with money when you die or it can be used as a savings plan to provide you with a lump sum (or income) on a fixed date. There are three basic types of life assurance: whole-life policies, term policies and endowment policies:

- *Whole-life policies* are designed to pay out on your death. You pay a premium every year and, when you die, your beneficiaries receive the money. With some policies you can stop when you reach a certain age.

- *Term policies* involve a definite commitment. As opposed to paying premiums every year, you elect to make regular payments for an agreed period, for example until such time as your children have completed their education or other important life event such as retirement, or for when you pay off your mortgage. If you die during this period, your family will be paid the agreed sum in full. If you die after the end of the term (when you have stopped making payments) your family will normally receive nothing.

- *Endowment policies* are savings products with some life cover. You pay regular premiums over a number of years and in exchange receive a lump sum on a specific date, which could be from 10 to 25 years.

An important feature of endowment policies is that they are linked to death cover. If you die before the policy matures, the remaining payments are excused and your successors will be paid a lump sum on your death. The amount of money you stand to receive, however, can vary hugely, depending on the charges and how generous a bonus the insurance company feels it can afford on the policy's maturity. If you wish to surrender an endowment policy before the date of the agreement you can request a 'surrender value' from the product provider, but shop around as you may be able to sell the policy for a sum that is higher than its surrender value. See the Association of Policy Market Makers (www.apmm.org).

Both whole-life policies and endowment policies offer three basic options:

- *Without profits*: sometimes known as 'guaranteed sum assured'. The insurance company guarantees you a specific fixed sum, you know the amount in advance and this is the sum you – or your successors – will be paid.

- *With profits*: you are paid a guaranteed fixed sum plus an addition, based on the profits that the insurance company has made by investing your annual or monthly payments. The basic premiums are higher and the profits element is not known in advance.

- *Unit linked*: a refinement of the 'with profits' policy, in that the investment element of the policy is linked in with a unit trust.

The size of premium varies depending on the type of policy you choose, the amount of cover you want and any health underwriting that may be required (medical checks may be involved). Under current legislation, the proceeds of a qualifying policy – whether taken as a lump sum or in regular income payments – are free of all tax.

Top tip

If you have assets above £325,000 and potentially another £175,000, if you have a house being left to a child (more in Chapter 6 – Tax), you may be able to avoid significant Inheritance Tax by having your life insurance policy or endowment written into a trust so that the payment falls outside your estate on death. Instead payment will be made to the trustees to distribute to the beneficiaries of the trust. Your solicitor or financial adviser should be able to arrange this for very little cost.

Income protection and critical illness benefit

These can assist if you are still earning and do not have sick pay from your employer as they will pay a monthly income (income protection) or lump sum (critical illness benefit) if you suffer a serious illness and/or cannot work due to a serious illness. There may be age restrictions, although cover can last to 75 with some providers, and medical screening questions will be required. If you have a challenging health history the premiums will increase. In return for regular monthly premiums it may provide added peace of mind. If you stop paying the premiums the cover stops. The payments you receive are normally tax free under the current rules.

Simple accident protection

This cover usually is very restricted in the events it will pay out for but it can give some peace of mind in the event of an accidental injury. It is fairly cheap, can be arranged with immediate effect and you may find insurers who will cover you up to 81 years of age. It does not require you to attend a medical and no medical questions are asked, although UK providers do usually require your main place of residence to be in the UK. It is often overlooked but in the event of an accident and injury or death it could provide you or your partner with vital funds at a time of need.

Investor protection

Most financial transactions involving banks, investments, pensions and insurance take place without any problems but sometimes things go wrong. This is where the UK's regulatory regime steps in. This is covered in Chapter 3 and, as it is vitally important to your protection, part of that chapter is repeated here.

The **Financial Conduct Authority (FCA)** is accountable to the Treasury and aims to make sure the UK financial markets work well so that consumers get a fair deal. It registers individuals and companies that are suitable to work in the industry, checks that they are doing their job properly and fines them if they do a bad job. The FCA has a range of helpful guides and factsheets to help consumers understand the UK financial markets and the role of the FCA (www.fca.org.uk).

The **Financial Ombudsman Service (FOS)** is a free service set up by law with the power to sort out problems between consumers and registered financial businesses. It is an impartial service and will investigate your complaint if you have been unable to resolve matters with the registered individual or company (ie registered with the FCA, as above). If the ombudsman considers the complaint justified it can award compensation (www.financial-ombudsman.org.uk).

The **Financial Services Compensation Scheme (FSCS)** is the body that can pay you compensation if your financial services provider goes bust. The FSCS is independent and free to access. The financial services industry funds the FSCS and the compensation it pays. There are limits on how much compensation it pays and these are different for different types of financial products. To be eligible for compensation the person or company must have been registered by the FCA (www.fscs.org.uk).

Building your good retirement plan

There are plenty of hints and tips in this chapter and hopefully your own good retirement plan at the end of the book is now starting to build up as you read through the 'plan more' sections of this book. We deal more with tax and tax planning in Chapter 6 (Tax) but you will have seen already that pensions, savings and tax are all interlinked and can help you save more, live better and be happier. As we draw this chapter to a close the final note is about being more investment and tax savvy in your retirement. Martin Gorvett concludes:

> There are plenty of allowances for you to utilize to create 'tax-free' income in retirement. Indeed, these can be doubled if you involve your spouse in the planning phase. You each have a Personal Allowance of £11,850, a savings allowance of £1,000 (£500), the dividend allowance of £2,000 and a Capital Gains Tax Allowance of £11,700 (all are 2018/19 amounts). This is £26,550 each a year, doubled to £53,100 per annum if planned correctly between two people. When you add in the tax-free element of your pension (25 per cent of the fund value), investment bond withdrawals of 5 per cent (or original capital) and income from your ISA (tax free), the payment of tax in retirement could be a preventable obligation with an investment in knowledge and planning.

Useful reading

How the Stock Market Works (2017) by Michael Becket of the *Daily Telegraph*, published by Kogan Page

Money Advice Service: www.moneyadviceservice.org.uk

Inspired? Remember to fill in your plan for a good retirement at the end of the book.

CHAPTER SIX

Tax

I like to pay taxes. With them I buy civilization.

OLIVER WENDELL HOLMES JR

Benjamin Franklin said the only things certain in life are death and taxes. So there is no avoiding this chapter, especially as tax in the UK is unnecessarily complicated and, therefore, it is a tough job making sense of it all. Readers who work their way through the chapter will find key information on retirement and tax planning and this knowledge will give you an advantage and you will save more, live better and be happier.

The UK tax rulebook is now – wait for it – 12 times the length of the Bible and has reached over 20,000 pages. We have the most complex tax system in the world and successive governments just accept it. Surely there is a better way? In the meantime 'it is what it is', so let's start with the four basics.

First, taxes are necessary. Oliver Wendell Holmes Jr (one of the most widely cited US Supreme Court Justices) famously said 'I like to pay taxes. With them I buy civilization.' Surely very few would want to disown the schooling, roads, health service, security and rescue services that our taxes pay for (in one way or another).

Second, we currently have a low-interest-rate environment and, therefore, financing your retirement from savings has been difficult ground on which to find crumbs of comfort. However, there has been some good news in recent budgets for savers and pensioners. Tax reliefs on interest and dividends have been introduced for most people; the tax-free limit on ISAs has risen to £20,000 per annum and there is the new Lifetime ISA (LISA) introduced in

April 2017 for adults aged under 40. There is also some useful tax-free money for those earning £1,000 or less from a small business or property letting. Also, recent changes in Inheritance Tax (IHT) mean that only a small minority of married couples will end up with the massive 40 per cent tax charge eating into their estates.

Third, the biggest tax opportunity lies in the world of pensions and flattening your tax bands by deferring income received today to some point in the future – too many people miss this point or find out too late. Allied to the third point are the benefits now being gained from new and significant access arrangements on defined contribution pension schemes.

The problem, and worth repeating, is simply that the UK has the longest tax book in the world and, therefore, tax knowledge and planning remains essential and saves you money. This is not 'dodgy' – it is simply knowing the rules and applying them.

Finally there is the problem of tax evasion, which you can always remember because E is for evasion, which is 'E-legal' (got it – 'illegal'). That is the work of the tradesperson who takes cash above £1,000 and does not declare it to the taxman. It is also the individual who forgets that the reason they had a few flights to some offshore tax jurisdiction was to hide money away to try to evade tax on the interest they were earning. HMRC's own definition of tax evasion is: 'When people or businesses deliberately do not pay the taxes that they owe' (source: www.gov.uk).

Another term to explain upfront is 'tax avoidance' and this is HMRC's own definition:

> Bending the rules of the tax system to gain a tax advantage that Parliament never intended. It often involves contrived, artificial transactions that serve little or no purpose other than to produce tax advantage. It involves operating within the letter – but not the spirit – of the law.

It is the person who resides in the UK and takes an income and routes it round the world, writes it off through loans and puts it in and out of trusts and (somehow?) ends up spending the very same money in the UK and pays little or no tax. Hey presto, there is a rich lifestyle and no tax paid. The individual concerned would probably dismiss Oliver Wendell Holmes Jr's quote at the head of this chapter, while still enjoying the free benefits their society provides. HMRC is targeting this sort of person with increased resources and commitment (and powers) – more later.

Importantly, this chapter is only a guide and it is neither legal nor taxation advice. Any potential tax advantages may be subject to change from the time of writing (summer 2018) and will depend upon your individual circumstances, so individual professional advice should be obtained. The information outlined in this chapter may, however, assist you in understanding some of the issues you may face and the terminology used, helping you in planning for and achieving a more financially rewarding retirement.

This chapter at a glance

- The main Income Tax bands for zero tax, basic rate 20 per cent tax, higher rate (40 per cent) and upper rate (45 per cent) are explained (as are the small differences in tax bands now used in Scotland). National Insurance, Inheritance Tax (IHT) and Capital Gains Tax are explained and the way they interact is outlined. This will help you get a better understanding of the issues and impact of tax planning in the world's most complex tax regime.

- Potential opportunities are outlined to help you understand and then consider with professional help the use of your pension allowances to contribute to your pension pot and receive extra Income Tax relief. But be careful about drawing down your pension pot too early as once you access the private pension pot there are rules that may restrict tax relief to only £4,000 of contributions a year. This is to stop people recycling pension withdrawals and getting double tax relief.

- Reminders that you cannot access pension pots before the age of 55 without incurring massive tax penalties, so beware of anyone who says you can. Ensure any adviser is registered with the Financial Conduct Authority (FCA) and call the FCA to check that they are, indeed, registered.

- For 2018/19 'big earners', the loss of your tax-free Personal Allowance is explained if your income is between £100,000 and £123,700. This is the tax 'kill zone' where income is effectively taxed at 60 per cent due to the gradual loss of the personal allowance. But did you know that you can shift the tax to being taxed at less than 20 per cent if you make the appropriate pension contributions?

- If you do not use your £20,000 ISA allowance by 5 April 2019 the tax shelter for that amount will be lost forever. If you have a spouse or civil partner the amount doubles. So open up and start funding your 2019/20 ISA and you can start saving more tax from 6 April 2019.

- Use Capital Gains Tax breaks if you have shares or assets that have soared in value by selling some that have gained by £11,700 by 5 April

2019 without paying tax on the gain. This is especially important on shares that are not 'protected' from tax by one of the special tax wrappers (like an ISA or SIPP). Consider selling them and using the proceeds to fund an ISA, LISA (if eligible) or SIPP.

- Reduce your Inheritance Tax (IHT) liability by gifting using the reliefs set out in this chapter. Larger gifts are normally IHT-free if the giver survives a further seven years. Watch out for Capital Gains Tax on the giver if they have made a large gain at the date they give the asset away (over its original cost or value at 31 March 1982). New IHT rules can allow the IHT limit to increase from £650,000 to £1 million when a house is involved and money is left to your children.

- Tax reliefs allow you £2,000 of dividend Income Tax-free and £1,000 of interest tax free (for basic-rate taxpayers and for higher-rate taxpayers the amount reduces to £500 and nil for upper-rate taxpayers). If married or in a civil partnership you should consider how best to structure who holds investments and bank deposits.

- If you are both basic-rate taxpayers you may be able to transfer part of your Personal Allowance to make you jointly more 'tax efficient' if you are a married couple or in a civil partnership.

But it is all so complicated – and what about Betty down the road?

This book will try to help you cope with the challenges of the UK tax system. If someone cannot follow the information in this chapter and cannot afford to pay for professional advice they are not alone. Here is the pick of free further help for those who may be elderly, recently bereaved (losing vital help and support) and find tax challenging. Don't keep these tips to yourself and try to remember people like 'Betty down the road':

Tax Help for Older People (TOP) is a charity that provides independent, free tax advice for vulnerable and unrepresented people on low incomes – www.taxvol.org.uk

Tax Aid is a charity that advises only those people on low incomes whose problems cannot be resolved by HMRC – www.taxaid.org.uk

Citizens Advice is very useful if someone does not meet the 'low income' criteria of the above two recommendations. It has a very useful website to help you understand tax and how it is collected and what to do if you have a tax problem. They can also provide face-to-face and telephone support – www.citizensadvice.org.uk

Self-assessment

Self-assessment is the system that HMRC uses to collect tax from individuals. Income Tax is usually deducted automatically from wages and occupational and private pensions (but, significantly, not from the State Pension). Those people with other taxable income and capital gains must report it on the self-assessment return once a year. The tax you have to pay depends on allowances you have and the tax band you are in; there are also different rates for Capital Gains Tax (CGT) and Inheritance Tax (IHT).

Self-assessment notices to complete the form are sent out in April each year. The details you need to enter on the form you receive in April 2019 are those relating to the 2018/19 tax year, which is 6 April 2018 to 5 April 2019. Not everyone has to complete a self-assessment form but one is required for a number of specified circumstances, which include: the self-employed; being a company director; having income from savings and investments of £10,000 or more; having employment income on PAYE above £100,000; and having CGT to pay. If you don't receive a self-assessment request but owe tax to HMRC you are required to notify HMRC. Do this initially by writing to HMRC at: Self-Assessment, HM Revenue & Customs, BX9 1AX.

All taxpayers have an obligation to keep records of all their different sources of income and capital gains. These include:

- details of earnings plus any bonus, expenses and benefits in kind received;
- bank and building society interest;
- dividend vouchers and/or other documentation showing gains from investments;
- pension payments (state and occupational or private pensions);
- income and costs of any trading or other business activity;
- rental income from letting a property and associated costs;
- taxable social security benefits (for instance Jobseeker's Allowance and Carer's Allowance);
- gains or losses made on selling investments or a second home;
- payments against which tax relief can be claimed (eg charitable donations or contributions to a personal pension).

If you don't voluntarily disclose the fact that you may owe tax and HMRC finds out about untaxed income and launches an investigation into your tax affairs you could face stiff penalties, as well as paying any tax due and interest (more on this later). Ignorance is no defence.

Income Tax

This is calculated on all (or nearly all) of your income, after deduction of your tax allowances. The reason for saying 'nearly all' is that some income you may receive is tax free (a list of the main ones appears later in this chapter).

The tax year runs from 6 April to the following 5 April so the amount of tax you pay in any one year is calculated on the income you receive between these two dates. The tax bands are as follows:

- The point at which most people start paying Income Tax will be the Personal Allowance of £11,850 (this will change from 6 April 2019). Up to this level of income you will not pay Income Tax and you are a 'zero rate taxpayer'.
- The 20 per cent basic rate of income tax is payable on income beyond the Personal Allowance up to a further £34,500 (this will change from 6 April 2019). The 'shorthand' for a taxpayer who pays a top rate of tax at 20 per cent is a 'basic-rate taxpayer'.
- The combined effect of the above measures is that the 40 per cent higher-rate Income Tax threshold then starts at £46,350 for 2018/19. The taxpayer who pays a top rate of tax in this band is a 'higher-rate taxpayer', but remember you only pay tax at 40 per cent on the taxable income above £46,350.
- The very top rate of 45 per cent is levied on incomes in excess of £150,000. This person is called an 'additional-rate taxpayer' and again, remember, the 45 per cent additional rate only applies to taxable income above £150,000.

The rates are slightly different in Scotland where there is a slightly lower tax rate of 19 per cent Income Tax for income between £11,850 and £13,850; the 20 per cent rate applies from £13,850 to £24,000 and then there is a 21 per cent rate between £24,000 and £43,430. The rates then step up to 41 per cent for £43,430 to £150,000 and over £150,000 is 46 per cent. The cumulative effect of the changes seen in Scotland is to help lower earners pay a bit less tax and higher earners pay a bit more tax to balance the Scottish government's books.

A knowledge of the bands is vital to understanding some of the tax-planning opportunities that lie ahead and which could help you save more, live better and be happier in retirement. So far so good? If so, you are ready for the next vital piece of knowledge.

Tax allowances

Personal Allowance

Your Personal Allowance is the amount of money you are allowed to retain before Income Tax becomes applicable. For big earners the Personal Allowance is reduced by £1 for every £2 of income over £100,000. The Personal Allowance will therefore disappear completely if your income in 2017/18 is above £123,700 in the tax year 2018/19.

For 2018/19 'big earners' you may still be able to preserve part or all of your Personal Allowance if your income is between £100,000 and £123,700 by making pension contributions – as such contributions (subject to certain limited allowance) can, effectively, extend the personal allowance. This can extend the £100,000 income 'barrier' and is worth considering as income in this tax 'kill zone' is taxed, effectively, at 60 per cent. The effect can be positive as income deferred into a pension may then be accessed more tax efficiently and, if you get your planning right, it may be 25 per cent tax free and the remainder taxed at 20 per cent basic rate. So it is either tax at 60 per cent or about 15 per cent on that slice of £23,700 – take your pick.

Tax tip

For 2018/19 'big earners' you may still be able to preserve part or all of your Personal Allowance if your income is between £100,000 and £123,700 by making pension contributions if your pension allowances allow this.

In much the same way individuals that end up as higher-rate taxpayers can also make pension contributions to shift income from being taxed at 40 per cent to receiving 25 per cent tax free and the remainder taxed at the 20 per cent basic rate if you get your planning right.

Tax tip

For 2018/19 higher-rate taxpayers may still be able to shift income being taxed at 40 per cent to some being tax free and the remainder at 20 per cent by making pension contributions.

Other tax allowances to which you may be entitled include:

- **Married Couple's Allowance** of £8,695 (2018/19) is available if at least one partner was born before 6 April 1935. Tax relief for this allowance is restricted to 10 per cent of the £8,695 and you get this in tax relief. The £8,695 is reduced by £1 for every £2 over £28,900 until you reach £3,360.
- A widowed partner, where the couple at the time of death were entitled to Married Couple's Allowance, can claim any unused portion of the allowance in the year he or she became widowed.
- Registered blind people can claim an allowance (the **Blind Person's Allowance**) of £2,390 per year (2018/19). If both husband and wife are registered as blind, they can each claim the allowance.

Tax tip

Transferable tax allowances between married couples and civil partnership came into effect in April 2015 and this could reduce your tax in 2018/19 where you have two basic-rate tax payers who are married or in a civil partnership and one does not use up all of that brilliant tax-free allowance known as your Personal Allowance. This is called the Marriage Tax Allowance and works by the partner who is not earning above £11,850 transferring £1,190 of their Personal Allowance to their partner (to be a basic-rate taxpayer in 2018/19 their partner could be earning up to £46,350). It is the non-taxpayer who must apply and you do this online at www.gov. uk (go to 'marriage allowance') or call HMRC on 0300 200 3300. One final thing – you both must have been born on or after 6 April 1935. If you were born before that date your own extra tax break is found at the Married Couple's Allowance summarized above.

Same-sex partners

Same-sex couples in a civil partnership are treated the same as married couples for tax purposes.

Tax-free income

Not all income is taxable and the following list indicates some of the more common sources of income that are free of tax:

- Attendance allowance.
- Child benefit: there is a partial tax clawback if one parent earns more than £50,000 and child benefit was received, and results in all child benefit being repayable via a tax assessment for those on £60,000 or more.
- Child tax credit.
- Disability living allowance and personal independence payment.
- Housing benefit.
- Industrial injuries disablement pension.
- Income-related employment and support allowance.
- Income support (in some circumstances, such as when the recipient is also getting jobseeker's allowance, income support will be taxable).
- Pensions paid to war widows (plus any additions for children).
- Certain disablement pensions from the armed forces, police, fire brigade and merchant navy.
- The winter fuel payment (paid to pensioners).
- Working tax credit.
- National Savings premium bond prizes.
- Winnings on the National Lottery and other forms of betting.
- Income received from certain insurance policies (mortgage payment protection, permanent health insurance, creditor insurance for loans and utility bills, various approved long-term care policies) if the recipient is sick, disabled or unemployed at the time the benefits become payable.
- Income and dividends received from savings in an ISA.

- The bonus on contributions to a LISA.
- Dividend income from investments in VCTs.
- Virtually all gifts (in certain circumstances you could have to pay tax if the gift is above £3,000 or if, as may occasionally be the case, the money from the donor has not been previously taxed).
- Certain redundancy payments up to the value of £30,000.
- A lump sum commuted from a pension.
- A matured endowment policy.

> **Tax tip**
>
> If you are still in doubt about whether income is taxable, don't stick your head in the sand. Either take professional advice on any 'unusual' income that you have received or find further free information at the Citizens Advice website: www.citizensadvice.org.uk – taxable and non-taxable income.

Income Tax on savings and investments

Savings

Most people can earn some interest from their savings without paying tax due to the **Personal Savings Allowance** of £1,000 for basic-rate taxpayers (£500 for higher-rate taxpayers). There is no allowance for additional-rate (45 per cent) taxpayers.

So far so good, but it then gets complicated. For 2018/19 there is a £5,000 tax-free (0 per cent) savings income band on top of the Personal Allowance, so if you earn less than £17,850 a year in income plus savings interest you won't have to pay tax on the interest paid on saving. This comes from the £11,850 personal allowance (this increases a bit if you have Blind Person's Allowance or Married Couple's Allowance), £5,000 savings income band and then the £1,000 Personal Savings Allowance.

> **Tax tip**
>
> There is a tax-planning opportunity for a husband and wife (or partners in a civil partnership) on different tax bands (ie zero rate, basic rate, higher rate or additional rate). Review who holds the money and, therefore, who earns the interest and who can therefore benefit the most from the Personal Savings Allowance.

Investments

There is a £2,000 dividend allowance in 2018/19 that allows dividends up to this value to be taken 'tax free'. Higher-dividend taxes would then be levied on amounts above £2,000. Dividend tax then increases from 7.5 per cent to 32.5 per cent as you move from the basic-rate tax band to higher-rate tax band. It increases further to 38.1 per cent for additional-rate tax-payers.

> **Tax tip**
>
> A husband and wife (or partners in a civil partnership) on different tax rates should review and realign who holds what in terms of shares and their dividends. If you own your own company and can control the level of dividends should you limit your dividends (if finances allow) to keep your income within the basic-rate band?

> **Tax tip**
>
> Check out any opportunities to invest in your employer. Shares acquired under share incentive plans or sharesave schemes usually provide price discounts and tax breaks for taking part. Think about and plan your annual contribution limits so that there could be a steady flow of share sales in the future and you can maximize your Capital Gains Tax exemption.

Reclaiming tax on savings income

You can reclaim tax paid on savings interest within four years of the end of the relevant tax year by filling in form R40 and sending it to HMRC. It normally takes about six weeks to get the tax back.

Mis-sold PPI compensation 'interest'

Millions of consumers have been receiving refunds after being mis-sold payment protection insurance (PPI) with credit cards and personal loans. Successful claimants are also being paid interest on the refunds to compensate for being without their money all that time. But, while there is no tax to pay on the refund element, which simply returns your own money to you, you may have to pay tax on the interest, just as you do on earned interest in a savings account if your interest is above the tax-free personal savings allowance. If you have received a compensation payment, check what the lender advises and whether they have deducted basic tax at 20 per cent already (which non-taxpayers can reclaim and higher-rate payers report to HMRC on their self-assessment).

Mistakes by HMRC

HMRC does sometimes make mistakes. Normally, if it has charged you insufficient tax and later discovers the error, it will send you a supplementary demand requesting the balance owing. However, a provision previously known as the 'Official Error Concession' and now labelled 'Extra Statutory Concession A19' provides that, if the mistake was due to HMRC's failure 'to make proper and timely use' of information it received, it is possible that you may be excused the arrears.

Undercharging is not the only type of error. It is equally possible that you may have been overcharged and either do not owe as much as has been stated or, not having spotted the mistake, have paid more than you needed to previously. If you think there has been a mistake, write to HMRC explaining why you think the amount is too high. If a large sum is involved it could well be worth asking an accountant to help you. If HMRC has acted incorrectly you may also be able to claim repayment of some or all of the accountant's fees (your accountant will be able to advise you on this).

As part of the Citizen's Charter, HMRC has appointed an independent adjudicator to examine taxpayers' complaints about their dealings with HMRC and, if considered valid, to determine what action would be fair. Complaints appropriate to the adjudicator are mainly limited to the way that HMRC has handled someone's tax affairs (perhaps undue delays, errors and discourtesy). Before approaching the adjudicator, taxpayers are expected to have tried to resolve the matter with HMRC directly.

Important dates to remember

The deadline for filing paper self-assessment forms for the 2018/19 tax year is 31 October 2019. Those filing online will have until 31 January 2020. The penalty for breaching these deadlines is £100.

If your return is more than three months late an automatic penalty from 1 May of £10 per day commences, up to a maximum of £900 in addition to the initial £100 penalty. If your return is still outstanding after a year another penalty arises based on the greater of £300 or 5 per cent of the tax due. In serious cases of delay a higher penalty of up to 100 per cent of the tax due can be imposed. You have 30 days to lodge an appeal with HMRC against a penalty if you believe you have a reasonable excuse. If you remain dissatisfied with HMRC's review of its decision you can ask a tax tribunal to hear your appeal.

In addition, if the payment is 30 days late from 31 January there is a further penalty of 5 per cent of the tax due and then a further 5 per cent if six months late and a further 5 per cent if 12 months late.

If you are in financial difficulties, engage with HMRC and request a formal 'time to pay agreement'. The late payment penalty is suspended but the taxpayer will become liable to the penalty if the agreement is broken. If it is your first instance of requesting a 'time to pay agreement' you should find that HMRC is approachable albeit they will want to know how you got into the situation and something about your assets and debts.

One final key date – you can amend your self-assessment at any time in the 12-month period after the latest 31 January deadline.

Tax tip

Submit a 'best efforts' self-assessment tax return rather than a late one. Explain any figures that are provisional in the additional notes section, apologize and explain that you will rectify matters as a priority (and do so!).

The late payment penalties can be worse than the late filing penalties and start just 30 days after 31 January. If you cannot pay your tax contact HMRC and see if you can enter into a 'time to pay agreement' – and then stick to the agreement.

Tax rebates

When you retire, you may be due a tax rebate because tax has been collected using PAYE assuming you will earn your salary for a whole year. Rebates can often arise for summer or autumn retirees. The tax overpayment would normally be resolved automatically, especially if you are getting a pension from your last employer or move into part-time employment. The P45 (tax form for leavers) should be used by the pension payer or new employer and, normally, the tax sorts itself out. If not, and the potential reclaim is for a previous tax year, HMRC may be ahead of you as they may spot it (usually by the end of July following the tax year) and send you a P800 tax calculation if they know you have paid too much tax. You will then get your refund automatically within 14 days of the P800.

If you have not received a P800 or cannot wait to the end of the tax year you may make a claim to HMRC for any of the four previous tax years. You will need to know your National Insurance number and have your P45 if you have one and details of the jobs or state benefits you were getting at the time. HMRC will process the payment or explain what further information they need. Use this address for all Income Tax correspondence: Pay As You Earn and Self-Assessment, HM Revenue & Customs, BX9 1AS.

Capital Gains Tax

You may have to pay Capital Gains Tax (CGT) if you make a profit (or, to use the proper term, 'gain') on the sale, exchange or other disposal of an asset and this includes giving it away. The usual assets are a second home, a valuable painting or a share investment that soars in price. CGT applies only to the actual gain you make after deducting a significant tax break known as the annual exemption from CGT. This is currently £11,700 for 2018/19. This means that in 2018/19 a married couple or a couple in a civil partnership can make gains of up to £23,400 that are free of CGT. However, it is not possible to use the losses of one spouse to cover the gains of the other. On the other hand, transfers of shares or assets between husband and wife or civil partners usually remain tax free, so should you be rethinking how your investments are held in this situation so that future gains are spread between the two of you?

Any gains you make are taxed at 10 per cent for basic-rate taxpayers and 20 per cent for higher-rate and additional-rate taxpayers; however, sales of a second interest in a residential property (mainly aimed at people with second homes) remain at older rates of 18 per cent for basic-rate taxpayers and 28 per cent for higher-rate and additional-rate taxpayers.

Following the same logic as immediately above, remember, transfers between husband and wife or civil partners usually remain tax free, so should you also be rethinking how your investments are held in this situation so that more of any future gains (after the annual exemption) are taxed as a basic-rate rather than higher/additional-rate taxpayer? If your husband, wife or civil partner later sells or otherwise disposes of the asset, they will have to pay the tax on any gain made over the total period of ownership (after 31 March 1982, see below for more on this 'special' CGT date).

The following assets are not subject to CGT and do not count towards the gains you are allowed to make:

- your main home (see below);
- most private-use cars;
- personal belongings up to the value of £6,000 each, such as jewellery, paintings or antiques;
- proceeds of a life assurance policy (in most circumstances);
- profits on UK government loan stock issued by HM Treasury;
- National Savings certificates;
- gains from assets held in an ISA (and older PEPs);
- premium bond winnings: the maximum holding is £50,000 per person aged over 16 and under that age they may be held in the name of under-16s by parents or guardians;
- betting and lottery winnings and life insurance policies if you are the original owner;
- gifts to registered charities;
- usually small part-disposals of land (limited to 5 per cent of the total holding, with a maximum value of £20,000 (but the amount you receive is taken off your cost for any future disposal);
- gains on the disposal of qualifying shares in a venture capital trust or within the Enterprise Investment Scheme (EIS) and Seed Enterprise Investment Scheme (SEIS), provided these have been held for the necessary holding period. These are complex and tax-efficient investment schemes and they carry risk and are outside the scope of this book, so professional advice should be sought. Find further information at www.gov.uk and go to 'enterprise investment scheme' and 'venture capital trusts'.

You work out the profit on disposal of an asset by comparing the sale proceeds with the original cost of the asset. If it was bought before 31 March 1982 you use the market value at that date. If you dispose of an asset left to you by the will of a relative you use the market value on the date of death of the relative. If you give away an asset to a child or other close relative you use the market value on the date of the gift as the proceeds instead of any amount received. To bring clarity to potential complex situations you can agree the valuation with HMRC before you submit your tax return by completing form CG 34 – professional advice may prove beneficial.

You can add other allowable costs that were incurred when acquiring the asset – such as Stamp Duty, solicitor's costs and valuation fees on a second home. You add these to the original cost so remember to keep the receipts in a safe place. Improvement costs, such as adding a conservatory or converting a garage, also can be added to the cost on, say, a second property that may be subject to CGT but not maintenance costs such as decorating and repairs.

Your main home and Capital Gains Tax

Your main home is usually exempt from CGT and for that reason individuals who buy small and extend tend to be tax efficient in using their funds to build up a tax-free asset if it remains their main residence. Perhaps the strategy of buying the smallest, most run-down property in an expensive or up and coming area makes sense now! There are only a few trip points. One is if you convert part of your home into a dedicated office with, for instance, a separate entrance. Or into separate self-contained accommodation on which you charge rent. Both of these examples show how you may taint part of the CGT exemption for the relevant portion of the house over the relevant period and some CGT may be payable when you come to sell it.

If you leave your home to someone else who retains it for a while (as a property speculation or to rent out) and later decides to sell it then they may be liable for CGT when the property is later sold (although only on the gain since the date of death). If you own two homes, only one of them is exempt from CGT, namely the one you designate as your 'main residence'. There may be some overlap opportunities and, providing a dwelling home has been your only or main home for a period, the final period of ownership that qualifies for relief can be useful. The final period of ownership of a private residence that potentially could qualify for relief is currently 18 months. HMRC's helpsheet HS283, 'Private residence relief' (available from www.gov.uk), provides more information.

> ## Tax tip
>
> If you have two homes and have lived in both, consider taking professional advice on whether to make a main residence election for your second home if it is standing at a large gain or you are thinking of selling it first. One of the tests used by HMRC when considering the availability of such reliefs is the actual period of residence and the quality rather than quantity of that residence.

Selling a family business

CGT is payable if you are selling a family business, and is 20 per cent for higher-rate and additional-rate taxpayers, but the reduced level of 10 per cent for basic-rate taxpayers. There are a number of CGT reduction opportunities or deferral reliefs available, including the potential to attain entrepreneurs' relief, which could produce a tax rate of 10 per cent. This, however, is a complex area and timing could be vital, so well before either retiring or selling your business or shares you should seek professional advice. You will want to do so anyway as the buyer will probably be getting professional advice and you could find yourself down on the deal pretty quickly if you don't obtain advice yourself (irrespective of any tax advantages).

Inheritance Tax

Inheritance Tax (IHT) is the tax paid on assets (the estate) that are left when someone dies. It is at a high rate of 40 per cent and applies to the value of assets on death (property, bank funds, investments, cars and payouts from life insurance companies) but there are many important exemptions and reliefs, which may mean that no tax is payable on the estate. No one knows precisely what is around the corner so this should be talked about sooner rather than later to help manage, wherever possible, the IHT to be paid on your 'estate'. Above all else there is the straightforward wish of not wanting ambiguity about what should happen after you die. So, time to take a deep breath and read on and then promise to talk to those who matter to you or put a large circle around the sub-headings 'Inheritance Tax' and 'Wills' and pass this book to them with two words: 'Let's talk.'

The tax threshold (the level at which you will need to pay tax) is set at £325,000 and is currently frozen at this rate until 2020/21. The threshold amount for married couples and civil partners is twice this, so £650,000, and this can be stretched to £1 million with the Main Residence Nil Rate Band (more below). The value of estates over and above this sum are taxed at 40 per cent. So the starting point is for you and your partner to sit down and make a list of your assets and then deduct all outstanding liabilities.

Tax tip

Many people underestimate how much they are worth and forget assets like pensions in a defined contribution pension pot (see Chapter 4, Pensions) – that is why this is a two-person job as it is easy to overlook assets acquired over a long time.

Some people mistakenly think that giving away your wealth gets around IHT. This is where the clouds of confusion sometimes arise from 'pub talk'. Yes there are some detailed points where this can be true, such as gifts for the national benefit. There are also other exemptions that have been brought into the debate, which are correct, such as service personnel dying on active service being exempt from IHT. There are then grey areas such as war service hastening a veteran's death, which found, upon challenge, that the estate could be exempt from IHT.

However, the root of the confusion referred to above is that there is no immediate IHT on lifetime gifts between individuals – it is only deferred. The gifts can then become wholly exempt if the donor survives for seven years. So when the donor dies, any gifts made within the previous seven years become chargeable as their value is added to the estate for IHT reasons. For this reason, in the seven-year period they are known as 'potentially exempt transfers' or PETs for short. Where gifts exceed the nil rate band there is a tapering relief that begins to soften any resulting tax charge, on a sliding scale between years three and seven following the gift. Gifts with strings attached are treated as if they did not happen, so if you try to 'give away' your house to the kids but still live in it the 'gift' probably will not be a gift in the eyes of HMRC, so it falls back into your assets pot with IHT due. The basic rule is that gifts 'with strings attached' probably will not work. Extreme care must be taken here, as not only might you fail to secure the desired IHT saving, you might also inadvertently create a CGT liability that would otherwise not have existed. Linked to 'give away' tactics are various schemes that seek to lock away the home in some form of a trust.

Trusts

A trust is a relationship between persons and property under which property is invested in persons known as trustees, who hold the property for the benefit of other persons known as beneficiaries. The settlor is the person who provides the property to be held on trust. The golden rule is that the terms of the trust must be certain and to be valid there must be three certainties: certainty of what was intended; certainty of what was going into the trust; and certainty of the beneficiaries (who they were). Trusts are complex and are usually created by family solicitors who are experienced in the relevant jurisdiction and can help with potential complexities such as conflicts of interest between generations and care around the settlor retaining sufficient assets to continue to live on to a standard that is acceptable. The jurisdiction point reflects England and Wales having a common system; minor differences in Northern Ireland; and other differences in Scotland.

Certainly, some very old and established trusts have sheltered significant family estates from IHT as the occupier never actually owns the property; they are merely allowed to live there subject to conditions. This sort of thing was used by the wealthy to stop their children and subsequent grandchildren disposing of the main assets within a family estate and, instead, simply being allowed to live in or use the asset and receive some income. Trusts were also used to keep the family money within the bloodline (in the case of divorce and remarriage). This allowed the big family estate to be passed down intact from generation to generation.

In recent years, firms have tried to market tax saving schemes to 'protect your assets from the tax office' or schemes to shelter assets from 'claims for care-home fees' based loosely on schemes involving trusts. These may include fancy seminars with free coffee and biscuits and smiling salespeople, but tread carefully. The ideal scenario is that you would want to be dealing with the trusted family solicitor regulated by the Law Society in your jurisdiction (for instance in England and Wales at www.lawsociety.org.uk) and you would want a solicitor accredited on their Wills and Inheritance Quality Scheme (WIQS). If you depart from this route the following questions may help your selection process:

- What are the specific legal and tax qualifications and regulating body of the individual that will be responsible for talking with you, understanding your position and then advising you? Then check their name on that organization's register. This could be one of the biggest transactions you make so obtain at least two quotations if you are treading into the unknown and also seek recommendations from trusted family members or friends.

- Does the trust documentation provide certainty of what was intended, certainty of what was going into the trust, and certainty of the beneficiaries (who they were)? Ask what happens if the scheme does not work. It may be several years until the scheme comes under challenge. How big is the firm advising you and how long have they been around? What professional indemnity insurance cover do they have?

- Extras? Have the total costs of all aspects from start to finish been set out in advance in writing so that you have clarity before proceeding? If changes are needed, what are their hourly rates? This avoids the issue of cost creep as things are added in – perhaps the cost of setting up a trust, any trust administration costs and so on.

- What are the pros and cons? There will always be some risks to any scheme – how well are these set out and how prominent are they?

- What are the tax charges –what types of tax will the trust incur and when?

- What happens if the government rules change? Are the schemes amended and updated and at what hourly rate or other cost?

Tax tip

There is no such thing as a magic wand that makes IHT disappear on your main home if you continue to live in it or guarantees that local authorities will not chase down assets deliberately given away to avoid claims for care-home fees. Tread carefully if someone offers you a magic wand for a fat fee – and satisfy yourself on the above questions.

Tax tip

Proceeds from life insurance policies will form part of your estate unless you take steps to divert the proceeds, perhaps using a trust, directly to another party – perhaps children or grandchildren. This is not a complex area of tax planning and many life assurance companies can provide simple trust forms for you to complete to shelter the funds from IHT – consult a financial adviser or solicitor if you remain unsure.

Tax treatment of trusts

There may be IHT to pay when assets – such as money, land or buildings – are transferred into or out of trusts or when they reach a 10-year anniversary. There are complex rules that determine whether a trust needs to pay IHT in such situations, so ensure you have clarity on the tax consequences and if unsure get further clarity on this with professional advice (usually a financial adviser, solicitor or chartered accountant could help: see Chapter 3). Further information is available on the website: www.hmrc.gov.uk – 'inheritance tax and trusts'.

Main residence nil rate band and IHT

The 'main residence nil rate band' is a relatively new and a very significant tax break that will remove the IHT worry for the vast majority of UK married couples. Here is how it works. Remember the £325,000 threshold allows married couples or civil partners to transfer the unused element of their IHT-free allowance to their spouse or civil partner when they die, giving an effective threshold of £650,000 before any IHT will become payable. Then remember that IHT will be levied at 40 per cent above the IHT threshold (£650,000 for a couple or £325,000 on the estate of anyone who is single or divorced when they die).

Then along came one of the biggest fanfares in the UK taxation system in the summer 2015 Budget with the announcement of the 'main residence nil rate band', which started being implemented on 6 April 2017. It is an extra relief available where the value of the estate is above the IHT threshold and contains a main residence that is being passed on to 'lineal descendants'. It will raise the IHT-free allowance to from £325,000 to £500,000 per person by 2020/21 where married couples jointly own a family home (worth less than £2 million) and want to leave this to their children. The joint IHT exemption between the married couple will be £1 million.

The key aspects are:

- The relief was introduced on 6 April 2017, for deaths on or after that date.
- It was phased in, starting at £100,000 in 2017/18, now rising to £125,000 in 2018/19, £150,000 in 2019/20 and £175,000 in 2020/21. For a couple, the £175,000 each, plus the existing £325,000 each, makes up the £1 million maximum relief that will be achievable by 2020/21.
- The relief will then increase in line with Consumer Price Index (CPI) from 2021/22 onwards.
- The relief applies only on death, not on lifetime transfers.
- The amount available will be the lower of the net value of the property and the maximum amount of the main residence nil rate band. The net value of the property is after deducting liabilities such as a mortgage.
- The property will qualify if it has been the deceased's residence at some point.
- The property must be left to lineal descendants: children, grandchildren, great-grandchildren etc or the spouses of the same. Children include step-children and adopted children.
- The relief is transferable, so the estate of the second spouse to die can benefit from the main residence nil rate band of their deceased spouse, regardless of when that spouse died.
- The relief will be tapered away for estates with a net value over £2 million, at the rate of £1 for every £2 over that limit, so will be reduced to zero on an estate of £2.35 million.

IHT and pensions

The transfer of pension pots from a deceased's estate can either be simple or complex and can be paid out tax free or taxed (sometimes at rates of up to 55 per cent for unauthorized payments). There are complex rules depending on age at death, type of pension and whether it is a lump sum or an annuity and so on. Individuals or couples with an estate (before taking account of any pension pots) worth more than the IHT exempt amounts should consider their pension pot strategy, especially in the years up to age 75, and professional advice usually proves beneficial in such circumstances.

For basic information there is more at www.gov.uk ('tax on pension death benefits').

> ### Tax tip
>
> The transfer of pension pots from a deceased's estate can result in tax anywhere between tax free to 55 per cent. To an extent this is down to your choice and planning. The savings involved can be substantial for those who benefit from the wishes in your will, so consider finding out more and then taking professional advice.

Other IHT planning

Other IHT planning includes the charitable donations exemption, with a reduced rate of IHT payable on estates that give at least 10 per cent of the value of their estate above the nil rate band (£325,000) to charity. The remainder is taxed at 36 per cent against the usual 40 per cent IHT rate.

Gifts or money up to the value of £3,000 can be given annually free of tax. If you didn't use last year's allowance you can carry it forward and use it this year to give £6,000 away to your children, for example. The allowance is per donor, not per child.

Additionally, it is possible to make small gifts to any number of individuals free of tax, provided the amount to each does not exceed £250. You cannot combine this with the £3,000 allowance.

Another opportunity for gifting in a way that does not see the money caught by the IHT trap is gifts to mark a wedding or civil partnership. The limits for these gifts are up to £5,000 given to a child, £2,500 given to a grandchild or great-grandchild or £1,000 given to anyone else.

Perhaps the most generous of these reliefs, though, is that gifts made out of surplus income and that have a degree of regularity and do not detract from the donor's standard of living or capital worth may be made free from IHT without any fixed monetary limit. The greater your income and lower your living costs, the more can be given away in this fashion.

> ### Tax tip
>
> Planning and longevity go hand in hand, as most lifetime gifts to individuals (who are not covered by one of the exemptions mentioned) do not trigger IHT if you survive for seven years.

Recent Budgets also created new and welcome provisions to enable the tax and other advantages of ISAs and pensions to be passed on to the deceased's spouse (for instance in the case of ISAs that funds could remain in the ISA tax-effective wrapper). Could it be tax efficient to ensure that your spouse inherits your ISA under your will rather than the investments passing to other family members? Remember that the government can change the tax rules without notice and exemptions can be withdrawn or reduced.

Wills

Finally, as we draw this important section to a close, please remember the importance of a will and how it ties into IHT. Without a will in place it will be the intestacy laws that decide how your estate is distributed, not you. Having a will allows you to state precisely who your beneficiaries are and what they receive, and allows you to appoint administrators who will administer the estate after your death. So make a will either through an online or postal service or, if your affairs are more complicated, with a face-to-face professional adviser, and consider a power of attorney. Keep them up to date so that they are effective and efficient from both a legal and a tax perspective. For further information, see 'Wills' in Chapter 17, and also find more at www.gov.uk (search for 'probate and inheritance tax').

Help in dealing with a tax investigation

HMRC is increasing its investigation capability, arming itself with more staff and more power. If HMRC believes your errors were deliberate they can go back 20 years. Add in interest on any late tax and further additional penalties of up to 200 per cent of the tax shortfall and you could be facing an eye-watering tax assessment.

HMRC will listen carefully to facts that may mitigate any penalty due – and if you are looking at serious amounts of tax due then early discussion with a professional adviser will assist you in dealing with the unwelcome situation you may find yourself in. You should also check whether any insurance or professional association memberships that you have could provide free tax investigation cover, which is very useful.

Graham Boar is a tax partner from UHY Hacker Young. We asked him for his views on the compliance landscape and how HMRC has been performing:

Tax investigation trends have changed remarkably over recent years. In part this is a by-product of the merger of HM Customs and Excise with Inland Revenue to form HM Revenue & Customs back in 2005. In the years that followed that merger there was a huge amount of activity not only to integrate the staff and systems of the two predecessor entities but also to align more closely the investigation, penalty and compliance processes, powers and time limits.

Examples at a high level include the replacement of the Commissioners for the Inland Revenue when escalating a tax dispute with the First Tier and Upper Tier Tax Tribunal system, and the infamous 'Schedule 36 powers' under which HMRC was given explicit and legally enforceable powers to demand information held both by taxpayers themselves and also by third parties.

The new powers and processes necessarily brought about a change in the conduct of tax investigations, and the increasing centralization of resources with the closure of most local tax offices has further impacted on that. With centralization comes systematization and the decline of discretion on the part of HMRC staff. In 2008 the system of penalties, which until that point had been largely a discretionary affair, was put on a statutory footing with four categories of behaviour, fixed maximum and minimum percentages for each, and mitigation for perceived taxpayer 'telling, helping and giving'.

Then came the sea change – the introduction of the Connect IT system. Before Connect, selection for a tax investigation relied on things like tip-offs by a disgruntled former spouse or colleague, human consideration of 'odd-looking' entries in tax returns and accounts, and a healthy dose of random selection. These are now things of the past as Connect interrogates vast amounts of data, cross-referencing and flagging potential anomalies for investigation. Using, amongst other things, Schedule 36 powers, HMRC is collecting bulk data from banks and building societies, Land Registry, Stamp Duty Land Tax returns, employers, insurance companies, letting agents, online marketplaces and many others. These can all be cross-checked with taxpayer records in the blink of an eye.

In the simplest cases this makes HMRC interventions very short-lived affairs. The taxpayer is told that HMRC believe the tax return is wrong: you have reported bank interest of x and we have information suggesting it is y – 95 times out of 100 HMRC's information is correct, the additional tax is due, and all that is left is to see whether HMRC consider a behaviourally related penalty to be appropriate.

In the more in-depth cases HMRC is also using technology and online resources to do its homework, meaning that by the time HMRC turns up for a meeting staff will already have checked your social media and online presence to see what fee-paying school your family attend, where you spent your summer holiday, and what car is sitting on your driveway in that Google earth picture.

At this point it would be easy to bemoan our Big Brother society and scaremonger about what HMRC might 'pin on you'. But that is not my view. I see the changes in HMRC's tactics as being overwhelmingly positive. The elimination of random enquiries (or fishing trips, as they are termed in our business) and their replacement with informed, risk-assessed and targeted compliance activity has not only enabled HMRC to collect increasing amounts of tax through compliance activity against a backdrop of austerity and staff cuts, it has also significantly insulated the innocent and honest taxpayer from the risk of a stressful and disruptive intervention into their tax affairs.

These days, the chances are that if HMRC wants to look into your tax affairs there is either a simple explanation that will explain the perceived risk or else there is a good reason for them doing so.

The landscape has therefore changed significantly and HMRC has the intention to narrow the 'tax gap' and target resources with a much more focused capability.

We sought Graham's views on what we should be looking out for in the year ahead:

> HMRC's goal is still to shift from current self-assessment data reporting by taxpayers to a validation and correction exercise on data already gathered by HMRC. As that happens, the focus of interaction between the taxpayer and HMRC will increasingly change. A simple example is where the taxpayer considers data, from a bank or pension provider for example, to be inaccurate; it is HMRC's intention that the taxpayer will need to resolve the dispute directly with that third party, the third party then updating the figures it provided to HMRC. As the staff numbers at HMRC continue to reduce, this pattern of pushing the compliance burden on to taxpayers themselves can only continue. In the short term, however, the plan appears to have suffered at the hands of HMRC resources being diverted towards Brexit and for the time being HMRC is spending its limited budget elsewhere.
>
> An area that should not be impacted by these cuts, though, is the use of Common Reporting Standard (CRS) data. Effective as of September 2018 the CRS sees vast swathes of automated cross-border financial data exchange between a whole host of participating countries. Coupling these new data sources with HMRC's existing Connect interrogation system, and the promise not only of undeclared tax but of penalties between 100 per cent and 200 per cent, HMRC can be expected to pursue with some vigour those taxpayers with undeclared overseas tax affairs.

If HMRC discovers an error during an investigation, they can reopen other closed years as well. For example, if a careless error is discovered, HMRC can include up to six years within any settlement negotiations. If a deliberate error is uncovered, HMRC can include up to 20 years in the most serious cases. In addition to settling any tax owed you will have to pay interest on that tax and a penalty, which can be up to 200 per cent of the tax owed. Needless to say, tax investigations can prove to be extremely stressful and very expensive. So we turned to Graham for his hints and tips relating to tax investigations:

1 *Engage an accountant.* If you are the subject of anything but the simplest of HMRC interventions, find an accountant who holds themselves out as a specialist in this area and take some advice, even if it is only some tips and help in dealing with the enquiry yourself, and ensuring that HMRC is playing by the rules.

2 *Get tax investigation insurance cover.* Many accountants will offer this type of insurance; specialist providers such as Abbey Tax do too, as well as trade membership bodies such as the Federation of Small Businesses. But if you get an enquiry and don't have a specific policy, it is worth checking things like your house insurance in case it provides some level of assistance.

3 *Keep good records.* When HMRC comes knocking and you have contemporary written evidence supporting your position you will immediately be on the front foot and the onus will be on HMRC to undermine your stance. If you are relying on advice, get it in writing. Certainly don't think that a recollection of something an HMRC staff member told you on the phone will hold water if the inspector in front of you thinks differently.

4 *Consider disclosing interpretations.* If you are declaring your taxes based on an interpretation of a grey area or otherwise in circumstances that HMRC may not agree with, consider offering a full explanation in the tax-return white space. The 'discovery' assessment provisions allow HMRC to look back six (careless) or 20 (deliberate) years, but a full set of details on your return should limit their enquiry window to 12 months post-filing, giving you tax certainty a lot earlier.

Graham also provided his personal top five tax-planning tips for a better retirement:

1 *Get an early start.* It is never too early to start planning for the future, but particularly in the four or five years preceding your retirement it

might be possible to significantly change your behaviour towards savings, earnings, pension contributions and similar to achieve significant tax efficiencies.

2 *Don't let the tail wag the dog.* In other words, consider your tax position and take reasonable steps to mitigate charges that might arise. But don't let tax be the be all and end all, and certainly don't take tax-planning measures that risk leaving you struggling for money, worried or unhappy. Find a solution that ticks all the boxes, not just the tax box.

3 *Keep it under review.* Tax rules change all the time, and many of the measures affecting the retired are intended as a stimulus to behaviour. Don't just make a plan once and then rigidly stick to it; have a think about your tax position once a year (February is a good time) and consider any changes that could benefit you in the coming 12 months.

4 *'I'm going to' and not 'I've just'.* As a tax adviser, my heart sinks when a client calls me to ask about the tax implications of what they have just done and whether the position can be improved. Almost invariably the tax outcome of a transaction can only be improved in advance of committing to it and not once it is completed. So ask questions at the right time, especially where big life events are concerned.

5 *Don't be pressured into things.* Lifetime succession planning is a fantastic way of managing Inheritance Tax burdens, but it is disheartening when clients feel a guilty sense of obligation to provide an inheritance and worse still when children appear to be grasping after 'their inheritance'.

Retiring abroad

A vital question for some readers is the taxation effects of living overseas. There are examples of people who retired abroad in the expectation of being able to afford a higher standard of living and who returned home a few years later, thoroughly disillusioned as they had not planned through the costs and implications – more in Chapter 11, 'Your home'. Part of the plan has to be a consideration of tax.

Tax rates vary from one country to another; a prime example is VAT, which varies considerably in Europe. Additionally, many countries levy taxes that don't apply in the UK and complications can usually be expected from wealth taxes and estate duty on overseas property, and localized and national property taxes can also combine to trip up well-laid plans.

The starting point is therefore the free and quality information, available on most countries from our own Foreign and Commonwealth Office – access via www.gov.uk and search for 'living in [country]'. The World Factbook by the US Central Intelligence Agency is also a useful source of quality information on every country in the world.

As things advance, legal advice when buying property overseas is essential (again, more in Chapter 11).

Many intending emigrants cheerfully imagine that, once they have settled themselves in a dream villa overseas, they are safely out of the clutches of the HMRC. This is not so and your first step is to work out your residence status. Whether you are a UK resident usually depends on how many days you spend in the UK in the tax year, which runs from 6 April to 5 April the following year. According to HMRC: 'You are automatically resident in the UK if either you spent 183 or more days in the tax year or your only home was in the UK – you must have owned, rented or lived in it for at least 91 days in total – and you spent at least 30 days there in the tax year.' On the other hand, HMRC states that you are automatically non-resident 'if either you spent fewer than 16 days in the UK (or 46 days if you haven't been classed as UK resident for the three previous tax years) or you work abroad full-time (averaging at least 35 hours a week) and spent fewer than 91 days in the UK, of which no more than 30 were spent working'. In the year you move out of the UK (or back in) the year is usually split into two – a non-resident part and a resident part. More information is at www.gov.uk – go to 'statutory residence test' – and you can also use HMRC's tax residence indicator toolkit and go to 'check your residence status'.

So why is this 'residence' status so important for tax? Well, residents pay UK tax on all their income, whether it is from the UK or abroad. Non-residents only pay tax on their UK income and they do not pay UK tax on their foreign income. In addition, non-residents only pay UK Capital Gains Tax either on UK residential property or if they return to the UK.

The usual scenarios that may require non-residents to complete a self-assessment tax return include:

- if you are in receipt of UK rental income;
- if you make capital gains from the sale or disposal of assets in the UK;
- if you are a director of a UK company;
- if you receive profits from a UK partnership;
- if you earn an income in the UK through self-employment;

- if you do not live in the UK, but you do some or all of your work in the UK.

In addition, HMRC's Non-Resident Landlord Scheme requires landlords with a usual place of abode outside the UK to have the tax on their UK rentals collected by their UK letting agent or tenant and the tax is due for payment within 30 days of each quarter ending 30 June, 30 September, 31 December and 31 March. Where property is owned jointly, the share of each joint owner is considered separately. If you want to pay tax on your rental income through self-assessment, fill in HMRC form NRL1 and send it to HMRC.

You must tell HMRC if you are either leaving the UK to live abroad permanently or going to work abroad full-time for at least one full tax year. You do this by HMRC's Form P85 and send it to Self-Assessment, HM Revenue and Customs, BX9 1AS, United Kingdom.

Double tax agreement

The country where you live might also seek to tax you on your UK income. This is where a double taxation agreement between the country you live in and the UK may save you being taxed twice, by claiming tax relief in the UK for foreign tax paid. The conditions for tax relief vary from agreement to agreement; find more at www.gov.uk and go to 'double taxation treaties: non-UK resident with UK income'.

> **Tax tip**
>
> Tax is one of the most complex twists of moving overseas. Don't guess or listen to pub talk. Research the issue thoroughly or get professional advice both in the UK and the country you are moving to.

Planning your retirement and tax

This chapter concludes Part One (Plan more) of the book, where knowledge is vital. You will have gained a better understanding of the three phases of retirement; the special challenges facing the 'sandwich generation' of 50- and 60-year-olds; how you can get good professional help;

and then a barrowload of tips on pensions, savings, investments and protection intertwined with tax hints and tips. The backdrop is worth mentioning again – in the UK we have the world's most complex tax regime, so knowledge and planning are even more important. Grasping all this and making some changes will help you save more, live better and be happier.

Important information

This chapter is only a guide and it is neither legal nor taxation advice. Any potential tax advantages may be subject to change from the time of writing (as at summer 2018) and will depend upon your individual circumstances, so individual professional advice should be obtained.

Further information

HMRC has closed all of its enquiry centres that provided face-to-face help to people with tax queries. This service has been replaced by an enhanced information service via www.gov.uk and a telephone support service. The most frequently used telephone line is the self-assessment general enquiries number: 0300 200 3310.

Use this address for all Income Tax correspondence with HMRC: Pay As You Earn and Self-Assessment, HM Revenue & Customs, BX9 1AS

Contact the Adjudicator's Office for information about referring a complaint about HMRC: www.adjudicatorsoffice.gov.uk

The TaxPayers' Alliance campaigns towards achieving a low-tax society: www.taxpayersalliance.com

Tax Help for Older People (TOP) is a charity that is an independent, free tax-advice service for vulnerable and unrepresented people on low incomes: www.taxvol.org.uk

Tax Aid is a charity that advises only those people on low incomes whose problems cannot be resolved by HMRC: www.taxaid.org.uk

Citizens Advice has a very useful website to help you understand tax, how it is collected and what to do if you have a tax problem. They can also provide face-to-face and telephone support: www.citizensadvice. org.uk

Useful reading

The Daily Telegraph Tax Guide 2018, by David Genders, published annually by Kogan Page.

Inspired? Remember to fill in your plan for a good retirement at the end of the book.

PART TWO

Save More and Earn Better

CHAPTER SEVEN

Cutting costs and getting better at complaining

Competition is the keen cutting edge of business always shaving away at costs.
HENRY FORD

We are now switching focus for the next four chapters, which should help you save more or earn better. Both, of course, are vital to helping you make your retirement numbers add up and meet your retirement aspirations. The first of these chapters focuses on the easiest pickings and will help you save more, live better and be happier.

We seem to have a problem in the UK as it seems we may be complacent and overpay for things – as Henry Ford quotes at the head of this chapter we need to get better at stirring up a bit of competition, save more and have more to spend on other things in our active retirement years. But then we British have another problem that makes matters worse – we are not very good at complaining – or should we say complaining effectively and then upping the ante if we feel we are being fobbed off.

This chapter at a glance

- There is not much law around overcharging. Whilst internet online scams present threats, the flip side should be recognized, as there are now massive opportunities to use the internet to turn information into power for yourself. So why do we so often end up accepting the price and overpaying? But no longer – welcome to a cold, wet winter day that can save you, potentially, hundreds of pounds on services that you may have been overpaying. You will save £££s – guaranteed.

- Inevitably in life things do sometimes go wrong. If you do lose out and someone is clearly at fault you may wish to complain. The complaint process can be frustrating and some people and organizations may not have the time or ability to deal with your concerns. Worse still, they may try to suppress complaints or be deliberately obstructive. Tips are provided on how to be heard, how to spell out what you want and then what you can do to up the ante.

- Millions were mis-sold PPI by banks and other financial organizations and billions have been paid out in compensation but the deadline to complain is 29 August 2019 and it is fast approaching. Tips will help you act now and not pay a penny to any claims firm.

A day's work on a wet winter day will save you money

Let's face it, there is, in reality, little protection against overcharging, and the buck usually stops with you on what you choose to pay for utilities, insurance, phone and TV contracts, and even big transactions like estate agency fees and those university loans that we encourage our children to take out.

Quite often, suppliers rely on lethargy, as there just never seems to be enough time to sit back, start thinking straight and review your main financial transactions. The automatic renewal comes through and you pay up (yet again). Choose any cold, wet winter day (maybe in February after the Christmas spending rush and the January credit-card bills!) and dedicate it to checking all your current deals and contracts and seeing what you can save. If you get good at this it will pay for another holiday. So get stuck in: here is how it works.

Insurance

This is potentially one of the biggest areas for a saving. Log your insurance renewal dates: home buildings, home contents, car, pet and any others. Contact them and ask what discounts can be applied to a renewal and then check out their biggest competitor (remember Henry Ford!) with equivalent policies. Be careful, however, about life and health insurance policies and pet insurance so you don't lose any existing cover for pre-existing conditions.

Utilities

Check with your supplier if you are on their best tariff and compare this to other options via Ofgem-approved comparison sites such as uswitch.com or theenergyshop.com.

TV and broadband bundles

So, who is paying more than £75 a month? This is a hugely competitive market, with Sky, Virgin Media and BT all bidding for your money and Amazon and Netflix providing great entertainment platforms. Better still are the freeview TVs that now come with a built-in recording, storage and pause/rewind facility so you can ditch the satellite or cable or, at the very least, negotiate a half-price bundle for another year. Compare the deals and make the switch, and remember there will be dramatic price drops when you tell them you are leaving (good old Henry and his competition motto comes in again).

Mobile phones

The costs can mount up if you are paying for the mobiles of yourself, children and/or parents – and providers can rely on lethargy. So it is a case of holding back from the early upgrade offer and then using a website such as www.uswitch.com to compare all the current offers on handset, calls and that vital data package – and then you call the shots. A simple five-minute call explaining you have found a better deal will usually see you passed through to the business retention department and you may receive a matched or bettered deal. You should also check for mobile providers who offer data-sharing facilities across several mobile phones if you find that children keep going over their data limits: some providers offer this facility, which can save you money.

Cash back and air-mile credit cards

A quick look at moneysavingexpert.com could find you cutting your existing card in half and shifting to someone who will reward you properly. Some even come with neat little complimentary extras.

The 'oops, I forgot about that direct debit' moment

Get your bank statements and credit-card statements together and sit down with your partner and check you recognize and can account for all those direct debits and standing orders. Most online banks can generate a list at the press of a button. If you don't use that club or gym membership, stop paying for it. Definitely do this review with an elderly relative once a year – pounds will be saved.

Savings

Contact your bank and ask what upgrades are available on your savings – this could be a quick win. If it all looks a little average check out a few of the money comparison websites – we like www.moneysavingexpert.com. Account switching is a lot easier than you would imagine and as interest rates rise the competition will become greater.

Lost premium bonds or other National Savings and investment

These can be traced via mylostaccount.org.uk.

Overpay your mortgage

Mortgages cost more than savings interest can earn. Assess whether you can start overpaying on your monthly mortgage payments without penalty – and save money. Another trick is to move your monthly payment earlier in the month and the effect can be dramatic and again save you more so you can live better.

Student loans

If you have children going through university or who have completed their studies and now have large student loans, do a review and think about the debt and interest. The 2012 jump in annual tuition fees from around £3,000 to around £9,000 per annum brought a sudden and dramatic change to the level of debt most of our young people may end up carrying. Up to then, UK higher-education fees were 'cheap' as they were heavily subsidized (and still are in Northern Ireland and Scotland for their home-grown and non-UK EU students).

So the first step is to think about the level of debt now being carried by many of our young people who were entrants in 2012 and later. The second and equally important point is to add in the interest on their student loans. Pre-2012 loans get the benefit of interest being calculated at the lower of two alternatives, RPI or the Bank of England base rate (the latter is currently 0.5 per cent as of summer 2018) plus 1 per cent. So that makes an interest payable rate of just 1.5 per cent. But, and it is a big but, the 2012 and later loans will be paying much more as their interest is RPI (at March) plus up to 3 per cent interest, which takes these students to 6.3 per cent from September 2018 (policy at Summer 2018). If the student ends up with a £50,000 loan just pause, sit down and start adding that interest and maybe think if cheaper money could be found. For instance, a seven-year fixed-rate remortgage could free up significant money at around 2.5 per cent and could offer considerable savings if the student is likely to ultimately pay off their loans, and if you have the equity in your home.

Estate agent fees

If selling your home use an online estate agent to slash your costs.

If you can't save money, try a change and vote with your feet

Even if savings are marginal, remember that business is all about making money and if you are dissatisfied with customer service vote with your feet. That alone can be quite satisfying.

Complaints and 'how to complain'

Things in life inevitably go wrong and sometimes you lose out when it was not your fault. It is always satisfying when you explain your complaint and an organization says:

> We are really sorry for the inconvenience we have caused you. Thank you for taking the time to set out your concerns. We have now fixed the issue and it will not happen again and we would like you to accept a bunch of flowers as our way of saying sorry.

This sort of response is rare and we find it irritating the way more and more companies hide behind websites and make it almost impossible to find someone to speak to directly. Perhaps some businesses will see the benefit of reverting to two-way communications and proper customer care. Many consumers are willing to pay that little bit more for decent service and the assurance that when something goes wrong there will be someone there to do something about it. You should expect justice, fairness, equality and accountability – the mantra of the radical lawyer Michael Mansfield, QC. This chapter will help you achieve this.

Top tip

As the trailblazing punk band The Clash said in 1982… know your rights (and, yes, it is hard to recognize that this was indeed 37 years ago!). They sang about three rights and, using this vision, the three rights you may want to cling to are, first, you have the right to complain. Second, your rights under Section 75 of the Consumer Credit Act 1974 (credit-card rights) are massively powerful when things go wrong. Third, you have rights within the Consumer Rights Act 2015.

You have the right to complain and expect justice, fairness, equality and accountability

When something goes wrong, contact the firm or organization responsible straightaway and give them a chance to sort out the problem. It is only fair that they have a chance to look into your complaint as there are usually two sides to any story and perhaps you have simply misunderstood the situation. Clearly state your complaint. Spend time thinking about this beforehand so that you can be concise about what has happened and, more importantly, what you expect. If you are vague when you complain then you can expect a vague reply. If you want an apology, say this and say why. If you want compensation, state how much and why.

Your first port of call for assistance and back-up is usually the Consumer Rights Act 2015. It came into effect on 1 October 2015 and covers what should happen when goods are faulty, services don't match up to what was agreed, or the service was not handled with reasonable care and skill. It also covers unfair terms in a contract, and extensions to existing laws brought in coverage of digital content (such as online films and games). For more details, including summaries of your rights, use www.citizensadvice.org.uk and go to 'Consumer Rights Act 2015'.

Up the ante: 'formal complaint'

When you complain, keep a note of who you spoke to, the date and time, and what they said will happen next and by when. Ask whether it would help if you put your complaint in writing. If the issue is not resolved, take steps to make it a formal complaint. Ask the organization for the name, address, telephone number and e-mail of the person or department that deals with complaints. Write a letter or e-mail and head it 'FORMAL COMPLAINT' in capitals, quoting any reference you have. Spend time getting it factually correct and attach supporting evidence. If it goes beyond two pages it sounds like you could be rambling. Don't worry – we all do this when we feel aggrieved. But it probably means you need to set it aside and come back to it with a clearer head, reread it and relegate some information to an attachment. Send it by e-mail and ask for confirmation of receipt by return, or send by recorded delivery and keep a copy, together with the post-office tracking receipt.

Take the case further if the organization rejects your complaint and you believe they have not addressed your concerns. Unfortunately, some customer relations teams really don't seem to care what you say or how unfairly you have been treated and will just go through a formula approach, so you may need to significantly escalate things and show you mean business.

Do not be fobbed off at this stage; escalate matters and get more clarity by trying something like:

Dear

FORMAL COMPLAINT: Your ref [reference]

X weeks have now passed and I am dissatisfied with the way you have handled my complaint. Please let me have a copy of your complaints policy and if you have not got one please let me know how I may escalate my complaint within your organization. Please also let me know of any ombudsman scheme, arbitration service or suchlike that I may go to outside your organization if I continue to remain dissatisfied about the complaint that I first put to you on [date].

Yours
[your name]

Top tip

If you remain dissatisfied, say so, and ask for a copy of their complaints policy. This should show you how you may escalate your complaint within the organization and, if you continue to remain dissatisfied, any external organization that you may go to (for instance an ombudsman or external arbitration service).

Some organizations will try to get rid of you by sending you a 'go away' letter. This needs some explanation. They will say that they have 'fully considered' your complaint and have now exhausted all opportunities to reach a conclusion. The punchline is that they will no longer respond to any further letters or communications from you and they will close their file. At this stage it is up to you to decide whether to give up (that is what they want) or take them to an arbitration service or ombudsman or even court (but court could be expensive and is it really worth it?).

Up the ante again: 'obtain your complaint file'

There is a very useful route that few people know about and most big companies have to sign up to. This should help you exert pressure and probe a little further before considering the next step. It really is simple. Just ask for a copy of your complaint file, including all internal notes, telephone transcripts, manager review notes and any other document bearing your name. State the request is made under the General Data Protection Regulations (basically a new improved Data Protection Act 1988) and is a subject access request. State that your request should be passed immediately to their Data Protection Officer. The information has to be supplied to you within one month and provided for free (under the old Data Protection Act you could be asked for a fee of £10 and it could take up to 40 calendar days). When you have your complaint file, review how they have considered your complaint; have they gone back to get the store's side of the story to ensure 'fairness' and is it correct? Has the store said anything that is unfair or untrue? If they have not gone back to get the store's version of events this may mean they have just assumed things and handled your complaint unfairly. Check if there are derogatory statements made about you. This process helps you achieve more accountability from the firm if they seek to fob you off; it shouldn't really be needed if they deal with you openly and fairly – but at least you now have a route to up the ante.

Sometimes firms may blank out (or 'redact') parts of their files and there are strict rules about what can and cannot be redacted. If you believe information has been unfairly redacted you have a right of appeal to the organization that oversees fair play. The Information Commissioner's Office (ICO) has lots of helpful information and template letters that can help you access your personal information: visit www.ico.org.uk – 'for the public'.

Up the ante again: 'pull in some free help with clout'

There are some final routes to consider if you feel you are not receiving justice, fairness, equality and accountability. Some organizations have independent assessors and their service is completely free (for instance, Companies House and other quasi-government agencies). Some have a free ombudsman service (banks, financial advisers and estate agents, as we have signposted below). Others have regulating bodies (solicitors, surveyors and chartered accountants) that may be able to intervene on your behalf. Others have oversight organizations such as Ofcom (mobile phones) or Ofgem (utilities). The route to accessing the relevant organization should be in the firm's complaint policy. If not, try googling complaints about [name of firm] to see if that can provide a pointer.

Estate agents and letting agents: the Property Ombudsman

Some of the biggest financial transactions we entrust to professional advisers are around possibly the biggest asset we own – the house. Things can go wrong, and protection and industry standards have been hit and miss in the past. The Property Ombudsman is penetrating into this area and has the power to make awards of compensation for loss and/or aggravation, distress and inconvenience. The service is free of charge for the public. Its website at www.tpos.co.uk contains all the information you need for making a complaint to an agent and then bringing that complaint to the Property Ombudsman if you remain dissatisfied. The website also lists all agents that are members. If an agent is not a member then you are not covered.

The consumer ombudsman: utilities, phone, internet and property

The consumer ombudsman, Ombudsman Services, will assist with unresolved complaints about your internet or telephone provider, a gas or electricity provider and some property matters, including chartered surveyors and surveyors, agents and valuers (more at www.ombudsman-services.org).

Complaints about the NHS

There is information in Chapter 13 (Health) on what to do if things go wrong.

Professional advisers and financial services

Things can go wrong and there is comprehensive information in Chapter 3 (Professional advisers) on what to expect and what to do if this happens.

Other help

Another useful route is to consider if mediation, arbitration or conciliation services are possible. These routes are referred to as 'alternative dispute resolution'. For instance, the National Conciliation Service handles issues about vehicles (including service and repairs) and can be found at www.nationalconciliationservice.co.uk (there is also www.themotorombudsman.org for resolving motor disputes). Then there is the ABTA arbitration scheme, which deals with alleged breaches of contract and/or negligence between consumers and members of ABTA, the travel organization, which has been in operation for over 40 years.

These schemes are provided so that consumers can have disputes resolved without having to go to court and without having to go to the expense of instructing solicitors. It is important to understand that some are a legal process, which means that if you do go through the process but are not happy with the outcome you cannot then go to court. You have to choose one or the other when pursuing your complaint. Alternative dispute resolution is extending its reach following the Consumer Rights Act 2015 and if you are in dispute with a business they will now need to make you aware of the relevant certified alternative dispute resolution provider.

You are not alone; Citizens Advice may know if there is an alternative dispute resolution process available for your complaint and it also has very useful template letters and advice for complainants at www.citizensadvice. org.uk, or give them a call on 03454 040506.

If there is no external organization you could choose to use a complaints management service. These charge a fee so make sure you understand the costs you will have to pay. You could also consider legal proceedings, but remember that the costs you will pay include the other side's costs if the court decides you are wrong. There is a 'do-it-yourself' service via the County Court online (www.gov.uk – 'make a court claim for money').

Finally: vote with your feet

The final tip is to consider whether or not your complaint is really worth the effort of pursuing. Perhaps an organization has been wrong and you have been dealt with unfairly. You should, of course, think about taking the first few steps as outlined above. But then do you just vote with your feet and go elsewhere – and tell your friends about it? Sadly, some complainants just go on and on (and on) making the same points that have been dealt with by the organization they are complaining against. The complainants then avail themselves of all appeal mechanisms, including involving their MPs. Perhaps they just don't fully understand the issues or have too much time on their hands and dig themselves into a rut. On the other hand, some organizations create havoc with their 'customer don't care' attitude and lack of fairness, and they may side-step any difficult questions. They may ignore or mishandle your requests to focus on the evidence you have supplied and try to fob you off with vague 'standard paragraphs' and, quite simply, you may find there is no accountability for the further distress and inconvenience they cause. In fact, the original incident or cause for complaint may now be minor when compared to the time and effort you have spent trying to right the wrong. The organizations that suppress complaints or act in a deliberately obstructive way really deserve to be held to account. When the evidence mounts up against them, regulators may levy heavy fines, which may prompt them to be accountable and handle complaints with fairness.

We hope this section tunes up your ability to complain more effectively (or helps you perhaps to drop the matter and move on). If there is an action point or something to research further, remember to include it in your own plan for a good retirement (at the end of the book).

Useful reading

Our top recommendations for further help, guidance and support on saving yourself money, scams and complaints are:

- Martin Lewis's website – www.moneysavingexpert.com – which helps you weigh up the best deals on phones, gas, banking products, travel, motoring and shopping.
- The Information Commissioner's Office at www.ico.org.uk and the 'for the public' section.
- The Financial Ombudsman Service website and their 'How to complain' section can help you tackle financial organizations that cause you loss, inconvenience and distress: go to www.financial-ombudsman.org.uk and search for 'complaints'.
- There are many useful template letters and advice for complainants at www.citizensadvice.org.uk – or give them a call on 03454 040506.
- The Property Ombudsman Service and their consumer guide, which sets out what estate agents and letting agents should do and what you can do if they cause you loss, inconvenience and distress: www.tpos.co.uk and search for their consumer guide.
- Ombudsman Services, the Consumer Ombudsman, for guidance on unresolved complaints about your internet or telephone provider, a gas or electricity provider and some property matters, including chartered surveyors and surveyor, agents and valuers (www.ombudsman-services.org).

Inspired? Remember to fill in your plan for a good retirement at the end of the book.

CHAPTER EIGHT

Avoid being scammed

A fool and his money are soon parted.

THOMAS TUSSER

Having worked so long to build up a wealth and asset base we want to protect it and enjoy the benefits of our decades of hard work or, perhaps, some lucky opportunities we have had over the years. At the end of the day this book is all about planning more, saving more, living better and being happier in retirement. This chapter sits within Part Two (Save more and earn better) of the book, which runs to four chapters; however, this particular chapter could be just about the best thing you read this year if it saves you or a loved one from being scammed.

Sadly there are predators out there who may want a slice of our cake. Scammers are basically clever crooks who deploy sleight of hand, fast talk and a few back-up techniques such as vanity and knowing that people never want to admit to being stupid. You may not spot a scammer in action or be able to work out how they pulled it off, in the same way as a good magician really will leave you believing that they made someone 'float' on stage. The equivalent of smoke, mirrors and sleight of hand can make anything look possible. With the help of friends in the know this chapter serves as your common-sense approach to help you ignore the smoke and mirrors deployed by the scammers and stay safer.

> **This chapter at a glance**
>
> - Five simple golden rules for staying safe from scammers. Follow them and you will be safer.
> - Scams tend to follow a pattern and just get dressed up in different guises each year. The common scams are set out and you will learn the pattern and spot the next one that comes along.
> - Further tips are provided on staying safe on the phone and online. Both routes are like leaving the door open to your house, but there are some straightforward steps that are the equivalent of a door lock or tach and will keep you safer.
> - Tips from the best in the industry – the Police and the Financial Ombudsman.

The five golden rules for staying safe from scammers

Trust your instincts

It is a simple common-sense approach: ignore the smoke and mirrors and sleight of hand that crooks and scammers are so capable of pulling off that are used to distract you from the real issue. Does it look, feel and 'smell' like something is not quite right? Does it get your hackles up? If so, trust your instincts and walk away, put the letter in the bin or put down the phone, shut the door or make an excuse and walk away/leave. Instincts have been honed in the human species over thousands of years – if they have served you well in the past, learn to trust them.

Actions speak louder than words

Scammers, generally, are all talk (unsurprisingly, they are very good at it) and no action. It should also come as no surprise that they are also charming and 'nice and friendly'. So here's the nub of the issue as, quite simply, any reasonable person should be able to deliver against what they promise or apologize and explain before you have to ask, 'what's going on?' If the actions don't happen then just walk away and don't give them a second chance to take advantage of you. If some reasonable questions (it's good to ask and ask) provoke a hint of aggression or anything to put you down then that should tell you all you need to know. Remember the motto – it is actions that count, not words.

Too good to be true?

Scammers know that greed often gets the better of many people and so they employ it to their advantage. If it sounds too good to be true, it is probably a scam. Put down the phone, shut the door or make an excuse and walk away/leave.

Thank you, but I'll just check with...

We have great financial institutions in the United Kingdom and this goes to the very heart of the UK economy. Our regulatory system is sound. You should therefore check precisely who you are dealing with, and if it involves big money or risk then ensure you are dealing with professional advisers – check out the information in Chapter 3 (Professional advisers) where you can verify who they are and if they really are a 'professional adviser'. For anything to do with savings, investments and pensions you must check that the firm is regulated by the Financial Conduct Authority (www.fca.org.uk).

Sometimes individuals hide behind the cloak of a firm or a company. If it is a professional advisory firm the same rules apply – check them out as per the advice in Chapter 3. If the company is not a high-street name you can do some straightforward, free research at Companies House (www.gov.uk). Go to 'Companies House' then 'find company information', then 'start' and enter the company name or unique number in the 'search the register' box, then look at the filing history documents, which have lots of juicy detail. Check how long the company has been in existence and whether it has filed its accounts on time. Both can flag up warning signs and accessing the service is completely free and really easy to do.

Also linked to the 'I'll just check with...' tip is the simple fact that crooks have one other objective in addition to taking your hard-earned cash – and that is not getting caught out. This is where nosy neighbours are brilliant – a stroll in their direction, a smile, a look in the eye and a few questions (after talking about the weather for 10 seconds!) can be of great assistance armed with tip number one, 'trust your instincts'.

If in doubt, stay out

Over the last decade the online world has gained a reach into our lives, our information and our wealth. Regulation has not been able to keep up to date to protect us as, literally, anyone, anywhere in the world can reach us and interact with us online. We really must accept that, to a large extent, it is up to us how much we use the online world, acknowledging that everyone (including the government) is encouraging us to use it. For safety follow the golden rule – if in doubt stay out. That means if your browser does not display the 'secure' green padlock on the site you are looking at then you have no protection. It means you keep people out by knowing and checking your profile settings on social media.

Share this with granny

If you only do one thing as a result of this chapter, do this: require any elderly friend or relative to learn the above tips and read this chapter as the scammers prey on those who are alone or vulnerable – and giving them the knowledge and confidence of your complete support is one of the best things you could give. Giving is good, and perhaps this could feature in your plan for a good retirement at the end of the book.

Some common scams

Amazing concert tickets, beautiful holiday cottage – and it's all make believe

You probably already know the reputable ticket sale sites and bona fide sites where you can get holiday accommodation. So why do people sometimes think they have found a bargain, send their money and then, hey presto, just like a magician, the scammer, concert ticket and holiday accommodation has disappeared? Stick to the reputable sites. If you do think you have a found a bargain and it really is too good to be true, the acid test is in the payment route.

The warning bells have a range of sounds. They range from a non-bank transfer overseas (the alarm bells are sounding so loudly we cannot sleep) to a bank transfer (still not good and a very uncomfortable night's sleep) and we only really settle down when they take a credit card payment and it is over the value of £100 (great, a good night's sleep). This is because if you pay for something costing between £100 and £30,000 on credit then the credit provider is equally liable if something goes wrong. If you want the details this comes from Section 75 of the Consumer Credit Act 1974, which gives us the shorthand of a 'Section 75 claim'.

Payments by debit card get an honourable mention due to a process called 'chargeback'. It works by you contacting the bank and stating: 'I want to chargeback the (describe transaction, amount and date of the original debit-card payment)'. Importantly the request must be made within 120 days of the original transaction (this may not work for holiday accommodation or tickets booked more than 120 days in advance and you find out too late that it was all a scam). Chargeback is usually used where goods do not show up, are damaged or differ from the description (ie breach of contract-type claims). If the bank rejects your claim you can appeal to the Financial Ombudsman to have your case reviewed.

Hackers

Your bank, solicitor or other trusted professional will e-mail you to finalize payment of a transaction you currently have in progress. You diligently follow their instructions but end up being scammed and losing it all – perhaps a six-figure sum if it was a house deposit. So how did that happen? The world of the internet had been hacked and someone, somewhere in the world identified your transaction was in progress and the parties involved. They simply created bogus e-mails drawing on the publicly accessible information of the bank, solicitor or other professionals and, with a bit of clever graphic design, amended their real e-mail so that it somehow displayed in your e-mail account as having come from the bank, solicitor or other professional. In some cases the individual's account has been hacked so it comes from their genuine account. You duly make the payment. Unfortunately the scammer has set up bank accounts in the UK with false ID and the payment is cleared out and 'gone' before anyone has worked out what has really happened.

A variant is a scammer impersonating a regular supplier (to you individually or to your business), stating that they have changed their bank details and requesting the recipient amend their records. To counter these attacks ensure your anti-virus software is up to date, use extra-secure passwords (see below for more on this) and on e-mailed bank details call the firm and secure confirmation from two different people.

Other e-mail scammers

The ingenuity and creativity of e-mail scammers is reaching new heights. Someone somewhere has gathered thousands of e-mail addresses, including yours, and mass-mails them with a piece of information – designed with only one purpose in mind. That purpose is to gain your attention and engagement and a 'click' on their planted dodgy button/link etc. All scam e-mails end up the same way, which is you losing out. Maybe they offer a refund from HMRC or purport to be a bank indicating that the security of your account has been compromised. It could be a fairly credible-looking court summons or something that looks like a Facebook friend request (but you are already Facebook friends so that seems a bit strange). The e-mails all have one purpose and one purpose only and that is to get you to 'click on a link'. Unfortunately, the reality is that the message you received has been built by scammers and they want to steal your money – the link you are asked to click or document you are asked to open could contain a harmful virus intended to monitor the activity on your computer or cause other security problems.

> **Top tip**
>
> Never, never, never click on any links from strange e-mail accounts, and if in doubt check it out with the organization directly – hover over the displayed e-mail address to show the actual e-mail account the scammer may be using.

Generally try to protect yourself by restricting yourself to known organizations and deal directly with their websites and look for the secure 'padlock' symbol in the browser. If it is a UK business they must clearly show the company or business operating the website (usually in the 'contact us' or 'about us' section), which you can then check out. If it is a company and it is not a high-street name check out the company at Companies House as suggested in the 'Thank you, but I'll just check with…' section above – the service is free. The watchwords here are 'If in doubt, stay out'.

The surprise prize-ballot win

There is usually a premium-rate telephone number to call in order to claim the prize or a fairly small-value payment to make, but at the end of the day, and after much excitement, the ultimate actual prize is probably worthless or trivial. File anything like this under 'B' for bin. It is, however, sometimes fun to read the small print in such 'prizes' in order to spot the scam or the impossibility of winning the supposed big prize. This is how it works: there will be a few flashy big prizes (always something eye-catching to get you excited) and then other prizes for which there may be 5,000 or more 'winners' and will probably take you more than £10 in phone or other 'processing' charges to 'win'. In reality your chances of winning are remote and cunningly the scammers do not state the odds of actually winning. Watch out for words such as 'your assigned numbers could match', which means you may not have won anything at all and what you have is just a chance to enter some sort of ballot. The scammers rely on you getting distracted by the official-looking paperwork and the mention of prizes – the equivalent of the magician's smoke-and-mirror distractions mentioned earlier. As a final deterrent, if you are foolish enough to reply to something you didn't enter in the first place you are likely to be put on a 'suckers list' (the term the scammers use) and will be bombarded by even more junk ballots and scams.

Top tip

File mystery ballot wins under 'B' for bin and don't let your greed get in the way.

Credit- and bank-card cloning or snatching

This can be the jackpot for the scammers, but how can they actually get your credit or bank card? The cloning devices that they attach to a bank's cash machine are not so far-fetched these days. But how about the scammer who calls you and pretends to be from the police, explaining they have just arrested someone who 'apparently' was caught with a clone of your card? They arrange for a courier to call and collect your actual card as part of their investigations. Unfortunately, it is all just another scam and the supposed police officer is just another scammer. These guys really do have guts but the bottom line is never, ever, be worried about feeling made to look silly. Just play it slow, play it confused, take time out and confide in someone.

Top tip

Don't be worried about being made to look silly – play it as if you are just confused, ask them to write down exactly what they want so you can show it to your son/daughter/neighbour etc. If they won't and they tell you it's a secret then they are lying.

Advance fee fraud

This is one of the scammers' favourites and has been dressed up in a hundred different guises. The scam is remarkably simple. A payment is made by you with the promise of a bigger payout in return. Perhaps it is cloaked in terms of funds left to you by a mystery relative, where you pay a processing fee of £50, then maybe you are asked to pay another release fee of £150 and on it goes with a promise of £10,000 sucking you in (which, of course, you will never actually receive). Walk away.

Doorstep scams

National Trading Standards tell us that 85 per cent of victims of doorstep scams are aged 65 or over. These scams follow a regular routine. A knock on the door and a stranger. There is a request (Can I use the phone as it is an emergency? I noticed a broken window/broken roof tile/there is a gas leak or water leak, etc). Once inside, the crook will distract you whilst their sidekick steals something, or else they provide some emergency service and then overcharge you. Remember, you don't have to answer the door. Always use a door chain and fit a spy hole on solid doors. Trust your instincts, ask for ID, and if unsure ask them to return at a later time when someone will be with you. Again, this is where 'nosy neighbours' are brilliant, so look out for each other.

Romance and dating fraud

The new lover, or someone showing you interest, gives you attention you crave just when you may need it (maybe you are at a low point – remember, these scammers are clever and will make sure they look the part). After a while the sob stories start – maybe money for a sick mother or child. Scammers know how to manipulate you to get the response they want. They usually want you to keep things 'secret' as they know that any friend you confide in will tell you to run a mile. Sadly, emotional involvement and shame prevent some people from acting rationally – and the scammers know this. Charming chat, sleight of hand and, just like a magician, your money is gone before you know it.

> **Top tip**
>
> Romance scams – trust your instincts when you smell a rat. Be brave and confide in someone you really trust – and show them this page!

Sextortion

Sextortion involves the scammers duping you into some form of act or contact over some form of sex-related activity (either via fake online-dating profiles or content viewed online) and then blackmailing you. The *Daily Express* reported the upsurge in this new type of crime in 2017, highlighting 'the National Crime Agency statement of 1,245 cases of "financially motivated webcam blackmail" had been reported to their Anti-Kidnap and Extortion Unit in 2016, up more than threefold on 2015. But experts believe the true figure could be as much as 10 times higher. One NCA investigator said victims range from 14 to 82 but are mostly 21 to 30 years old.'

You may feel embarrassed but the police have seen it all before so don't pay the blackmailer and call the police instead, as this type of crime is usually perpetrated by organized crime and the police will take it seriously. Remember, with both romance scams and sextortion there are caring organizations you should use in order to help talk things through from the point of view of your own welfare:

- Sane: www.sane.org.uk or call 0300 304 7000.
- CALM – Campaign Against Living Miserably: call 0800 585858.
- Samaritans: www.samaritans.org or call 116 123.

Call in the police

If you spot a scam or have been scammed, report it and get help. Contact the Police Action Fraud contact centre on 0300 123 2040 or online at www.actionfraud.police.uk – or contact the police in your area. If a crime is in progress or about to happen, the suspect is known or can be easily identified, or the crime involves a vulnerable victim, then dial 999 if it is an emergency or 101 if it isn't.

For more information, take a look at the police guidance the *Little Book of Big Scams*: visit www.met.police.uk and go to 'The Little Book of Big Scams' – we think it is an absolutely top piece of work (advice about scam mail can also be found at www.thinkjessica.com).

Keeping safe from telephone cold calls and online fraud

The above examples are just some of the higher-profile and potentially higher-value scams, but there are many more. Some of them you may encounter over the phone and internet on a weekly basis.

Cold callers on the telephone can be irritating at best and sometimes downright scary. They may not take 'no' for an answer. The way these calls are intruding into our lives is becoming a real problem.

Top tip

Use the magic words, 'I am signed up to the Telephone Preference Service and you should not be calling this number', which helps make them 'go away'.

The Telephone Preference Service (TPS) is a free service. It is the official central opt-out register on which you can record your preference not to receive unsolicited sales or marketing calls. It is a legal requirement that all organizations (including charities, voluntary organizations and political parties) do not make such calls to numbers registered on the TPS unless they have your consent to do so. You can register both your landline phone number and any mobile phone number via the TPS; more information is available at www.tpsonline.org.uk. If you are worried about an elderly relative, neighbour or friend who is on their own and could be vulnerable, the best thing you could do is talk to them and buy them a telephone that displays the inbound number and, even better, blocks certain numbers, including overseas numbers (other than those they want to receive).

Premium-rate phone-call scams

A text message, e-mail or even a missed parcel note or debt-collector note through the door (clever eh!) asks you to call a phone number (and then inserts some words that lure you – a threat (debt collector), a prize, free holiday, free meal, free shopping voucher, missed parcel etc). Always google the precise phone number, as thankfully people report scam numbers and log why and what happened on the internet, so you can find out fairly quickly and can put it in either the genuine pot (rare) or scam bin. The scam numbers are at extortionate rates and you will lose out.

Top tip

Rule 1 – if it is important they will call back, so don't worry. Rule 2 – if it is not important then who cares? Rule 3 – always google any number before calling it if the number is not known to you.

The padlock symbol means secure (usually)

When buying online a secure website starts with the prefix 'https' where the 's' means secure. Happy? Well almost, as you need to be absolutely sure you are on the real website you were looking for. The scammers may have created a similar site, changing only one letter of the website name so the webpage you are buying from does not belong to the shop you expected but the scammer (albeit you are connected securely).

So don't rush transactions, check the website name, the 's' for secure in the prefix and the green padlock and you will be safer (and happier!).

Anti-virus software

Keep your anti-virus software up to date. There are free options such as AVG free (www.avg.com). For free online security advice, visit www. getsafeonline.org.

Have a backup

What happens if your laptop/other device is stolen or you get hacked and your data is stolen and then wiped? That made you think. The loss of photos and memories is one thing but what about everything else – your contacts, files and other vital information. Take a secure back up on devices such as Apple's iCloud, an external hard drive or a USB flash drive.

Review and change your social media profile settings

We expose a massive amount of personal information on social media without locking out the bad boys and girls. Ensure your privacy settings are as you would want – usually friends only. Don't overlook this for your good retirement plan at the end of the book, especially if you are about to post photos online showing you are thousands of miles from your home on holiday. If you don't know how to do this ask any younger relative to help.

The worst passwords

This almost beggars belief, but Time reported the worst passwords of 2017 as revealed by a password management security firm. The worst and most-used nightmare password was 123456, followed by 'password'. In 2016 the worst were 123456, followed by 111111, password, qwerty and 123qwe.

Nightmare passwords, as reported in previous editions of this guide, were 'welcome', 'letmein' and 'princess'.

Your password should be, where allowed, at least 12 digits long, contain a mix of upper- and lower-case letters, numbers and a special character. Remember to password-protect your smartphone as there is probably more information on that device than can be obtained from breaking into your house.

Only download apps from trusted sites such as Apple (www.apple.com/uk). If you sell or dispose of your phone, always clean it by restoring factory settings to blank it and remove media cards (younger relatives can show you how to do this if need be), or smash it to pieces.

Top tip

For free online security advice, visit www.getsafeonline.org.

Tips from the police on online fraud

The online world offers rich pickings for crooks as the criminal can engage with the victim without having to meet them. They can be sitting in an internet cafe on the other side of the world! This makes it increasingly difficult for law enforcement to trace the suspects' victims, who are frequently scammed when trying to make purchases online, including vehicles, event tickets and holiday lettings.

Scam online purchases continue to be rich pickings for the criminals. Typically the scammer lures people into buying a vehicle or some other valuable item (maybe a ticket to a prized event), which never turns up. As knowledge is the key in the fight against the scammers a Metropolitan Police spokesperson explained:

> **Metropolitan Police:** Often, there is a series of e-mails going between the suspect and the victim when the victim believes they are building a relationship with the suspect and levels of trust are increased. The criminal uses a name they think will engender trust and a scripted cover story as to why the victim cannot see the vehicle before they buy, eg it is in storage in Scotland. Often the victim is persuaded that any money will go into an escrow/holding account and will only be released once the vehicle has been delivered. They want you to believe the money is safe in the event that anything goes wrong. In reality, the bank account the victim pays into has been opened purely for the purpose of receiving fraudulent funds. The victim pays the money but the vehicle is never delivered.

When the victim realizes their mistake, the money is gone as it gets withdrawn from the account on the same day, and it will eventually be revealed it was opened with false documents using a false address.

Good Retirement Guide: So what can we do to protect ourselves?

Metropolitan Police: Read and follow the fraud-prevention advice given on the auction websites themselves. Do not be tempted to stray from that advice. Pay by credit card, as that offers some degree of protection for amounts over £100. If the seller refuses to talk over the phone and/or meet with you, walk away from the deal. Two of the techniques of the scammers are rushing you (so don't rush – take time out and think) and wanting you to keep things secret (so don't keep it to yourself – talk it over with a trusted friend). Never let the excitement of a bargain get in the way of applying good common sense and caution. Our most important tip: wealth can be replaced or insured but always consider your personal safety before meeting with someone you have had contact with over the internet – take a friend along or walk away.

Good Retirement Guide: We have packed this chapter with hints and tips. From your experience over the last year do you have any other tips?

Metropolitan Police: Your tip about reviewing and changing the privacy setting on social media is vital to 'lock out' potential scammers from your life. This really is non-negotiable in 2019. Another tip we can share is around the nasty side of romance and dating fraud where crooks steal other people's images and pretend to be them. If someone interacts with you online remember you can search the image online to see if it has been used elsewhere. You can check if images are held elsewhere on the internet through websites such as Google's reverse image search at reverse.photos or the reverse image search at www.tineye.com – this can give a good indication if the picture has been taken from the internet and is being used fraudulently.

Reporting fraud can be done online at www.actionfraud.police.uk or call Action Fraud on 0300 123 2040. In an emergency, dial 999. Be assured that the most effective method to combat fraud is to prevent it in the first place. Awareness of common frauds and taking simple actions to prevent yourself from falling victim are the most vital things you can do. Pass on your copy of this book to an elderly friend or relative so we can all keep people that little bit safer, as knowledge is the key to protecting yourself.

The Financial Ombudsman's top tips to fight back against the scammers

David Cresswell is Director of Strategy at the Financial Ombudsman Service and is a well-known and trusted voice on radio and television. His knowledge on keeping your wealth safe is second to none. David's top tips for our readers are listed below and will help keep you safe:

1 *Are they regulated?* The Financial Ombudsman Service and Financial Services Compensation Scheme are there to help if the person or company you are dealing with is on the official Financial Conduct Authority (FCA) register and things go wrong. Because of this added protection you should always check, if you are offered investments or pension products or advice, whether the company is on the register: go to www.fca.org.uk and go to 'register' or phone 0800 111 6768. It is unlikely that either organization will be able to help if the business you think you have been scammed by is not regulated, but if you are not sure, call the ombudsman to ask. Prevention is better than cure, so the tips below will help you steer a safer course.

2 *Out of the blue.* They say you have more chance of being repeatedly struck by lightning than you have of winning the lottery. Yet every day hundreds of us receive e-mails claiming that we have won money from a mysterious foreign country, or that we have been selected by a strange organization for a random prize.

   Most of us know better than to fall for this, but in recent years, fraudsters have invested time and effort into making fake e-mails and letters look more convincing. They look like messages from official organizations such as your bank, HMRC or even the ombudsman, and ask you to confirm your personal details. Recently, we have even seen pleas for help that look like they have been sent to you by friends in trouble who need you to send them cash. Don't fall for them. Watch out for questionable e-mail addresses that are either from personal accounts (Gmail, Hotmail) or other countries (check the letters after the 'dot' – as in '.ru' for Russia) and e-mails or letters that fail to address you by your name.

3 *Vishing and smishing.* In recent years, the ombudsman has seen a rise in new telephone scams that can be devastatingly effective. Vishing (using the telephone) and smishing (using text messages) are scams where the fraudster pretends to be from your bank (or another official organization) and tricks you into transferring or handing over your savings by pretending your account security has been breached. These scams work in a range of ways so it is simpler to remember this one fact – *your bank will never ask you to transfer or hand over your money because of a threat of fraud, and they will not ask you for your online or telephone banking passwords.* If someone asks you to do this, be suspicious. These scams are horrifically effective and some people have lost over £100,000.

4 *Too much information*. Phone or online banking passwords are often the source of much frustration – but they are a necessary hassle in many ways. Your bank will ask you for random letters, numbers or characters from your password. But they will not ask you to confirm your full password on the phone or ask for your PIN. If you are asked for this information, this should be a clear warning that something is wrong. If you are struggling to remember a password, or you are worried your existing ones are too simple, try getting creative, like taking the first letter of each word in a line from your favourite song.

Many people are concerned about 'chip and PIN' cards – the ombudsman gets lots of enquiries from people suggesting their card has been cloned. This is extremely unusual. In fact, the most common form of PIN fraud is the most low-tech – 'shoulder surfing', or peering over your shoulder at an ATM or when typing in your PIN at the local supermarket.

5 *Pry before you buy*. Every year, the number of things we buy online increases dramatically. Crowded shopping centres mean many of us are going online and bargain hunting. But sometimes we let down our guard when surfing the web. Websites are always competing to offer you the best possible price and it is tempting to think that 'cheapest is best'.

If you are accessing a website for the first time, before you confirm the purchase you should run a quick internet search to check out reviews and see what your fellow consumers are saying. If it seems too good to be true, be sceptical. Regardless, use a form of payment that offers you some protection, such as PayPal or MoneyGram. Alternatively, if you are making a larger payment, your credit card gives you some rights under the Consumer Credit Act if something goes wrong.

6 *Look after yourself*. The easiest way to spot something untoward with your money is to know your finances inside out. Reading your bank statements and knowing what you have got coming in and going out each month is the best way to avoid any cashflow surprises. Most importantly, trust your instincts. If something doesn't feel right, it's probably because it isn't.

Hopefully, these tips will help you keep one step ahead of the scammers. But if something does go wrong, the most important thing is to keep calm. Contact your bank straightaway and it may be able to sort things out. If you don't think your bank is being helpful, or you are not sure what it should be doing to help, call the ombudsman – they might be able to help. Financial Ombudsman Service: 0800 023 4567 (www.financial-ombudsman. org.uk).

> **Top tip**
>
> Trust your instincts. If something doesn't feel right it's probably because it isn't.

Useful reading

Our top recommendations for further help, guidance and support on saving yourself money, scams and complaints are:

- *The Little Book of Big Scams*, published by the Metropolitan Police Service, PSNI and other forces. You can download the booklet at www.met.police.uk – go to 'The Little Book of Big Scams'.
- BBC's *Rip Off Britain* – go to www.bbc.co.uk and search for 'Rip Off Britain', then go to their section on consumer advice.
- Visit www.getsafeonline.org for free online security advice.
- Citizens Advice: www.citizensadvice.org.uk and their 'scams' section.

Inspired? Remember to fill in your plan for a good retirement at the end of the book.

CHAPTER NINE

Career transition and paid work

We need to do a better job of putting ourselves higher on our own 'to do' list.

MICHELLE OBAMA

The first reaction of many people approaching retirement is often 'great, no more work' and they are puzzled at a whole chapter on career transition and other paid work. So here is how it works in a 'nutshell'.

High-responsibility, high-stress jobs with perhaps lots of travel within the UK or internationally can work right up to retirement. This may keep you busy and provide the finances you need. But is there another way, perhaps starting about 10 years from retirement, which provides more of a glide-path into retirement rather than a bump landing? Put another way, can you 'rightsize' your employment?

Even if you enjoy your work and find it satisfying it may be restrictive in ways you don't see. You stick to the rules – specific tasks, regular timekeeping – and have limited personal freedom to do as you want. Have you heard people say that 'their life isn't their own' due to the demands of the job? So can the pressure be turned down or even off? Can you get rid of the ball and chain and start following your own guiding star to a better retirement? Career transition describes the process of reassessing what you can offer and what you really want, and exploring opportunities to achieve a better last decade of employment. Perhaps the employment may last beyond state retirement age if things work out really well and you are able to 'rightsize' your job.

Working beyond your present intended retirement age can be so much more than just work. It can provide a boost to your self-esteem, a social life and much-appreciated mental stimulation. Wanting to have something to do to avoid boredom, and a desire to feel useful, are other key reasons that many people continue working, whether paid or unpaid. And why not? If you enjoy it, feel you are too young to stop, or want to try your hand at something new why not give it a go with a new and fresh perspective? So this chapter sits very well within the 'save more/earn better' section of the book and could well inspire one of the most important follow-up points in your own plan for a good retirement at the end of the book. If so, you should, in turn, live better and be happier.

Alternatively your needs may be financial as, quite simply, having reviewed your retirement plans in Chapter 1 (Doing the sums) you now need to supplement your present anticipated or actual retirement income. Or perhaps you are in an industry that traditionally has 'early retirement' and you are not yet ready to leave the working world behind.

The other key readers for this chapter are those looking to take on the role of a non-executive board member of a business, a position on a public body, or routine part-time work to provide some interest and extra finance.

This chapter at a glance

- Employment 'rightsizing' and using career transition to help you change career to provide a smoother glide-path into retirement.
- How to assess yourself and find the right position.
- Tips to help you get that role.
- Tips on redundancy situations.
- Help on getting full- or part-time employment in retirement.
- There is also information and advice on training opportunities and other employment ideas, including finding public appointments, which can be satisfying and financially rewarding. Once you start reading, you will be on the way to finding the ideal occupation for you.

Career transition

This comes down to blue-sky thinking on a blank sheet of paper. You have worked for decades and probably have seen all sorts of positive and negative work experiences. Added to this, your knowledge of work experiences of those close to you can be illuminating.

This career review has five broad components: what type of job I would like and where; what I bring; how I can make the best impression; what opportunities are out there; and, finally, whether or not the package is sufficient.

What type of job I would like and where

It begins with a review of what you value in life – list this in order of importance. This is the big stuff in your life – your wants and desires. Is it remaining close to family and perhaps caring responsibilities, a location or community or more freedom to pursue your passion in life (sailing, riding, refurbishing a cottage etc)? Conversely, what do you want to avoid? Is the role to be full-time or part-time? What travel limits would you like to see?

Next, assess how you respond best in a work situation and with what sort of management style above you. What causes you to thrive and what causes you stress? What really motivates you and, conversely, what demotivates you? Learn from past experiences – both the best and worst. Is it team working that you enjoy, and dealing with people, or do you prefer to get on with things on your own?

Then think about the types of work you could do and whether they are in a declining, stable or increasing market. How does this influence the breadth of choice you should be looking at?

Everyone is different and there is no right or wrong answer here. It is about reassessing what is best for you at this stage in life and as you move on from here.

What I bring

Identify the skills you have and especially how they are transferable to other roles – don't forget those learnt through hobbies or voluntary work. Talk to people who know you about the potential jobs you can do – this can yield great intelligence and trigger 'I'd never have thought of that' moments. Ignore the importance of these discussions at your peril: try to set aside at least an hour for each discussion, and have a structure (maybe the points in this section) so that you deal with specifics rather than vague notions. Generally, the more experienced your confidants, the better the output.

A trusted and structured form of career analysis is the 'Birkman method', which measures through a long questionnaire four main areas: your usual behaviour in the context of tasks and relationships; what you require in the environment and people around you in order to be at your best; your behaviours in stress situations when your needs are not met; your interests (the tasks and activities that offer you the greatest attraction and satisfaction). Your present employer may arrange for you to do this questionnaire as part of a career review or you can access it via a number of HR-type consultancies throughout the UK (try googling 'Birkman method' and your location).

How can I make the best impression?

This is all about translating what you know about yourself into a credible statement that underlines your experience, skills and knowledge and how you can add value to the company or organization in meeting the challenges they have.

Take care with application forms In addition to your CV some firms may also ask you to complete an application form relating to the job in question. Read carefully the questions they ask and in your responses try to play to your own strengths and experience. Remember that in a competitive job market firms will use the application form to shortlist those candidates they want to take a further look at through interview. Shortlisting decisions will be made solely on the quality of the application.

CV writing This is so important, and presentation is key. If it is a few years since you have updated your CV, make sure it is current and contains the following sections: personal and contact information; education and qualifications; work history and/or experience and relevant skills to the job in question. Personal interests, achievements and hobbies can be covered briefly if relevant to the job. Use assertive, positive language, emphasizing the skills you have gained from past work. The CV should not run to more than two pages of A4 paper.

Doing an interview You may be called for an interview. Take time to prepare for this and research the firm itself and the job vacancy. Study the attributes required for the role – you will find these on the job profile – and decide how you can show you meet them. You may be asked to do a presentation and, if so, you should receive guidance on the subject, slide length and time allocation for the presentation and then the time for questions. Prepare a mental checklist of your own strengths and experience that might enable you to do the job in question – the interview panel will almost certainly want to explore this with you during the actual interview. Your decades of experience and loyalty will set you apart from youngsters so emphasize this with examples of extra work you did on the job and how you can add value. To do yourself justice – prepare, prepare, prepare – and then, in the interview, try to relax and be yourself.

Referees These will not be required until you are at the point of receiving an offer. Have them ready: one should be a previous employer and the other someone who can vouch for you personally.

What opportunities are out there?

Get organized Your career transition/job-hunting campaign needs planning. Don't leave something so important to chance. Set aside a study area in your home and devote a number of hours each day to job searching.

Let the internet force be with you The ability to use the internet to get a job is vital. Familiarity with social media sites such as Twitter, LinkedIn and Facebook will show that you are up to speed with technology. It will also show interviewers that you are able to connect with younger colleagues and keep abreast of the ever-changing technological advances.

Make use of your contacts Within the network of people you know there are bound to be some who, whilst not actually able to get you a job, can give some advice, information and potential job leads. Decide what the best means of approach will be for each one of them – personal contact, e-mail, telephone or letter.

Former colleagues and finder fees – a win-win Introductions to prospective employers from a former colleague or a friend you know who already works for the target organization can work well. It gives you a 'warm in' and may give the former colleague or friend a finder fee, which can be significant. It cuts out the recruitment agencies and the fee they would otherwise get and can be a great win for all concerned. You may want to explore these routes before signing up with recruitment agencies.

Recruitment agencies Identify the recruitment agencies who operate in your targeted career areas. These can vary in size and quality so ask around for recommendations on the good and the bad.

Remember the '3 Rs' While looking for paid work, regularly review results. Check how much progress you make each week on your work-seeking campaign: how many contacts you have added to your network, what results these have yielded and how you plan to follow them up.

Is the package sufficient?

The numbers are important and will be dealt with in a moment, but now that we are more experienced there are other vital factors:

- The new boss and prospective colleagues. Did you like and respect them?
- What is their spirit and ethos? Do they support volunteering and community work and, from an ethics point of view, did you feel they fit with you?
- You will be listening and looking during any interview and perhaps tour the office. What do your instincts tell you? Trust them as they are usually well honed and tailored, of course, to you.
- What are the travel and overtime expectations? Are these clear and understood?
- Do they offer a gym and other wellness activities?

Then on to the numbers. Make sure you are clear on the package – salary; any bonus expectations; health care, life cover; holiday entitlement, ability to buy extra days' holiday (increasingly important as you glide into retirement); pensions (what you contribute and what they contribute – the latter can be significant); and any share-purchase plans.

Employment rightsizing

The traditional view is that people press onwards and upwards in employment – and in the old days of final salary pension schemes (see Chapter 4) this had a logic. Today the model is turned on its head and the final decade or years of employment is more about a glide-path. So can you re-engineer with your current employer less stress, less travel and less responsibility for the same or similar headline pay but perhaps sacrificing some of the bonus by agreement? If not, is it time to 'blue-sky' think and find that other role that meets your values and skills and provides a smoother glide-path into retirement? This is employment 'rightsizing'.

Redundancy

Managers feel that one of the worst jobs they will have to deal with is making someone redundant. Hopefully it will be handled with care and compassion with outplacement support ('outplacement' is the term the industry uses for the process to help move employees on when there is restructuring). The outplacement support can vary in length and quality but broadly may include a one-to-one relationship with a career counsellor who will assist you in the transition from one career into another or into early retirement. The process may include workbooks, seminars and work-shops, webinars – and the process should cover career research, the job application process, CV preparation and interview techniques. Other options such as early retirement or starting your own business may also be available.

Generally, employers will want to handle this well – as cost cutting and redundancies can involve several rounds as a business restructures. If the first round goes badly then motivation and productivity can decrease and the business continues to decline.

If redundancy is likely then the following pointers may assist:

- If your employer's pension scheme allows it can you take your pension early in lieu of part or all of the severance package?

- Up to £30,000 of redundancy can be tax free and anything above that is taxed at your highest rate of tax, so could it help if it fell in the next tax year if this was an option?

- Review with your human resources manager whether you can ask for part of any termination payment beyond the £30,000 tax-free sum to be paid into your pension. This can be tax efficient and professional advice should be sought (see Chapter 3, Professional advisers).

- If you have share options these may lapse on the date you leave (your employment contract and options offer will clarify this point). If you feel the options are likely to increase substantially see if you can extend the period so that they are spread over two tax years or more. This may give you more than one year of Capital Gains Tax exemption if you can spread the sale of options (see Chapter 6 for information on Capital Gains Tax).

- Check out your rights and follow this through with any legal expenses insurance that you have, which can help you understand your rights. Legal expenses insurance often comes as an extra to home insurance or professional association membership so check your policies. There are strict rules about consulting with trade unions or employee representatives before redundancy notices are handed out and you should also be consulted individually. If this does not happen you may have a case for unfair dismissal and any legal expenses insurance you have could be valuable to help you enforce your rights. If the business is insolvent and an insolvency practitioner is appointed in control of the business the rules are different and there is less protection (but a government safety net still exists for unpaid salary and redundancy payments).

- Don't agree to anything verbally – ask for all proposals to be put in writing and review it via any legal expenses insurance you may have, or consider taking legal advice.

- Check what happens to your benefits during any notice period that you are not required to work. What is the value of these and how will you be compensated?

- Check specifically if life cover and health cover can continue during any notice period that you are not required to work whilst you find a new job, especially if you have a challenging medical history as these can be costly to implement for a short period and can take time to arrange in such circumstances.

- Ask about retaining office equipment you may have been supplied with as it is usually more bother for the employer to gather these in. Ask also about any mobile phone or laptop, but these may need to be restored to the original state to remove company confidential information.

Paid employment into retirement

You may feel the need to supplement your retirement income with a full- or part-time job. The good news is that job opportunities for people in the traditional retirement years are increasing. There are a number of global companies becoming known for employing people beyond the normal age of retirement, including Ikea, B&Q, Tesco and Asda. But some people find that having retired it is then difficult to get re-employed. It is a fact: the longer that people are out of work the harder it is to get back into it. If this is a situation you are facing, Chapter 14 (Volunteering) is particularly relevant, as showing that you have worked as a volunteer, rather than remaining unoccupied whilst unemployed, effectively and efficiently fills a gap in your CV. Indeed, volunteering roles can, on occasion, lead to paid jobs within the organization or charity – it is like a simple 'try before you buy' arrangement.

Once employed again never turn down the chance of any sort of training. Opportunities to refresh skills or add new ones will make you a valuable resource whatever you do.

If you are looking for a full- or part-time job you will need to give some thought to how best to go about it. If it is some time since you last tried the job market you may find that things have changed a little. Firms now tend to pay very little regard to informal contacts but rather go to the market to get the most suitable people. You will therefore need to keep a very close eye on the jobs section of your local newspaper. Also, many firms now have a vacancy/recruitment section on their websites, so if you are interested in a particular firm then check it out online.

Training opportunities

Knowing what you want to do is one thing, but before starting a new job you may want to brush up existing skills or possibly acquire new ones. Most professional bodies have a full programme of training events, ranging from one-day seminars to courses lasting a week or longer. Additionally, adult education institutes run a vast range of courses or, if you are still in your present job, a more practical solution might be to investigate open and flexible learning, which you can do from home. There are a number of vocational education and training opportunities offering such training for individuals of all ages. You are more likely to be successful if you learn at a time, place and pace best suited to your own particular circumstances. You should try to find out what is available locally; the following organizations offer advice and a wide range of courses:

For free online courses from universities and specialist organizations: www.futurelearn.com

Adult Education Finder: www.adulteducationfinder.co.uk

Home Learning College: www.homelearningcollege.com

Learn Direct: www.learndirect.co.uk

National Extension College: www.nec.ac.uk

Open and Distance Learning Quality Council: www.odlqc.org.uk

Open University: www.open.ac.uk

Other paid employment ideas

Consultancy and contracting

If the idea of hiring yourself out as a consultant or contractor appeals, you may be able to build up a steady stream of assignments and be recommended to other companies who could use your skills (there is more on this in Chapter 7, Starting your own business) or you may get placements through an agency; there is a vast choice through mainstream and niche agencies. If you are not sure about who's who in the world of agencies then ask around (former HR colleagues and other contractors/consultants are the usual starting places). More research and information can be obtained from:

Association of Independent Professionals and the Self-Employed: www ipse.co.uk

Consultancy UK: www.consultancy.uk

Interim management

Interim management is the temporary provision of senior- or director-level management resources and skills. It is a short-term assignment of a proven heavyweight interim executive manager to manage a period of transition, crisis or change within an organization. Assignments could be full-time or involve just one or two days' commitment per week. More research and information can be obtained from:

Alium Partners: www.aliumpartners.com

Institute of Interim Management: www.iim.org.uk

Interim Management Association: www.interimmanagement.uk.com

Interim Partners: www.interimpartners.com

Odgers Interim: www.odgersinterim.com

Non-executive directorships

A non-executive director, or external director, is a paid member of the board of directors of a company or organization who does not form part of the executive management team. They are not employees and they do not participate in the day-to-day management of the organization. Instead, they are expected to monitor and challenge the performance of the executive directors and the management. Such appointments carry heavy responsibilities and people who are qualified to take on such a role are usually chosen for their breadth of experience and personal qualities. See the following for information:

Executives Online: www.executivesonline.co.uk

FT Non-Executive Directors' Club: www.non-execs.com

First Flight: www.nonexecdirector.co.uk

NED on Board: www.nedonboard.com

Public appointments

There are a large number of advisory and other public bodies or quangos (quasi-autonomous non-government organizations) that have responsibility for a raft of public services at national, regional and local level. Those services cover a vast spectrum, including health, education, the environment, agriculture and food, defence, policing, legal/judicial, culture, media, sport, science and technology, and transport. The list is by no means exhaustive and further details can be found on the Cabinet Office website (publicappointments.cabinetoffice.gov.uk), which outlines opportunities throughout the whole of the UK.

Most of the bodies have a large staffing complement and a managing board or executive of senior administrative and professional staff. However, as public bodies, most are also required to have non-executive directors or board members drawn from the general public. The role of these external appointments is to bring outside experience and expertise to the table and also to bring a degree of external challenge to the work and decisions of the executive body or board. There are also purely advisory bodies designed to give external advice in a wide range of areas.

It is not necessary to have been in the public sector in order to be able to make a contribution. Indeed, in many instances the body will be looking for the sort of practical experience that people gain in business or commerce outside of the public sector. The skill set will vary from body to body and, in addition to a lay person's interest in the subject matter, experience in areas such as finance, human resources and change management, along, perhaps, with specialist knowledge, will often be seen as valuable.

The time commitment can vary, but on average it is probably one or two days per month. Likewise, the remuneration varies from body to body – from a very modest attendance allowance to several thousand pounds per year. But for some people the idea of being involved in an area of particular interest may be as attractive as any financial reward. For the post of chairperson, the time commitment is likely to be much greater, but so too will be the remuneration.

There is a rigorous and open appointments procedure for all posts, usually looking at the extent to which any candidate measures up to the specific competence-based criteria that the appointment requires. Full details of the appointment, the criteria relating to it and general advice on applying will be available to candidates. It is important that this information is looked at in detail as the shortlist for final interview will be based on an objective assessment of the extent to which the information provided in the application form meets the specific criteria relating to the post.

Virtually all posts are now publicly advertised in the national, regional or local press – so anyone interested should keep an eye on this. Further information, including vacancies, is also available on the Cabinet Office website mentioned above or at a regional level from www.gov.scot/public-bodies for Scotland, and www.nidirect.gov.uk/public-appointments for Northern Ireland.

Paid work for charities

There are some opportunities to work for money rather than as a volunteer in the charity sector, although it might be helpful to work as a volunteer before seeking a paid appointment. Anyone thinking of applying for a job with a charity must of course be sympathetic to its aims and style and it is likely that you may have already been involved with the charity before seeking paid employment with it. You can also keep an eye on job adverts in that sector.

Jobs with tourism and travel

The travel and tourism sector comprises many different industries such as tour operators, tourist boards, passenger transport (coach, aviation, waterways and rail) and visitor attractions such as museums, theme parks, zoos and heritage sites. This industry is not just for the young – mature and experienced people are also sought. If you have stamina, enjoy meeting the general public and like travelling, then working in the tourism sector could be interesting. It requires an active mind and involves a certain amount of study. Tour guides need an interest in history and culture, and in some cases an aptitude for languages can be an advantage. Some people with specialist knowledge sign on as a lecturer with one of the travel companies offering special interest holidays; others specialize in tourist attractions nearer to home. Air courier jobs are also good for people who like travelling abroad.

Teaching and tutoring

If you have experience of teaching, there are a number of possibilities open to you, both in the United Kingdom and abroad. With examinations becoming more competitive many parents require private tutors to help their children prepare for public examinations – and so there is always a demand for people to teach English to foreign students at the many language schools, and most UK universities offer language courses during the summer. You should keep in touch through your old networks to see what might be available.

House sitting

If you like the idea of saving money, having a paid holiday, enjoying new horizons, staying in a beautiful home and making friends with the family pets, why not consider house sitting? This is something that mature, responsible people can do, and there are opportunities throughout the United Kingdom and abroad. Agencies prefer car owners, non-smokers, with no children or pets of their own. Companies who specialize in this kind of work include:

House Sitters UK: www.housesittersuk.co.uk

Trusted House Sitters: www.trustedhousesitters.com

Caring for others

A good carer can make an immeasurable difference to someone's life. Caring for others includes working with young as well as old people, and those with mental or physical disabilities. If you are a good communicator, are patient, have excellent problem-solving skills and are physically fit, you will find numerous opportunities for paid work in this field. You may be required to have a full Disclosure and Barring Service (DBS) check if you are considering working with vulnerable people (young and old). For further information about DBS checks, see www.gov.uk – 'employing people'.

Keep a lookout locally to see what might be available. In addition, a number of agencies specialize in finding temporary or permanent companions and housekeepers for elderly or disabled people, or for those who are convalescing; a search on the web will find vast numbers of agencies and organizations with potential positions.

Useful help

It is down to you to recognize the employment position you are in and how that sits with where you would like it to be. That is why Michelle Obama's quote at the beginning of this chapter is so important to remember: 'We need to do a better job of putting ourselves higher on our own 'to do' list.'

Inspired? Remember to fill in your plan for a good retirement at the end of the book.

CHAPTER TEN

Starting your own business

Screw it – let's do it!

<small>SIR RICHARD BRANSON</small>

More and more people are setting up their own business and becoming their own boss. Whether it is earning £1,000 per annum to supplement your pension income or building a business that can keep you earning and occupied for years to come beyond your intended retirement date, this is the chapter for you.

If you have dived straight into this chapter looking to find your first piece of inspiration the biggest message of reassurance is, simply, you are not alone. According to the Department for Business, Innovation and Skills (Business Population Estimates for the UK and Regions 2017) there were 5.7 million private-sector businesses in 2017, which is a massive 2.2 million more than in 2000: 60 per cent trade as sole proprietorships (sometimes called the self-employed), 33 per cent trade as companies and 7 per cent are partnerships. These terms are explained in more detail in this chapter to help you decide which could be right for you. But for now the main message is that the one- or two-person businesses are the absolute backbone of the UK economy and are growing in number. Even better, there is plenty of help out there – you will not be alone and this chapter will signpost you to free help and support (it is just a matter of knowing where to look to find the quality material!).

This chapter goes to the heart of this book, as prosperity is not just about material wealth it is also about what we get out of everyday life through social and emotional benefits. It may also be a route to escaping corporate structures when there is still time to learn a new trick or two and, therefore, could be another option to help you save more/earn better.

This chapter at a glance

This chapter will give you the confidence to get started and provide plenty of straightforward advice. The key issues covered are:

- A quick-start guide on how to start a small business (you can get going today if you want!).

- Understanding the differences between starting a small business and employment, especially if both options are still open to you.

- Help with the question: 'Do I really need to bother with a business plan?'

- Getting off to a good start – some practical and emotional tips.

- Administration, finance and tax – keep on top of the paperwork or it will keep on top of you!

- Filling the diary with work, and some clever tips for marketing that will make a difference.

- The trading format – should you set up your own limited liability company, work as a sole trader or maybe go into partnership?

- Other ways of getting started and some operational issues.

- Where you can go to find further help – remember you are not alone and these are enterprising times in the United Kingdom.

- A summary checklist to help you tick off the key issues once you decide to get started in business.

Start a small business – quick guide to get you started today

This one section will get you on the way to starting a small business in the simplest of formats – as a sole trader – just follow this step-by-step guide and start earning straightaway:

- Find something you enjoy doing and/or goods or services that you know you can sell.

- Register as self-employed with HMRC via www.gov.uk (then go to 'working for yourself').

- You will then have to complete HMRC's self-assessment form each year and declare your business's taxable income (if it is above £1,000).

- Acquire some files and keep a list of your income and costs, sales invoices, purchases receipts, bank statements and cash books. If it 'proves' your business transactions, you must keep it (and keep it for six years).

- The big lesson: HMRC doesn't like people evading tax (it is illegal!). If you cannot prove your transactions then you will be charged the tax that HMRC believes was due, plus a penalty of up to an extra 200 per cent plus interest. HMRC can go back six years without much fuss, and even longer if they believe your errors were deliberate.

- If you are self-employed and keep good records you may be able to prepare the year-end accounts and self-assessment tax return by yourself. In time, your business may generate enough to pay an accountant or a bookkeeper for some assistance or to handle all accounts and tax on your behalf.

- Think really carefully about risk – as a self-employed person your personal wealth is backing your business and anything that goes wrong. If you are worried about risk then investigate and take out appropriate insurance and don't start trading until this is in place. If risk is potentially significant don't trade as self-employed but do look into the benefits of having a limited company (more in this chapter).

- Take a deep breath and start living your new business. Involve yourself with other people who run their own businesses and listen and learn from them. Join the best business club or organization that you can find – a Federation of Small Business membership should be on your shortlist but listen to other recommendations from other business owners who you know and respect.

- Make sure that you can sell your product or service for more than it costs – do the numbers and remember to think about marketing, packaging and transport costs/postage and then 'administration/office costs'. To help your business grow further just jump to the marketing section in this chapter. The tips should take you to the next level and, in time, you may benefit from delving into even more of this chapter and its hints and tips.

The secret ingredient and how to bag it

There is a secret ingredient for starting your own business and potentially bringing in a vital extra income and it is actually quite simple: it is the 'belief/can do' and positive attitude of the business owner. They have the ability to press on with their ambition and deliver on the goal they have set themselves. They involve others and are good at listening to those who can help (usually those who have experience of running their own successful businesses) and professional advisers (their accountant and solicitor). However, they recognize, at the end of the day, that it's 100 per cent down to them and get on with it using a timescale plan. The businesses that falter seem to do the opposite of this and thus never quite reach their potential.

Top tip

Don't just sit there thinking about it. Try and BAG IT for yourself.

Belief – **A**mbition – **G**oals – **I**nvolve – **T**ime

Some of the differences between starting a small business and employment

In some cases where there is an opportunity to start a small business there could be a similar opportunity to take a full- or part-time employed position. So which route is right for you?

Here are some of the main reasons for starting a small business:

- focusing on what you are best at or enjoy;
- being your own boss and therefore benefitting from very rapid decision making;
- flexibility (around other interests/responsibilities);
- freedom to organize things your way;
- no commuting;
- less involvement in internal politics and no more attending meetings that you have started to believe were becoming a bit pointless;
- being able to work on your own;

- developing a unique idea or delivering a better solution/product;
- providing a legacy for your children;
- the more you put in, the more you get out.

On the other hand, here are some of the reasons for seeking a part- or full-time employed position:

- having a local employer with known travel requirements;
- security of income;
- benefits of holiday pay, pension, paid sick leave, and perhaps private health and life cover;
- bonuses;
- having a team and the friendship of colleagues;
- no personal liability if things go badly wrong;
- staff discounts or other perks.

Do I really need to bother with a business plan?

Yes! There are thousands of success stories about those who took the plunge to build a business that provided involvement, enjoyment and a new or extra income. However, for every three success stories there is a business that does not work out and your money could disappear fast if you set up in the wrong way or overstretch yourself. Worst of all, you could lose your home if things go badly wrong. So, yes, you need some form of a plan – the information below and tips throughout this chapter should help you and also help you to understand and deal with the risks.

Why businesses fail – learning the lessons

Businesses can fail for many reasons. Learn from the mistakes of others. The number-one reason why businesses fail is that *the market moves on and you are left behind*. Take time out to think and keep abreast of what your customers really want (have you tried asking them?). Where are your competitors and what are they doing to keep on top of or ahead of the market and, overall, how is the market moving?

A second reason (and one that will continue to increase in 2019 as HMRC increases its resources on tackling tax evasion and avoidance) is the *failure to deal with tax affairs properly*. The implications of penalties and interest levied by HMRC are often ignored and only hit home when it is too late. Keep your books properly and retain all records for six years after the year end – in brief, if you cannot prove it, you may lose the tax benefit and pay additional tax, penalties and interest. If there is a problem, HMRC can go back and inspect previous years' accounts (for up to six years or even longer). If you fail to pay your tax fully when it is due, HMRC will pursue you vigorously and you are giving them a reason to take a closer look at you and your business. On the other hand, if you have genuine cash-flow difficulties and cannot pay your tax on the due date, talk to HMRC and you may find their attitude refreshing (especially if it is your first time of asking).

Other reasons include a failure to plan and also bad debts – if a customer goes bust and cannot pay your invoices, this will come off your bottom-line profit and can really hurt. There are a few simple steps that you can take to reduce the potential of taking such a hit. What are your credit terms and have you encouraged all customers to pay electronically? Do you contact them as soon as your invoices become overdue? Require cash on delivery or prepayment if there are some worrying signs emerging – and do trust your instincts here. PayPal and mobile credit-card machines are transforming payment services. In some cases it is worth remembering that a bad customer is sometimes worse than no customer at all.

Let's return to the question: 'Do I really need to bother with a business plan?' The answer is usually 'yes', even if it is just one page, as you are improving your chances of succeeding and may even do rather better than you first thought.

What goes into a plan?

'*I have always found that plans are useless but planning is indispensable.*' This is a quote from General Eisenhower and is about planning for battle. Pause and take in the wise words 'planning is indispensable', as too many people run a mile when the subject of a business plan comes up. Or, armed with confidence gained from a book on setting up a business, you may start a plan but never get it finished. The reason for this 'block' is usually fear of the planning process or feeling intimidated by daunting business-plan templates and spreadsheets seen in some books or banking literature.

So try this. If you want to travel somewhere you use a map. In business it is just the same except you get yourself a *plan*. Write it down and don't expect to get it right first time (no one does!). A few pages are fine to start with based on objectives, your market research and a budget for the year (accountants call this a profit-and-loss forecast). Review it with your accountant and/or a trusted friend who runs a business, then build it up.

Top tip

Have some sort of thought-out plan when you start and keep refreshing it. With experience you can tweak it and make it that bit slicker but you must put it down in writing.

Stage 1 of the plan: objectives

What, financially, do you need to set as objectives to bring you in that £2,000 or £20,000 or £60,000 you need to help reach and attain the lifestyle you desire? This takes a bit of thinking through but you should be able to come up with two or three simple objectives based on income, gross profit (if you sell stock) and overheads.

As an example for someone who sells advice-based services and who does not sell stock it is easy and you only need two objectives.

Objective 1: I aim to invoice £30,000 in my first year of trading based on working at least 100 days at an average billing rate of £300 per day. I will review my billing rates quarterly and my performance monthly.

Objective 2: I aim to keep my overheads (after expenses recharged to clients) in my first year to £5,000.

Then, for the more complicated businesses, for example one that trades in buying and selling stock, you will need a further objective based around the difference between sales price and purchase price. *Objective 3* will be something like: I aim to achieve the following gross profit percentages:

- product line A: 30 per cent;
- product line B: 40 per cent;
- product line C: 50 per cent;
- gross profit percentages are calculated using (sales price less cost of materials/product sold ÷ sales price) × 100.

The key point with objectives is that less gives more: you don't want a long list of objectives, instead try to ensure each objective is Specific, Measurable, Achievable, Realistic and Timed (or SMART) and you will improve your chances of success.

Stage 2 of the plan: your market research

The next page of your plan should be all about your marketing effort: this is a topic that is often misunderstood and mistaken for advertising. Think about approaching this section under the following three headings: products, customers and competitors.

Products

Start with your main product or service and think about the features and benefits of what you are selling. Understanding these and discussing them with your trusted advisers will allow you to start thinking about other related services or goods that you could offer.

Customers

For each main product area ask lots of questions to tease out your research. Who are my customers? Where are they based? When do they tend to buy? How and where do they tend to buy and at what price? How should I contact them? Keep asking those important questions of who, what, why, where, when and how – they tease out all sorts of quality research information that you can action.

Competitors

Again, ask yourself who, what, why, where, when and how? This should lead to a series of activities that you can do to help secure new quality work and customers (note that the marketing section later on in this chapter has further tips). If you end up with a jumble of unfocused ideas try ranking each idea on the basis of priority, impact and cost (free is good!).

Stage 3 of the plan: your income and expenditure forecast

This third stage is the tricky one but hang in there as it is worth pushing your plan to include this: your income and expenditure forecast for the year.

It is your financial map and will allow you to check your actual performance against the plan. You can then do something about it when you are off target. You should be able to do this yourself, but if it becomes a struggle ask your accountant or a friend who has their own business to help.

Is there more?

Once you have completed your first plan you need to keep it alive. Keep reviewing how you are doing against it and you should find that the planning process itself teases out what will make things that little bit better – guaranteed!

Practical and emotional tips

Your partner's attitude is crucial. Even if not directly involved, he or she may have to accept (at least initially) the loss of some space in the house to give you an office. Do you have space available to work from home initially? Or as an alternative would you need/prefer to rent accommodation? The rental market has transformed in the last decade with many 'serviced' office providers opening up and renting out space by the hour, day or month on flexible and economic rents. These offices can be great places to meet and network with like-minded small business owners. If you are selling products or crafts, try googling for craft and market events and try negotiating on a first attendance rate so you can try it out (as attendances, site pitch and quality can vary).

If you work from home will you need to spend some time managing the expectations of neighbours and/or friends about your new life and 'work hours'? There will be the added distractions of out-of-hours phone calls and, perhaps, suddenly cancelled social engagements, depending on your business. Can your family/partner cope or help?

Can you cope without the resources/back-up provided by an employer (IT/HR/training/marketing/legal and/or administrative support)? You will have to do it yourself or buy it in at a cost (a potential overhead cost for your business plan).

Running a small business means developing new networks. The network that provides vital practical and emotional support is other like-minded individuals who run their own business, so join the best trade or professional association you can find (there are some listed later in this chapter).

Keep on top of the paperwork

Generally, this one topic causes the most groans! But simple bookkeeping, if done properly, is just a by-product of your business and flows naturally, from raising sales invoices or receipts to tracking income and what you pay for, when and how. As a bonus, you will never miss an unpaid sales invoice if you are on top of your bookkeeping.

An even more compelling reason for doing your own bookkeeping is the HMRC 'prove it or lose it' viewpoint when enquiring into an aspect of your tax return. Under the system of self-assessment, HMRC relies on you completing your tax returns. In the case of an enquiry, HMRC tells you precisely what part of your tax return is under investigation and you are expected to be able to validate sample payments or receipts. If you are unable to prove the expenditure, you lose it as far as HMRC is concerned, resulting in, for example, fewer purchases being accepted as a deduction from your profits and more tax to pay. There will be penalties and interest to pay and the scope of HMRC's enquiries will be widened, which means more time, distraction from your business and, probably, stress.

Basic bookkeeping

All incoming and outgoing payments need to be recorded throughout the year. Records of outgoings need to be categorized according to type, and examples of some categories you might need to consider are stock, subscriptions/meeting fees, office equipment, office supplies, post and courier costs, travel fares, parking and subsistence, telephone and internet, sundry, accountancy and professional fees, and insurance.

Many small-business owners opt to do their own bookkeeping, with or without the help of computer software. If you opt for software choose one that your accountant understands as then their fees should be lower. For many small businesses your accountant should be able to provide Excel spreadsheets that will do the job, together with a bookkeeping guide to help get you started.

If you are really averse to bookkeeping yourself, consider hiring a bookkeeper. Bookkeepers currently charge about £15 to £25 per hour, depending on geographical location and experience, and can be found by recommendation from your accountant or business network contacts.

Finding a good accountant

Depending on qualifications and experience, accountants can charge from £35 to about £120 per hour (plus VAT) to assist you in setting up in business and to prepare your accounts and tax. But as anyone can call themselves an accountant it can be a bit hit and miss, with very variable quality when things go wrong. Unreturned calls and not dealing factually with enquiries and questions, vague verbal assurances, and not dealing with formal complaints are all part of the 'deal' when you end up with a low-quality accountant. If there are mistakes in your accounts and tax you will also find that you are very much on your own when it comes to dealing with HMRC enquiries.

Top tip

Don't end up with a low-quality accountant. What should you look for? The letters ACA or FCA after the accountant's name mean that you can be assured that you are dealing with a chartered accountant, but the key is that qualifications, professional indemnity held, any regulating body and complaints procedures should all be set out in writing for you at the start and before you sign up. If not, start shopping around.

Some accountancy firms offer a combination of bookkeeping, accountancy and tax services and, if so, you can expect to pay a premium on the bookkeeping hourly rates quoted above.

So how can I find a good accountant? Ask your trusted family members or friends if they can recommend one. Then ensure you get clarity on three things:

1 confirmation of the accountant's qualifications (the type of qualifications);

2 the professional body you would complain to if there is ever a problem;

3 confirmation that they hold professional indemnity insurance.

It is advisable to meet at least two accountants and see how you feel about rapport and the availability of proactive hints and tips. Make sure you believe you can get on with the accountant you select as it is likely to be a long and mutually beneficial relationship. Ask if the person you meet will be the person who does your accounts and tax and whether they will provide proactive advice. Get written confirmation of hourly rates plus an estimate of fees for the year, and get clarity on what happens if you decide to change accountants half-way through the year if fees are paid upfront or monthly. Most accountants should be used to providing clients with a 'retainer', clarifying the above and what you and the accountant will do and by when. Best of all is a good accountant who knows your industry area as they will be able to help with general guidance and offer input to your plan on marketing and pricing, drawing on experience beyond accounting and tax.

Finally, there is sometimes some confusion over the term 'audit of accounts'. Many years ago, smallish companies in the UK had to have an audit of their accounts. The turnover threshold (one of three thresholds) for being required to have an audit has been increased and currently stands at £10.2 million, so the vast majority of start-ups need not concern themselves with audited accounts.

Paying tax and National Insurance

Introduction on business taxes

There are quite significant differences in the taxes you will pay if you run a small business and, therefore, the different options are worth thinking through before getting started.

Sole traders

Self-employed individuals running their own businesses are usually called 'sole traders'. Nearly all new small businesses that trade as sole traders need to register as self-employed via www.gov.uk (then go to 'working for yourself').

First the good news if you just want to earn an extra £1,000 by doing odd jobs or gardens in the warmer months to help pay for a holiday. From 1 April 2017 HMRC introduced a new 'trading allowance' for individuals with trading income and you can keep the money and don't have to tell HMRC providing the total income (before costs) is £1,000 or less.

If your trading income is above £1,000 you must register for self-assessment with HMRC and complete a self-assessment tax form and submit this to HMRC each year (go to www.gov.uk and search for 'register for self-assessment'). While tax can be daunting, some sole traders with relatively straightforward billing and overheads do their own self-assessment and pay Income Tax on their profits. With Income Tax, you first have a Personal Allowance, which gives you a tax-free amount, and then any excess income (including your profits) is taxed at

20 per cent, then over a certain limit at 40 per cent and then 45 per cent. In very broad terms you currently (summer 2018) have a tax-free allowance of £11,850.

You are then taxed on the *next* £34,500 at 20 per cent, so for 2017/18 an individual will be able to earn £46,350 before having to pay tax at 40 per cent (ie £11,850 Personal Allowance at 0 per cent tax and then £34,500 at 20 per cent). Then 40 per cent tax applies to further taxable income up to £150,000. Anything above £150,000 gets taxed at 45 per cent. The rates are slightly different in Scotland where there is a slightly lower tax rate of 19 per cent for most between £11,850 and £13,850; the 20 per cent rate applies for £13,850 to £24,000 and then there is a 21 per cent rate between £24,000 and £43,430. The rates then step up to 41 per cent for £43,430 to £150,000 and over £150,000 is 46 per cent (which helps fund the lower-end tax cuts implemented in Scotland only). Many sole traders choose to run their bookkeeping for the year to 5 April to coincide with the tax year end (or 31 March, which HMRC effectively accepts as equivalent to 5 April).

If you are past the state retirement age there will be no National Insurance contributions (NICs) to pay. Subject to this, sole traders are liable for Class 2 NICs (currently a nominal amount of £2.95 per week, which will be abolished from 6 April 2019). You are also liable for the much more significant Class 4 NICs that are assessed and collected by HMRC at the same time as assessing your Income Tax on profits. Currently (summer 2018) Class 4 NICs are at 9 per cent on profits from £8,424 to £46,350, reducing to just 2 per cent on profits over £46,350.

The payment of sole-trader Income Tax is reasonably straightforward but there is a twist in your first year of trading. Assuming that you have a year end of 5 April 2020, the first payment will be due by 31 January 2021 so you have a long period of (effectively) interest-free credit, as some of the profits on which the tax is due may have been earned as long ago as May 2019. With the first payment, however, you get a 'double whammy' as you also have to pay on 31 January 2021 a payment on account of your second year's trading. Then on 31 July 2021 you have to make a second on-account payment of the second year's trading. Both on-account payments are set by default on the basis of your year-one profits. Underestimate this cash-flow impact at your peril as it can hit hard later. You can 'claim' a reduction if year two is proving to have lower profits than year one; your accountant will help you with this if it is appropriate.

After the initial tax famine, followed by (effectively) a double payment of tax, you will thereafter pay tax twice a year. Payments need to be made by 31 January (during the tax year) and then by 31 July after the end of that tax year, with any overpayment or underpayment sorted out by the following 31 January. Many sole-trader businesses set up a reserve bank account in addition to their current account, and place a percentage of their income aside, which is earning interest each month (albeit not amounting to much in the current climate). This tactic should help you resist the temptation to raid money that is not for spending – and ensure you can pay your tax on time.

Additionally, as a self-employed person you are allowed certain other reliefs. Ask your accountant, but the following expenses and allowances are usually tax deductible:

- *Business expenses*: these must be incurred 'wholly and exclusively' for the purposes of the trade. Office supplies that you buy will probably qualify; however, any business entertaining will not.

- *Partially allowable expenses*: these mainly apply if you are working from home. They include such items as the part of your rent (or mortgage interest), heating, lighting and telephone usage that you devote to business purposes, and also possibly some of the running expenses on your car, if you use your car for your business.

- *Spouse/partner's wages*: if you employ your spouse/partner in the business, his or her pay (provided this is reasonable) will usually qualify as a legitimate expense, in the same way as any other employee's, but must be accounted for through a pay-as-you-earn (PAYE) system.

- *Pension contributions*: tax relief is generally available for pension contributions of £3,600 (gross) or, if higher, 100 per cent of relevant earnings up to a maximum of £40,000 (this is subject to a tapered reduction for taxpayers with 'adjusted income' in excess of £150,000). You can go above the £40,000 'maximum' if you have not used the £40,000 maximum in the previous three years and have not reached the lifetime allowance on your pension pots (for most people this is £1,030,000 for 2018/19). You will probably benefit from getting professional advice if there is the potential to make very significant pension contributions and obtain the associated tax reliefs.

- *Capital allowances*: this is a tax break for expenditure on equipment.

Partnerships

Partnership tax is broadly similar to the process described above for a sole trader, with the exception of there being some more paperwork due to submit each partner's individual personal self-assessment tax return and a composite partnership tax return.

Limited company

Companies pay Corporation Tax on their profits (currently as of summer 2018 at 19 per cent and reducing to 17 per cent in April 2020). Your company accounts need to be finalized and any Corporation Tax paid nine months after your year end.

The key point with a company is that the money coming in is not your money – it is the company's money – so how do you extract your money?

The first option is salary and this means running a PAYE system: another form of tax with a rigorous calculation regime and payments that have to be made to HMRC. PAYE carries the Income Tax rates as featured for the sole trader, but NICs (National Insurance contributions) are much higher as these are a composite of employee *and* employer NICs (as the company is an employer). Currently these are 12 per cent employee NICs on £8,424 to £46,350, reducing to 2 per cent for amounts above £46,350 and then an additional 13.8 per cent employer NICs on everything above £8,424. The employer's National Insurance is the killer blow if you are a one-person company and it seems unfair but, currently, that's the way it is and it drives many to look to a different route to profit extraction, involving less salary and more dividends. Salary and employer's NICs are deductible when calculating corporation tax but dividends are not, which complicates the scenario and doing the numbers.

The second option for extracting funds is dividends but, repeating for emphasis, these are not deductible when calculating your Corporation Tax. From April 2016, significant changes were introduced to the dividend tax regime. The change is designed to reduce what the government perceived to be an incentive for companies to extract profits through a dividend. The following was implemented:

- A new annual dividend allowance, which has subsequently been reduced to £2,000 that is tax-free in 2018/19.
- The new rates of tax on dividend are 7.5 per cent if the dividend falls in the basic-rate tax band, 32.5 per cent if it falls in the higher-rate tax band (£46,350 to £150,000) and 38.1 per cent if it falls in the additional-rate tax band (£150,000 plus).

For some contracting or consultancy-type businesses that trade as companies there is a 'tax trap' for the unwary known as HMRC regulation number 35 (IR35) that came into force in April 2000. HMRC is particularly interested in ex-employees setting up service companies that work exclusively for their former employer or for just a few clients (sometimes called 'personal service companies' to use an HMRC term). This is an extremely wide-ranging and difficult subject but, in very simplified terms, IR35 is to be avoided if at all possible; it only applies to companies (not sole traders). Most contractors/ freelancers working on assignments with the public sector (or public-sector quasi-agencies) are likely to be caught by IR35.

There are many hints and tips and some urban myths about IR35, all of which are outside the scope of this guide. It is a big issue and one that you have first got to recognize and then, if potentially applicable, do something about. One of the key players in helping freelancers guide themselves through the minefield of IR35 is the Association of Independent Professionals and the Self-Employed (IPSE) (www.ipse.co.uk). This organization, working in conjunction with a chartered accountant who understands IR35, is probably your next step if you are concerned. Briefly, if you fall foul of IR35, the tax inspector will seek to set aside the dividends you have paid and treat the dividend payment as if it were subject to PAYE and NICs (including employer NICs) and the tax advantage you thought you may have had could disappear.

Registering for VAT

Value Added Tax (VAT) was introduced in 1973 and it seems that many people have lost sight of the name of this tax and especially the word 'added'. You are adding a tax to your supplies, collecting it on behalf of HMRC and paying it over to HMRC. In effect you are an unpaid tax collector.

If your taxable turnover is likely to be more than £85,000 in a 12-month period (summer 2018) you must register for VAT unless your supplies/services are outside the scope of VAT. Any expenses that you recharge to clients need to be included in the calculation of taxable turnover.

UK business clients are invariably registered for VAT so are not concerned about having VAT added to their invoices as they can reclaim it. For that reason, some businesses register for VAT before reaching the £85,000 compulsory registration limit so that they can claim VAT on their purchases – it is like buying equipment, supplies and services for 20 per cent off. If your turnover is less than £85,000, before voluntarily applying consider whether registration will really be of benefit to you; whether reclaiming the VAT paid on items needed for your business (such as office equipment) is worth the trouble of sending in mandatory, quarterly VAT returns and keeping separate VAT records.

You can claim back VAT on pre-start/pre-registration expenditure incurred in setting up the business so keep those VAT receipts. If you elect for 'cash accounting' status, this means that VAT only becomes payable or reclaimable when invoices are actually paid. It avoids having to pay the VAT on your own sales invoices before slow-paying clients pay you, which creates cash-flow problems. One final positive note, if you do register for VAT it seems to give you added credibility with clients.

VAT flat-rate scheme

HMRC introduced the flat-rate scheme in 2004, with the aim of simplifying record keeping for small businesses. This allows you to charge VAT to your clients at the standard rate of 20 per cent and to pay VAT as a percentage of your VAT-inclusive turnover (instead of having to work out the VAT payable on your sales less purchases). You can apply to join the scheme if your taxable turnover (excluding VAT) will not be more than £150,000 in the next 12 months.

HMRC publishes a list of business categories from which you need to decide which best describes your business. A further bonus is that you can deduct 1 per cent from the flat rate that you use for your first year of VAT registration. As a tip, do not do anything without checking it out with your accountant as there are a few twists and turns that could make the VAT flat-rate scheme unsuitable, especially since the introduction of a new 'limited cost trader' category, which many small businesses with low purchasing levels are forced to use.

Marketing tips to fill your diary

It is a sad fact that many new business owners believe that marketing simply means placing an advert in some well-known directory. This will achieve only a fraction of the sales of any comparable business with a decent grasp of marketing. So how can you generate sales for a new business? The following tips will get you started:

1 *Your own website and/or social media.* Business and the public now rely heavily on the internet and a presence is vital either through a website and/or harnessing social media. Is there a vital domain name that you need to secure and register? If this one question alone fills you with fear the solutions are nearer than you think – just try asking friends and don't ignore help that is right in front of your nose: young friends or relatives who may know more than you. It is also worth checking out websites run by trade or professional associations that may allow you to register and

set up a profile. You can set up profiles on various social media networking websites such as LinkedIn. Depending on your business, Facebook and Twitter can provide the benefits of building your online contacts and allow you to showcase your expertise in a certain area. Social media (very like networking, below) is about building relationships and trust with an ever-increasing contact list.

2 *Personal contacts and networking.* Once you decide to set up your own business, your personal contacts, ex-colleagues or other small business owners are a potential source of work. Too many small businesses forget that behind every contact there is another layer of potential contacts who are just one introduction away, so ignore this multiplier effect at your peril. In your first year you should be re-educating your contacts to think of you not as 'Jane who used to work at IBM' but 'Jane who now runs her own business advising small businesses on their IT needs'. Do not be afraid to pick up the phone or send business cards explaining your new business and what you can offer. Joining the best trade or professional association you can find will be a great way of developing your business contact network, with the added bonus of research facilities, information and other fringe benefits.

3 *Discounts and offers.* These can be used to great effect during seasonal dips, introducing a new service or clearing old stock. Whether it is 20 per cent off, a buy-one-get-one-free offer or the numerous variations of this basic approach, there are three golden rules:

   – always state the original or usual price (to show the value in the offer);

   – always specify an expiry date;

   – always explain that the offer is subject to availability.

4 *Flyers and business cards.* Generally speaking, a response rate of 1 per cent to a flyer is considered fairly good, but with some clever thinking you can improve this. Have you targeted the flyer? A good example would be a wedding-gown designer who neatly persuades a sought-after wedding location hotel to keep a flyer dispenser in their foyer. Are you able to include your professional or trade association logo on your flyer and business cards? Have you asked if this is possible? There are two sides to a flyer and business card – have you thought about putting information on the blank reverse side? Could this contain some useful tips or, perhaps, a special offer or discount? Anything that ensures the card or flyer is kept rather than dumped will help your business to edge ahead.

5 *Testimonials*. People generally buy on trust, and testimonials show prospective customers that you have done a good job and can be relied upon. Positive testimonials can be powerful and should never be underestimated.

6 *Agencies*. Agencies will be especially important for prospective consultants or contractors, as many recruitment agencies also place full- and part-time contracts (as opposed to employed positions). The contract market is growing and offers dynamic and fast-moving industries the opportunity to hire (and fire) swiftly. When marketing yourself through an agency the same rules apply as when marketing yourself to a potential employer. Good personal and written presentation will help the agency to sell you on to its clients – and it is in their interest to find you work, given the fee they receive for placing you.

7 *Advertising*. There are many options for advertising yourself and your business, such as website banners, and free and paid-for directory listings. Another approach could be 'free' advertising through a press release that you forward to local or trade press with an interesting story. A clever variant is advertising yourself and your skills by writing articles in professional or trade journals – what do you have that is news or novel or leading edge?

8 *Sponsorship*. Another subset of advertising is sponsorship. A driving instructor who sponsors the playing shirts of the local under-17s football team is a great example of cost-effective and rather clever sponsorship.

9 *Awards*. Business awards can offer new businesses an opportunity to make a splash in the local area, introduce you to other vibrant businesses, and there may even be a category for mature business owners newly starting up. These are often sponsored by local press and the Federation of Small Businesses (www.fsb.org.uk), where more information can be found.

Learn when to say 'no'

This is one of the hardest lessons to learn and comes with experience. The fear of losing a sale to a competitor, or the uncertainty of where the next piece of work or sale will come from if you reject this one, may induce you to overstretch or undercut yourself. If you continually face this dilemma the resulting stress means you may not survive in business for long. So learning how to say 'no' in a way that does not burn bridges is important.

Business alliances

Business alliances can work well and when you first start up in business all sorts of people and businesses may approach you. You will quickly learn that some are all talk and no action or seem more interested in accessing your contact network than building a mutually beneficial longer-term business relationship. Lord Alan Sugar's words on what makes an entrepreneur, in his book *The Way I See It: Rants, revelations and rules for life* (2011), give a clear and simple lesson on this: 'If you have partners, they have to bring something to the party.'

Trading formats

You need to choose a type of business format – each carries a different level of personal risk and a different level of bureaucracy. The following will help you decide which one is right for you.

Self-employed (sometimes called sole trader/ sole proprietor)

A self-employed person is someone who works for him/herself, instead of an employer, and draws an income from their personally run business. If the profits from the work are accounted for on one person's tax return, that person is known as a sole trader. If the profits are shared between two or more people, it is a partnership (see below).

There is no clear definition of self-employment. Defining an employee, on the other hand, is slightly easier as it can generally be assumed that if Income Tax and NICs are deducted from an individual's salary before they are paid, then that individual is an employee.

Importantly, the business has no separate existence from the owner and, therefore, all debts of the business are debts of the owner, who is personally liable for all amounts owed by the business. This strikes fear into the hearts of many business owners. You only need to think of the number of business owners who go bust every time a recession comes around – and lose their house as a result. Should this be a worry?

First and foremost, you must consider the risk to you in any work that you do. Could it go wrong and could you be sued? Is that a realistic prospect or so remote that it does not even warrant thinking about? Or is it somewhere in the middle? Can insurance help? (More on insurance later.) Remember that insurance is only as good as the disclosures you make and the levels of cover provided. At the end of the day you know your business, your customers and the work that you do, so the risk assessment can only be done by you.

How to start up as a sole trader

- You can start trading immediately.

- You can trade under virtually any name, subject to some restrictions that are mostly common sense, such as not suggesting something you are not (connection to government, royalty or international pre-eminence). A B Jones trading as Super Lawns, for example, is fine.

- The full name and address of the owner and any trading name must be disclosed on letters, orders and invoices.

- Register as self-employed by going to www.gov.uk and searching for 'working for yourself'.

Partnership

Two or more self-employed people who work together on a business and share the profits are trading in partnership. The profits from the work are accounted for on a partnership tax return and extracts from that partnership tax return are then copied into the partners' individual tax returns.

The business has no separate existence from the partners and, therefore, all debts of the business are debts of the partners, so they are personally liable for all amounts owed by the business. In addition, partners are jointly and severally liable for the debts of the business or, put more simply, the last person standing pays the lot. There is a saying that you need to trust your business partner better than your husband/wife/civil partner.

As with sole traders, the first consideration is the potential for business risk, since your personal wealth is backing the debts of the business. First and foremost, you must consider the risk to you in any work that you do and, given the 'joint and several liability' point explained above, the trust and faith you have in your business partner. Again, as with sole traders, can insurance help reduce the risk?

How to set up as a partnership

- You can start trading immediately.

- You can trade under virtually any name, subject to some restrictions that are mostly common sense, such as not suggesting something you are not (connection to government, royalty or international pre-eminence). As before, A B Jones and A B Smith trading as J & S Super Lawns is fine.

- You will need to consult a solicitor to assist with the preparation and signing of a partnership deed. The partnership deed is for your protection and is essential because it sets out the rules of the partnership, including, for example, the profit or loss split between partners, what happens if one partner wishes to leave or you wish to admit a new partner.

- The full name and address of the partners and any trading name must be disclosed on letters, orders and invoices.

- Register the partnership with HMRC with form SA400 via www.gov.uk (then go to 'register a partnership for self-assessment').

Limited company

A limited liability company (often the shorthand of 'limited company' is used to describe this trading format) is a company whose liability is limited by shares and is the most common form of trading format. The company is owned by its shareholders, and is run by directors who are appointed by the shareholders. This can be one and the same person and indeed many companies in the UK are one-person companies.

The shareholders are liable to contribute the amount remaining unpaid on the shares – usually zero, as most shares are issued fully paid up. The shareholders therefore achieve limited liability.

How to start up a limited company

- A company needs to be registered with Companies House and cannot trade until it is granted a Certificate of Incorporation. The registration process is quick and inexpensive using the Companies House web incorporation service (it currently costs £12 and is completed within 24 hours). Some people use a company formation agent (google this term to find such an agent – there are plenty of them) and the process should cost less than £50.

- The company name needs to be approved by Companies House. No two companies can have the same name and approval is usually completed in a day. Names that suggest, for instance, an international aspect will require evidence to support the claim and certain names are prohibited unless there is a dispensation (for example 'Royal').

- You must appoint a director and this 'officer' of the company carries responsibilities that can incur penalties and/or a fine. The appointment of directors should therefore not be done lightly. The full range of responsibilities is set out in the Companies Act; further guidance is available from the Companies House section of www.gov.uk (go to 'running a limited company'). Some examples of responsibilities include the duty to maintain the financial records of the company, to prepare accounts, to retain the paperwork and to avoid conflicts of interest. Small businesses no longer need to have a separate company secretary but it can be useful to have another office-holder signatory and the risks associated with this position are relatively light. In addition you will need to appoint a registered office, which is a designated address at which official notices and communications can be received. The company's main place of business is usually used as the registered office but you could also use the address of your accountant or solicitor (there may be a charge for this).

Top tip

A limited liability company costs just £12 to set up. It provides enormous protection in managing the risk due to limited liability.

Alternative ways of getting started

Umbrella company

This is not really running your own business but it is a quick and easy way to get work and earn without all the red tape and time involved in running your own business. The downside is there are fewer tax-planning opportunities. It is worth some description here as it may be an option for you or it may come up in conversation.

Essentially it is a company that offers you a shelter (umbrella) from administration. You are employed through the umbrella company and the end firm that actually uses your services keeps you at arm's length. You don't accrue the usual employment rights that will be available to employed staff in that end firm. The umbrella company is very limited in its function – almost 'just' processing your payroll, deducting PAYE and National Insurance, paying it over to HMRC and paying you the net salary. It can offer a win for both you and the end firm that uses your services. For example, for someone who wants flexibility and earnings – perhaps working ad hoc or a few days a week. It offers firms a flexible labour pool that is easy to hire and fire as their only obligation is to pay the umbrella company a fee to cover your wages. The tricky bit is the administration charges levied by the umbrella company for running the payroll and who pays the employer's National Insurance, and you will want to check out how that works – possibly in deductions and charges from what hits your pocket.

Overall the umbrella company is a useful route to earning some cash in a flexible way, but if you have ambitions for earning over the longer term and over about £250 per day the other options for setting up your own business in this chapter could be more rewarding and tax efficient.

Buying a business

Buying an established business can be an attractive route to becoming your own boss, as it eliminates many of the problems of start-ups. The enterprise is likely to come equipped with stock, suppliers, an order book, premises and possibly employees. It is also likely to have debtors and creditors. Take professional advice before buying any business, even one from friends. In particular, you should consider why the business is being sold. It may be for perfectly respectable reasons – for instance, a change of circumstances such as retirement. But, equally, it may be that the market is saturated, that the rent is about to go sky-high or that major competition has opened up nearby.

Before parting with your money, verify that the assets are owned by the business and get the stock professionally valued. You should also ensure that the debts are collectable and that the same credit terms will apply from existing suppliers. Get an accountant to look at the figures for the last three years and have a chartered surveyor check the premises. A solicitor should be engaged to vet any legal documents, including staff and other ongoing contracts.

The value of the company's assets will be reflected in its purchase price, as will the 'goodwill' (or reputation) that it has established. For more information, agents specializing in small business sales have useful guides (for instance, see www.christie.com).

Franchising

Franchising continues to be a popular form of business entry route with attractions for both franchisor and franchisee. The franchisor gains, as their 'brand' is able to expand quickly. The advantage to the franchisee is that there are normally fewer risks than with starting a business from scratch.

A franchisee buys into an established business and builds up his or her own enterprise under its wing. In return for the investment, plus regular royalty payments, he or she acquires the right to sell the franchisor's products or services within a specified geographic area and enjoys the benefits of its reputation, buying power and marketing expertise. As a franchisee you are effectively your own boss. You finance the business, employ the staff and retain the profits after the franchisor has had its cut. You are usually expected to maintain certain standards and conform to the broad corporate approach of the organization. In return, the franchisor should train you in the business, provide management support and give you access to a wide range of back-up services.

The amount of capital needed to buy a franchise varies enormously according to the type of business, and can be anywhere between a few hundred pounds and £500,000 or more. The franchisee is normally liable to pay an initial fee, covering both the entry cost and the initial support services provided by the franchisor, such as advice about location and market research.

The length of the agreement will depend on both the type of business involved and the front-end fee. Agreements can run for 3–20 years and many franchisors include an option to renew the agreement, which should be treated as a valuable asset.

Many franchises have built up a good track record and raising money to invest in good franchises may not be too difficult. Most of the leading high-street banks operate specialist franchise loan sections. The franchisors may also be able to help in raising the money and can sometimes arrange more advantageous terms through their connections with financial institutions.

The British Franchise Association (BFA) represents 'the responsible face' of franchising, and its members have to conform to a code of practice. When considering opportunities, a good franchisor will provide a great deal of invaluable help. However, some franchisors may be less helpful and this will usually tell its own story. Make careful enquiries before committing any money – as basic information, you should ask for a bank reference; review several years' accounts and appointments and resignations of directors (all available for free from Companies House); visit their head office, cost out and prepare a business plan and profit and loss forecast for at least the next year (see above on how to do this), and review this with the potential franchisor. Also check with the BFA whether the franchisor in question is a member and visit some of the other franchisees to find out what their experience has been. Before signing, seek advice from an accountant or solicitor. For more information, see the BFA website (www.thebfa.org).

Operational and other issues

Banking

If you operate through a limited company you have to set up a separate business bank account into which all income is paid and out of which you pay all costs. Most self-employed and partnerships will operate a separate bank account for their business as it can make the accounts easier and it can also help stop you muddling personal and business funds. Shop around for the best deal that suits your business (often a trade-off between the conveniences of a local 'bricks and mortar' branch accompanied by internet banking versus free or reduced charges for internet-only accounts), but often the convenience of maintaining business and personal bank accounts at one bank wins the day.

Inventions and intellectual property

If you have a clever idea that you would like to market you should ensure that your intellectual property is protected if you believe there is a special value in the name (trademark) or something special or unique about the product (patent). For information about patenting an invention, trademarks, copyright and much more, look at the UK Intellectual Property Office website at www.gov.uk (go to 'Intellectual Property Office').

Licences and permissions

Certain types of business require a licence or permit to trade; these include pubs, off-licences, nursing agencies, pet shops, kennels, minicabs or buses, driving instructors, betting shops, auction sale rooms, cinemas, street traders and, in some cases, travel agents and tour operators. You will also require a licence to import certain goods.

Depending on the nature of your business, other permissions may need to be obtained, including from the environmental health department, licensing authorities and the fire prevention officer. In particular, there are special requirements concerning the sale of food, and safety measures for hotels and guest houses.

Your local authority office will be able to advise you whether you require a licence, and in many cases your council will be the licensing authority. More information is available at www.gov.uk (go to 'licence finder').

Employing staff

Should you consider employing staff, you will immediately increase the complexity of your business. As well as paying salaries, you will have to account for PAYE, keep National Insurance records and conform to the multiple requirements of employment legislation. If you are worried or don't want the bother of doing the paperwork yourself, your accountant is likely to be able to introduce you to a payroll service, which will cost you money but will take some of the burden off your shoulders. Keeping personnel records will bring you into the scope of data protection (see ico.org.uk).

Employment legislation

As an employer you have certain legal obligations with respect to your staff. The most important of these cover such issues as health and safety at work, terms and conditions of employment, and the provision of employee rights, including, for example, parental leave, trade union activity and protection against unfair dismissal. Very small firms are exempt from some of the more onerous requirements, and the government is taking steps to reduce more of the red tape. However, it is important that you understand in general terms what legislation could affect you. You will usually find free support on this subject via membership of a trade association or organization such as the Federation of Small Businesses (www.fsb.org.uk). The Health and Safety Executive also has a useful website (www.hse.gov.uk).

An employer, however small the business, may not discriminate against someone on the grounds of sex, race, disability, religion, marital status, sexual orientation or age. This applies to all aspects of employment, including training, promotion, recruitment, company benefits and facilities (more information can be found at: www.equalityhumanrights.com).

Disputes

If you find yourself with a potential dispute on your hands, it is sensible to approach the Advisory, Conciliation and Arbitration Service (ACAS), which operates an effective information and advisory service for employers and employees on a variety of workplace problems, including employment legislation and employment relations. It also has a wide range of useful publications, giving practical guidance on employment matters (see www.acas.org.uk).

Insurance

Insurance is more than just a wise precaution. It is essential if you employ staff, have business premises or use your car regularly for commercial purposes. Many insurance companies now offer 'package insurance' for small businesses, which covers most of the main contingencies in a single policy. This usually works out cheaper than buying a collection of individual policies. An insurance broker should be able to guide you through the risks and the insurance products available:

- *Employers' liability*: this is compulsory if you employ staff. It provides indemnity against liability for death or bodily injury to employees and subcontractors arising in connection with the business.
- *Product and public liability*: this insures the business and its products against claims by customers or the public.
- *Professional indemnity*: this is essential if a client could suffer a mishap, loss or other damage in consequence of advice or services received.
- *House insurance*: if you operate your business from home, check that you have notified your house insurer of this fact.
- *Motor risks*: check that you have notified your insurer if you use your motor vehicle for your business.
- *Life assurance*: this ensures that funds are available to pay off any debts or to enable the business to continue in the event of your death.
- *Permanent health insurance*: otherwise known as 'income protection', it provides insurance against long-term loss of income as a result of severe illness or disability – by paying a regular income.
- *Critical illness insurance*: this provides insurance against long-term loss of income as a result of severe illness or disability – by paying a lump sum.
- *Key person insurance*: this applies to the loss of a key person through prolonged illness as well as death. In small companies, where the success or failure of the business is dependent upon the skills of one or two key executives, key person insurance may be demanded by lenders.

You should discuss these points with your insurance company or a broker. To find an insurance broker, see the British Insurance Brokers' Association (www.biba.org.uk) or the Association of British Insurers (www.abi.org.uk).

Top tip

If you work from home or use your car for work remember to notify your insurer. Check how you can reduce any risk in your business through insurance.

Property investment

A frequent avenue that some people explore when nearing retirement is property investment as a form of business income. This is dealt with in Chapter 5 (Savings).

Pensions

When you go into business on your own a whole new opportunity opens up to you to manage your remuneration and how you make provision for pensions. This can be dramatically effective but can also be complex and there are traps for the unwary. Whilst the excitement of getting a new business up and running will usually take priority, a reasonably early review should be undertaken of existing pension provision against pension aspirations with a suitably qualified financial adviser. But remember there are also pension predators out there so ensure your adviser is regulated by the Financial Conduct Authority. Don't do anything unless you have the right advice and recommendations in writing. More information on pensions is detailed in Chapter 4 (Pensions).

Top tip

Pensions planning can be dramatically effective and very tax efficient but there are traps for the unwary. Get an early pensions review with an adviser regulated by the Financial Conduct Authority.

Further help, advice and training

Small businesses are well served when it comes to general help and training. Some of the best available feature below.

Organizations providing free or subsidized help

Government resources

The government website (www.gov.uk) contains the government's online resource for businesses.

Regional or country-specific support is also available at:

England: The Local Enterprise Partnership at www.lepnetwork.net

Northern Ireland: www.nibusinessinfo.co.uk

Scotland: www.mygov.scot/business

Wales: www.business.wales.gov.uk

Business is Great

Business is Great has been set up by the government to help you with support, advice and inspiration for growing your business, including advice on imports and exports, finance, employment, intellectual property and regulation. It includes a 'business support tool' and after answering a few questions you get a report of resources and schemes to start to support your business (further information is available at www.greatbusiness.gov.uk).

Start-up Britain

Start-up Britain has been set up by the government to help you find information about starting a business and contains offers and discounts available to new business start-ups (further information is available at www.startupbritain. org).

Other useful organizations

- *Solicitors*: many solicitors offer a free initial consultation and advice can be sought on a range of issues. To find solicitors in your local area use the 'find a solicitor' section at the Law Society website (www.lawsociety.org).
- *The Federation of Small Businesses* (www.fsb.org.uk): the networking opportunities and benefits of the Federation of Small Businesses make it a 'must have' for most new small businesses.

- *Association of Independent Professionals and the Self Employed* (www. ipse.co.uk): its *Guide to Freelancing* is free and can be downloaded from its website. The organization's knowledge of and guidance on IR35 for freelancers and contractors are second to none.

- *Business start-up websites*: these are packed with free hints and tips and a useful one is www.bstartup.com – their exhibitions are free and well attended and they have some excellent free workshops and guest speakers.

Useful reading

An extensive list of books for small and start-up businesses is published by Kogan Page on their website (www.koganpage.com). These include *Starting a Business from Home* by Colin Barrow, *Starting a Successful Business* by Michael J Morris, and *The Daily Telegraph Tax Guide 2018* by David Genders.

Starting and running a business checklist

When starting or running a business you will encounter a vast range of information and this can lead to you feeling swamped. This checklist has been developed to help you on the journey. Try annotating each item – N: not applicable; W: work on now; A: review with accountant; C: complete.

- If you want to travel somewhere you use a map. In business it is just the same except you get yourself a *plan*. Commit it to writing and don't expect to get it right first time (no one does!). A few pages are fine to start with, based on objectives, your market research and a budget for the year (accountants call this a profit-and-loss forecast). Review it with your accountant and/or a trusted friend who runs a business, then build it up.

- Choose your *trading format*, ie company (usually signified by 'limited'), sole trader or partnership, or limited liability partnership. This is an important step and one to talk through with your accountant or a business adviser. You can set up a company for £12 at Companies House (www. gov.uk, then go to Companies House and then 'starting a company'). Understand the personal liability risks of sole trader/partnership and, indeed, joint and several liability if trading in partnership ('last person standing pays the lot'!). If things go badly wrong your personal wealth could be at risk – but perhaps insurance could help (see below).

- Choose your *accountant*. There are many accountancy organizations; chartered accountants can be found at www.icaew.co.uk (England and Wales), www.icas.org.uk (Scotland) and www.charteredaccountants.ie (Ireland). Accountants are usually prepared to see you for an initial 'no obligation' meeting. Be clear about who your regular contact will be, their qualifications and knowledge of your industry, their hourly rates and whether they have professional indemnity insurance.

- Make sure you have a source of *legal help*. Could your local solicitor help? Alternatively, your trade association may offer a free legal helpline that may suffice initially. An early legal question that will usually arise is about your terms and conditions of trade or contracts.

- There is some *free government help* that you can find at www.gov.uk, which contains the government's online resources for businesses.

- You should also check out the government-backed initiatives www.startupbritain.org and www.greatbusiness.gov.uk for inspiration and ideas. Regional or country-specific support is also available at:

  - England: The Local Enterprise Partnership at www.lepnetwork.net
  - Northern Ireland: www.nibusinessinfo.co.uk
  - Scotland: www.mygov.scot/business
  - Wales: www.business.wales.gov.uk

- Join the best *trade or professional association* that you can identify and consider the extra benefits each provides in the areas of research information, networking events, helplines, tax investigation help and insurance offerings.

- Choose and, if appropriate, protect your *business name*. There is some useful free help available on intellectual property (patents, brands, etc) at the Intellectual Property Office (www.gov.uk/government/organisations/intellectual-property-office).

- Choose a *business bank account*. Shop around for the best deal that suits your business (often a trade-off between the conveniences of a local 'bricks and mortar' branch accompanied by internet banking versus free or reduced charges for internet-only accounts).

- Assess your *pension* needs with a financial adviser regulated by the Financial Conduct Authority – this can afford significant tax efficiencies but there are traps for the unwary.

- Sort out your *tax and record keeping* (documents need to be kept for six years and you need to become a receipt/invoice hoarder with a logical 'system for filing'); as the taxman might say, 'Prove it or lose it.' Check with your accountant that your proposed bookkeeping and record-keeping systems are acceptable before you buy them.

- Understand the implications of failing to deal with your *tax* affairs properly. This can be penalties ranging from 30 per cent to 200 per cent plus interest. Some trade associations include 'free' tax investigation cover – a very useful benefit.

- Understand your key *tax obligations* and deadlines. For companies, you are obliged to file your annual accounts at Companies House nine months after your year end (your accountant will do this) and your *confirmation statement* on the anniversary of setting up a company each year (fairly easy – you should be able to do this). There is good-quality free help at Companies House.

- Understand your obligations on *VAT*. The current (summer 2018) registration threshold for compulsory registration is £85,000. Consider VAT schemes, especially the VAT flat-rate scheme for small businesses.

- Set up your *premises* so that you can work effectively. If you work from home, manage the expectations of your family and neighbours – suddenly the phrase 'time is money' takes on a new meaning.

- Set up your *suppliers* (set up contracts and bills in the company or business name) and, if appropriate, set up stock-control and delivery systems.

- Consider *insurance* policies for identified business risks (professional indemnity, public liability, product liability, etc). An insurance broker can advise on this and you should also consider policies available via trade associations as these can provide increased cover at less cost (don't forget to notify your home and car insurers if you use these for business).

- Consider protecting the income you take from your business (especially if you have dependants) in the event of long-term *illness* or *death* and if in doubt take advice from a financial adviser).

- *Marketing and selling* will be massively important to your success. If you are not from a selling/marketing background, talk to trusted friends who run their own business and your accountant/adviser or mentor about your market research and marketing plan. Understand your customers and what they need.

- Do not underestimate the importance of networking and the potentially massive multiplier effect of reaching through to the networks that sit behind your primary network contacts.

- Plan the *pricing* strategies for your product or service. A different package means a different price. How have you benchmarked your price and how have you differentiated your offering (features and benefits) to allow you to charge that little bit more? Conversely, what features and benefits have you stripped out to allow you to offer a headline price that comes in beneath the competition?

- Plan your *marketing promotion strategy*. Remember that 'folk are different' and that it is a bit like fishing – you use different hooks depending on what you are trying to catch.

- Get paid promptly for your sales. What are your *payment terms* (terms and conditions)? Follow up on outstanding debts. If you sell stock, have you included a reservation of title clause to help you retrieve unpaid stock if your client goes bust?

- Set up your *IT system* and support and have a system to back up your data securely. Check whether you need to notify the Information Commissioner under the *data protection* laws (ico.org.uk).

- Consider other *red tape*, especially if your area is a specialized sector (food, health and safety, etc). Investigate and apply for the licences and permits that your business may need.

- If this all appeals to you, you should be making a note of action in your own good retirement plan at the end of the book.

Top tip

Review and update your business plan in the light of experience and keep it a living, written document.

Inspired? Remember to fill in your plan for a good retirement at the end of the book.

PART THREE

Live Better

CHAPTER ELEVEN

Your home

Home is the place that goes where you go, yet it welcomes you upon your return. Like a dog overjoyed at the door. We've missed you is what you hear, no matter how long you have been gone.

MICHAEL J ROSEN

For most people their home will be a central part of their lives, for economic and sentimental reasons. This is emphasized by a number of old familiar sayings – 'An Englishman's home is his castle', 'Home is where the heart is', and 'There's no place like home'. Perhaps it is best summed up by Michael J Rosen: 'It welcomes you upon your return.' It is our space, our comfort, our shelter, our retreat and a place to welcome family and friends. That is not likely to alter once you retire, and if you are content with the place you call home you are more likely to live better and be happier in retirement.

Your home is likely to remain at the centre of your social and domestic life, and if you are a homeowner it is also likely to be a significant part of your overall estate. Many homeowners will have cleared their mortgage by the time they retire and this can be a real financial bonus. However, maintenance costs are not likely to change so don't forget that you will still need to set aside finance to preserve your greatest asset. Then again there is the opportunity to save more by downsizing or relocating. Perhaps this was a factor in your retirement planning to free up funds for a more active retirement or to free up funds as defined pension pots run out and you move from the active to the passive phase of retirement, as outlined in Chapter 1. Either way, the home is absolutely central to Part Three of this book (Live better).

Looking back on the previous chapters, you will see how things are coming together as we 'plan more' (Part One) and then 'save more/earn better' (Part Two). Add these to the 'Live better' chapters beginning here in Part Three and you are framing your own happier retirement. How is your good retirement plan at the back of the book progressing?

This chapter at a glance

As a quick guide, this chapter covers in detail a number of aspects of home and property that you should consider:

- Future proofing the place you call home is important. This means taking an in-depth look at where you currently live and deciding if it will work for you in your retirement.

- Downsizing in the area, staying put and moving to a completely new area all present pros and cons. Suggestions and help are provided.

- If you are keen on moving to a new home, there is a helpful list of the pros and cons of taking this course of action.

- Moving abroad or taking a second home abroad can look brilliant through rose-tinted glasses. Find out more and some options in this chapter.

- Doing the sums. Information is provided on saving money and avoiding a 'pig in a poke'.

- Should it be necessary or helpful to use your home to earn money, there are some great ideas on how you can do this.

- Finally, help is offered around safety, security and insurance, and even housing benefits.

Reassess your needs

When you are approaching retirement it is time to reassess what you really need as a home. You may decide to continue with your present housing arrangements. However, this is an apt time to think carefully about what your future housing needs might be in light of possibly changing circumstances over the next 10 years or even further ahead. With life expectancy rising in the UK on average to 86 years for men and 88 years for women, today's retirees are living longer and staying fitter than previous generations. Most are aware of the need to keep fit and are looking for opportunities to maintain an active and healthy lifestyle. Rather than assuming that retirement means you should contemplate 'downsizing', perhaps it would be more appropriate to suggest 'rightsizing'. The way we consider our living environment as we get older is changing. Is the property you live in right for you for the next phase of your life? The following questions should be taken into account:

- Can you get around your current home and garden safely and can you afford to manage its upkeep?

- Do you have good support networks in the area – family, friends and neighbours?

- Are you well connected? Can you get to the places you need and want to go easily – by car, on foot, or by public transport?

- Are you reasonably confident that this will still be the case in 10 or 15 years, or if your health and other circumstances change?

If the answer is 'no' to some of these questions, it might be sensible to investigate other options. Even if you don't want to move now, thinking about the possibility will make things easier if and when your circumstances change.

Downsizing nearby

Break out the champagne – is this the moment you have always been waiting for where you crack open the equity in your home, release part of it and start going on luxury holidays every year or buy that home abroad? Or could the capital be used to help your offspring get started on the property ladder? Is downsizing and perhaps continuing to live in your present general area – with all the support and convenience with which you are comfortable – a viable option? It may be that your existing house is larger than you need now that your family has moved on. A smaller house may make more sense, be cheaper to run, easier to get around and indeed may more adequately meet your longer-term requirements as you get older; it may also avoid the need for a later move. The smaller home may also be closer to the town centre or where amenities are clustered; it could prove a big win to have facilities within walking distance. Or, on the other hand, does bungalow living with a sea or other view appeal? Despite these potential advantages you still need to think carefully about it.

Top tip

While your family may have largely moved away they will in all likelihood want to return from time to time with their own expanding families and you may therefore still need the space. Is downsizing short-sighted?

Also, your own parents may be becoming increasingly frail and the extra space you have might be well utilized by them. So there is a list of positives and negatives to think carefully about before deciding what to do in terms of this one option; there are also more options to consider, as we discuss below.

Staying put and maybe even increasing the home size

Many people who retire choose to stay put in the same area where they have lived for years rather than being tempted to move to some apparently ideal new situation. These reasons include being close to where they used to work, or near their families for whom they provide 'grandsitting' support (enabling their adult children to work), and staying within reach of friends and their social networks. Many people also find it reassuring to remain with their local medical practice and other medical facilities, which could prove a blessing in later life when more support may be needed.

Even if staying put there may be adjustments to consider to take account of your new circumstances; if more space is required to accommodate boomerang kids (see Chapter 2, The sandwich generation) try reviewing these four options, ranging from economical to expensive:

- *Economical.* Invest in a garden room – these have boomed in quality and reduced in price in recent years and range from a glorified wooden shed to fully insulated and double-gazed structures. Some require no planning permission and some can be built in less than a week. They can provide accommodation solutions that range from simple storage to a hobby room to living accommodation.

- *Fairly economical.* A garage conversion is another popular way to increase space in your home; it is reasonably simple and can be surprisingly cost effective. If you propose to add a room above your garage, any scheme would be subject to appropriate planning permission being granted. This is needed because of the extra height and alteration to the roof line. Rooms above a detached garage make an ideal guest suite, office, study, granny annex or somewhere to carry on a noisy hobby. If you convert a garage you may worry about where you put your car but don't forget that modern cars seem quite capable of surviving without the protection of a garage. Otherwise, a cost-effective car port could be added in as part of the scheme.

- *Quite expensive.* One possibility might be to extend your existing property. If you are considering doing building works, check out both planning and building regulation controls. Some smaller extensions to the rear or side of a property can often be built without having to make a planning application, provided that the design complies with the rules for permitted development (see www.planningportal.gov.uk). But make sure you carefully check the particular rules for the area in which you live, as building without the necessary approval can have serious consequences. Expect tighter rules for conservation areas and listed properties. Obtain quotes from more than one contractor and ask for references or visit their last job. The lowest quote may not necessarily be the best one with regard to the vital quality factor. Friends or your professional adviser can assist with recommendations before you go ahead with any works. Keep things in proportion – extra bedrooms are not an advantage unless there are sufficient bathrooms or shower rooms and many now prefer the convenience of en-suite facilities. Remember to keep the planning paperwork and electrical certificates as these will be needed when you come to sell the house.

- *Expensive but provides radical new space and environment.* Buying the property next door: if your budget allows, becoming your own neighbour allows more space than an extension, without leaving the neighbourhood. This option is neither cheap nor simple and professional advice from an architect is essential. Even if you live in a flat you might be able to buy the adjoining unit or the one above or below, then knock through or install a staircase to achieve double living space. Any construction work being undertaken must, of course, adhere strictly to planning and building regulations. If you can continue to live at the property while work is progressing this can cut down costs as temporary rentals of less than six months can be hard to find; you will also be able to monitor security and work efficiency.

Top tip

Garden rooms have improved in quality and reduced in cost and may not need any planning permission – is this the solution to a need for space and a new outlook?

Moving to a new location

There may well be circumstances where it might be worth thinking about moving to a new home in a new location. For example, you may want to be closer to your children and their families or you may simply want a change and the possibility of a different lifestyle in a new environment, or be attracted to the facilities in a different area. Or it may simply be the economics of a cheaper home in a different area freeing up more of your wealth to spend now on an active retirement, or to help fund your retirement income when defined pension pots dry up (as outlined at Chapter 4, Pensions).

Take care, pause and always reflect. It is easy to get carried away by the emotional attractions of a change; you really do need to sit down and think rationally about the practical pros and cons and about the longer-term implications. It's not difficult – get a piece of paper, list out the pros and cons, and keep it under review.

If you are considering moving to be closer to your family don't overlook the fact that everyone is now more mobile than has been the case in the past. While they may appear settled just now, new opportunities or challenges may mean that they themselves may need to move again – leaving you stranded in your new home, away from both old friends and family, which can't be a great place.

If you are thinking about moving to a new area that seems more attractive then check it out very carefully. Don't place too much reliance on lists of so-called 'best places' to live. They may well have their attractions but you need to be sure they meet your particular requirements. Ideally, before moving it would be sensible to spend some quality time in the new area (ie weeks at a time over different seasons), checking out what it is really like, whether it will meet your changing needs and whether you would be comfortable there socially. Don't forget that the social aspect is likely to be even more important to you in retirement. Assess all those recreational and medical positives and negatives. Don't forget the hidden intelligence that is lying around on the internet, such as TripAdvisor reviews of restaurants and Facebook sites for local community groups, which can all be quite telling/reassuring. If you move from a high-cost area to a lower-cost area it is difficult to unwind the decision years later, due to house-price inflation (and how it accumulates and the gap widens) and paying Stamp Duty and other costs again. Could you rent out your property and rent in the new location to provide a solution to this possible issue whilst you give it a year?

Moving abroad: full-time or part-time

If you are planning to retire abroad, the complexities and risk of a property purchase increase due to the dual factors of dealing in a foreign language and with foreign law where rights and remedies differ to the UK. Just now there are added complications and uncertainties as the relationship between the UK and the rest of Europe has the potential to change dramatically as a result of the Brexit negotiations. Those negotiations could have implications for important areas such as finance, residency rights and health care. It is very difficult to assess the implications of this for those living abroad and if you are contemplating a move you will need to keep a very careful watch on developments. What you really need to look out for is definitive information from government sources as it emerges and it could be some time before that happens. You do, therefore, need to proceed cautiously. A great place for a holiday is not necessarily a good place to live permanently or part-time.

Some ways of protecting yourself when buying property abroad include:

- Spend an extended period in the area at high and low season before you commit yourself to a purchase.

- Get a good solicitor. This is easier said than done but take recommendations from trusted friends and their network and try to identify a solicitor with offices in both the UK and the country you are buying in, as this can smooth transactions (especially complex ones where there may be an extra risk factor). Get all documents translated if you are signing them and they are in a foreign language.

- Make sure the solicitor you use is independent and not involved in the sale in any way.

- In particular, keep a very careful watch on any changes affecting those living abroad emerging from the negotiations relating to the UK exit from the EU.

There are many websites offering advice and information on retiring abroad. Have a browse through the following:

Britons preparing to move or retire abroad – www.gov.uk

Section on advice on retiring abroad and homes abroad – www. buyassociation.co.uk

Section on retiring abroad and popular locations – www.retirementexpert. co.uk

Information on living abroad – www.shelteroffshore.com

Essential information and advice for a successful move abroad – www. expatfocus.com

If you have the necessary funds another option would be to continue to live at home and buy another property abroad, especially if you are downsizing. If you can afford it, this might give you the best of both worlds. You would still have all the comfort and security of your home base but be able to escape to the sun from time to time as the mood moves you. To ease the financial burden you might consider letting the property out, particularly at peak times. You would, however, need to carefully check the local rules and regulations relating to letting property – these can vary from country to country and indeed from area to area.

If you do go for that 'home in the sun' as a second property the following budget planner will help you put some flesh on the likely returns to help inform your decision:

- First off, assess the structure and accommodation set-up and assess the cost of one-off adaptation work – security system, en-suites, new kitchen, fencing, roof integrity and the like.

- Income – expected weekly rental x number of weeks. Use Owners Abroad or equivalent sites to assess potential weekly rentals (the amounts can vary in high season), less:

  - accountancy and tax (you may be able to do it yourself for UK taxation but returns may be required in the foreign country);

  - advertising;

  - bank charges;

  - cleaning and laundry between occupiers and annual deep clean;

  - electricity (higher if you have a heated pool and air conditioning);

  - annual safety testing;

  - gas/oil if appropriate;

- insurance – buildings and public liability (and loss of rental, ie utilities failure etc);
- maintenance – house;
- maintenance – pool;
- letting agent fees;
- property service charge (flats and holiday-type villages with communal land/facilities);
- property tax of foreign country;
- local tax/rates of the area the property is in;
- gardening;
- security – annual maintenance and call-out fees;
- telephone/broadband;
- satellite or cable television;
- water rates/charges;
- administration costs (post, stationery).

Top tip

That second home in the sun could cost a lot more than you think and restricts holiday getaway flexibility. But if you do the numbers first it could be a fantastic opportunity and make for a perfect retirement.

Counting the cost

In order to fund a house purchase remember to do the numbers and budget for costs of 4–14 per cent of the value of a new home (the higher the purchase price the higher the percentage due to Stamp duty). So add up Stamp duty, legal fees, search fees, removal charges, survey fees, estate agents' commission and a provision for decoration and furnishings and you can refine the cost of moving. Remember, agents' fees vary and range from hundreds of pounds via online offerings to thousands of pounds for the traditional high-street agents – and don't pay too much for your new house. An asking price is just that – an asking price. So do your homework on websites such as Rightmove and Zoopla, which list the actual selling price of all houses in the street or area for the last decade; consider additions and extensions undertaken by the seller and gain more intelligence on price. Overlaying this are the general market conditions – is it a buyers' or sellers' market? Look at the sales price divided by square feet of the accommodation – this gives a useful indicator. But overriding this and governed by the golden rule of 'location, location, location' is the fact that the truly wonderful properties are often hard to find and even harder to secure, so be prepared to research, graft and undergo a bumpy journey if you set your sights really high.

Finally, don't end up with a 'pig in a poke'. When buying a new home, especially an older property, a full building (structural) survey is essential before committing yourself. This costs upwards of £500 depending on the type and size of property but it may provide you with a comeback should things go wrong. Also, an early review of environmental surveys will help you avoid being sold 'a stinker' – a home built on historic landfill (check the Environment Agency website and search 'historic landfill') or a property in an area of high flood risk (search the Environment Agency website for 'flood map for planning'). Helpful to homebuyers, the Land Registry allows members of the public to seek information directly about the 23 million or so properties held on its register via the Land Registry website (www.gov.uk/government/organisations/land-registry).

Top tip

Shop around for agents and removal firms – you could save thousands and still uphold quality. And don't end up with a stinker – check out the free intelligence on the Environment Agency website before starting to spend money.

Your protection

The Property Ombudsman scheme provides an independent review service for buyers or sellers of UK residential property in the event of a complaint. It also covers lettings agents and residential leasehold management. As with most ombudsman schemes, action can be taken only against firms that are actually members of the scheme. See the Property Ombudsman website (www.tpos.co.uk).

Removals

A reputable firm of removers and shippers will eliminate many of the headaches. A full packing service can save much anxiety and a lot of your time. Costs can vary significantly depending on the type and size of furniture, the distance over which it is being moved and other factors, including insurance and seasonal troughs and peaks. Shop around and try a quote from just outside your local area as neighbouring removal firms are always keen to get a slice of the action. 'Special deals' offered by a removal firm aligned with your estate agent sometimes turn out to be rather unspecial. The British Association of Removers (BAR) promotes excellence in the removals industry (for approved member firms, all of whom work to a rigorous code of practice, see the website www.bar.co.uk).

Living in leasehold

An ever-increasing number of people move into a flat in retirement. If acquiring a leasehold flat, the freeholder of the building may be an investment company, a private investor, or ideally the leaseholders themselves in the form of a management company. With the advent of 'right to manage', leaseholders do not need to own the freehold but will be able to manage the building as if they were the freeholder.

Leaseholders should be aware of their responsibilities, such as keeping the inside of the property in good order, paying their share of the cost of maintaining and running the building, behaving in a neighbourly manner and not contravening things as set out in the lease, such as subletting their flat without the freeholder's prior consent, or keeping a pet when the lease clearly states this is not permitted.

The leaseholder has the right to expect the freeholder to maintain the building and common parts. The leaseholder will be required to pay a 'service charge' to the freeholder (or their managing agent) to maintain, repair and insure the building as well as to provide other services such as lifts, central heating or cleaners. These charges must at all times be 'reasonable'. Leaseholders have a right to challenge the service charge if they feel it is 'unreasonable' via the Leasehold Valuation Tribunal (LVT). For further information see the Leasehold Advisory Service (LAS) (www.lease-advice.org), and Association of Retirement Housing Managers (ARHM) (www.arhm.org).

Other options

Caravans or mobile homes

If you want to live in a caravan on land you own, or other private land, you should contact your local authority for information about any planning permission or site licensing requirements that may apply. If you want to keep it on an established site, there is a varied choice. Check carefully, whichever you choose, that the site owner has all the necessary permissions. All disputes since 30 April 2011 are, under the Mobile Homes Act 1983, being dealt with by residential property tribunals in place of the county court.

Retirement housing and sheltered accommodation

Hopefully you will still be in good physical health at the time of your retirement. However, as time moves on it is inevitable that you will start to slow down and may find it increasingly difficult to maintain your existing property. At that stage, you may need to start thinking about the need to move to retirement housing or sheltered accommodation. You probably do not need to take any direct action as you retire; rather it is something that you could usefully keep at the back of your mind. Of course, you also need to consider any potential changes in your partner's wellbeing.

The terms 'retirement housing' and 'sheltered accommodation' cover a wide variety of housing but are designed primarily to bridge the gap between the family home and residential care. There are many well-designed, high-quality private developments of 'retirement homes' on the market, for sale or rent, at prices to suit most pockets. As a general rule, you have to be over 55 when you buy property of this kind.

Positives include 24-hour emergency alarms or on-site wardens and built-in design features such as walk-in showers and raised plugs. There can be a positive social community. Some 'villages' have been developed to offer on-site amenities and some developers have identified a need for luxury-type units, including a swimming pool. Negatives may include a no-pets policy, high service charges (these must be factored into any decision), smaller space than you are used to and a closer proximity to neighbours. Banks normally do not lend on these properties.

Practical suggestions for reducing your energy bills

The chances are that it will become even more important to carefully watch your costs, as in all probability you will be on more or less a fixed income. In that respect, property costs and particularly energy costs can be very important.

According to the Department of Energy and Climate Change, about 11 million households could save £200 or more per year by simply switching suppliers. Comparison sites are quick and easy to use to find cheaper offers. Find more information at www.moneysavingexpert.com and www.which.co.uk. Simply doing a few hours' research could save you substantial amounts, as we discussed at greater length in Chapter 7.

Something else to watch out for is the advent of 'smart' electric or gas meters, which send readings digitally to your supplier to tell them (and you) how much electricity and gas you have used each day. There are three big advantages to having smart meters: consumers will have no more estimated bills; by having an 'in-home display' (IHD) consumption can be measured daily and, hopefully, energy use can be reduced; and energy suppliers will be able to charge tariffs that reflect demand.

Don't forget that many energy suppliers offer free annual gas safety checks for the over-60s and everyone can save energy costs as follows:

- A simple thing like turning down your thermostat can save you money. According to Age UK, 21 degrees centigrade is the magic number to keep your living room warm; the ideal bedroom temperature is 18 degrees centigrade. For more information see the Age UK website (www.ageuk. org.uk) and search for 'keeping warm'.

- Turning off the lights when you go out of a room and replacing light bulbs with energy-saving ones really can save you money.

- Close curtains to cut draughts. Check on windows, doors and chimneys and get draught blockers in place.

- Replacing an old gas boiler may be expensive, but it could save you money if it is uneconomical to repair it.

- If you were born before 5 May 1953 you are eligible to claim the Winter Fuel Payment. This is an annual, tax-free benefit and is non-means tested. A separate benefit, the Cold Weather Payment, is paid in the event of exceptionally cold weather (visit www.gov.uk and go to 'winter fuel payment').

Structural repairs and improvements

You may be someone who is very handy and loves DIY. In this case you will now have more time to indulge yourself in maintaining and improving your home. However, many of us don't have those skills and home improvement work can be a stressful, costly business. Whether the work you are contemplating is complex or simple, here are some top tips to help get the work done safely, efficiently, cost effectively and to avoid some of the common pitfalls:

- *If your house needs structural repairs*: the Royal Institution of Chartered Surveyors can help you find a reputable chartered surveyor. See their website (www.rics.org).

- *Before work starts*: don't forget to contact your local authority planning and building control departments to check if there are any restrictions on what changes can be made.

- *Budgeting, quotes and specifications*: make a detailed list of everything you would like to have included; compare quotes and check whether VAT is included in the final cost. Include costs for labour and parts in your overall budget and agree with contractors who will purchase items and have responsibility for their delivery.

- *Finding a trader*: check your local authority trading standards website for details of approved trader schemes. Be clear about whether you need building regulations certificates for any of the work you are doing. *Never* use anyone who comes to your door cold-calling.

- *Contractual information*: written quotations are essential, and should be broken down to itemize the prices of work and materials. List work you wish to have done and agree who is responsible if there are delays – and who pays. Agree a timetable for the work and how payments will be made.

- *During work*: agree a single point of contact for the project and raise issues as they arise. If your local authority building control department has to sign off key stages of the work, check they have done so.

- *Finishing work*: agreement must be clear as to when the project is completed, when the final payment is required and what it covers. Some money is usually withheld to cover snagging, which refers to the bits and pieces that become evident a week or two after the job finishes – the list is endless, from dripping pipes to new doors that don't close over the new carpets – and you will also hold the retention until you have all the paperwork, including electrical certifications and building control sign-off by the local authority.

Building work is a big deal and some builders are more reliable than others. You need to tread carefully and definitely trust your instincts, as we warned in Chapter 7. For those of you who remember the classic television show *Fawlty Towers*, the episode 'The Builders' gives a great reminder of the downsides of hiring the wrong builder!

> **Top tip**
>
> Get recommendations from trusted and knowledgeable friends and visit the builder's last job – a good tradesperson/builder should have no problems whatsoever with this and if they do then that tells its own story.

Safety in the home

Most people feel safe in their own homes but we should not overlook the fact that serious accidents often do occur there.

The Royal Society for the Prevention of Accidents (ROSPA) estimates that every year in the UK more than 6,000 people die in accidents in the home and a staggering 2.7 million people turn up at accident and emergency departments seeking treatment for accidents sustained in the home. So you cannot afford to be complacent, particularly as, let's face it, with increasing age you get just that bit slower and forgetful.

Accident prevention is easy, relatively inexpensive to deliver and can make a high impact – especially for the most vulnerable members of society. So it makes sense to spend some time checking that your home is as safe as possible. Excellent advice on general safety in the home can be found by visiting www.rospa.com and searching for 'home safety'.

Here are some sensible safety tips from ROSPA:

- *Fire*: having approved smoke detectors is vital.

- *Electricity*: wiring should be checked at least every five years by an approved contractor. If an appliance appears to be faulty, stop using it. When buying electrical equipment look for the CE mark. Never overload sockets.

- *Heating and cooking*: air vents or airbricks should be kept clean and clear. Did you know that a gas flame normally burns blue? If it burns orange, this indicates a build-up of carbon monoxide. Appliances should be regularly checked. Be aware of signs of carbon monoxide poisoning, such as drowsiness and flu-like symptoms. Purchase or renew a carbon monoxide alarm. If purchasing gas appliances, look for the BS safety mark. Should you suspect a gas leak, open windows, turn off supply and call your gas supplier.

If you smell gas or suspect a carbon monoxide leak, call the National Grid 24-hour emergency line: 0800 111 999.

Safety with medicines and cleaners

Medicines and chemicals should be kept in a safe, locked container or cupboard, where children can neither see nor reach them. Leftover medicines should be returned to the pharmacist.

DIY and garden safety

Enthusiasm and inexperience can be fatal as accidents can happen when you take shortcuts. Use appropriate protective gear, for instance protective glasses when hedge cutting. All electrical appliances and tools should be disconnected before working on them. *Never* pour petrol on a barbecue or fire. Remember that some plants and berries are poisonous or can cause an allergic reaction. There are now a very wide range of chemicals for use in the garden – weed killers, pesticides, fungicides etc. Most of these are potentially dangerous and should always be used according to the manufacturer's instructions and stored carefully, particularly out of the reach of children (sensible advice and help can be found at www.rospa.com).

Home security

Your local crime prevention officer should be able to advise you on home security arrangements and whether there are any local 'neighbourhood watch' schemes in operation.

Top tip

Why not have a street meeting and invite your local crime prevention officer along to give a talk – it helps to be able to connect that face to a name if you really do need help.

Should you be leaving your property empty for a time due to holidays it is worthwhile to get a relative or a trustworthy neighbour to keep an eye on your property and clear up your mail on a regular basis – piled-up mail at a letterbox is a clear signal to thieves that the house is empty. The Royal Mail's 'Keepsafe' service will store your mail until you return; there is a charge for this service. Some general tips on keeping your home safe are:

- *Social media*: check your privacy settings (or ask someone to help on this) before posting about your holiday or saying something about your lifestyle that lets the world know that you are away from home.
- *Home exterior*: check any broken windows or access via garages or conservatories. Tools and ladders should be locked away.
- *Door and window locks*: all windows and doors should have locks that are in good condition, properly fitted to comply with insurance requirements.
- *Beware opportunist thieves*: should your home look unoccupied, using time switches to control inside lighting is a good deterrent.
- *Sensor lights*: dusk-to-dawn or sensor lighting to the front and rear of your home will deter potential thieves.
- *Security alarms*: remember to regularly change the code in order to gain the maximum benefit – and get it serviced yearly.
- *Security grilles or bars*: these can protect side windows, or you can use reinforced glass if windows cannot be blocked.
- *Key replacement*: if you haven't replaced your locks recently it is possibly time you did. If you ask a professional locksmith to fit a patented system, you will have the reassurance that keys can only be copied with proof of ownership.
- *Garden shed*: a good-quality lock or padlock will protect your garden shed and its contents.
- *Car keys at risk*: statistics show that thieves are increasingly breaking into homes to steal car keys. Don't make it easy for them by leaving keys in view.

Age UK provides a helpful booklet, *Staying Safe*, which can be downloaded from their website (www.ageuk.org.uk).

Insurance

Apparently, about 6.8 million households in the UK are underinsured. Hopefully yours is not one of them. Reassessing your policy annually makes sense; you may have made improvements to your property, or added to your home contents. A number of insurance companies now give discounts on house contents premiums if proper security precautions have been installed.

If you are planning to move into accommodation that has been converted from one large house into several flats or maisonettes, check with the landlord or managing agent that the insurance on the structure of the total building is adequate. Owners of properties in flood-prone areas in the UK have difficulty getting insurance. Further information can be obtained from the National Flood Forum at www.nationalfloodforum.org.uk and from www.floodre.co.uk, a national scheme to help provide better access to affordable flood insurance cover and help in managing the risk.

On buildings insurance, revisit both the rebuilding costs and insurance value of your home. Does your policy provide money to meet architects' or surveyors' fees as well as alternative accommodation for you and your family if your home is destroyed?

At the same time, review the value of your home contents. With older possessions, you should assess the replacement cost and make sure you have a 'new for old' or 'replacement as new' policy. Cancel items on your contents policy that you no longer possess and add new high-value items that have been bought or received as presents. (Insurers normally set limits that require disclosure of high-value items – what is yours? If you undervalue your total contents and suffer a loss you will find that in all probability your insurer will proportionally reduce any compensation due to you.)

Where antiques and jewellery are concerned, a professional valuation is wise; the British Antique Dealers' Association (www.bada.org) can assist or point you in the right direction. Photographs of particularly valuable items can help in the assessment of premiums and settlement of claims. Property marking, for example with an ultraviolet marker, is another useful ploy, as it may help the police trace your possessions should any be stolen. Further advice can be obtained from the Association of British Insurers: www.abi.org.uk (go to 'home insurance').

Financial institutions are keen on 'loyalty marketing' but loyalty should work both ways, so shop around, as we advocate in Chapter 4. If you feel you have been unfairly treated by an insurer you can take your grievance to the Financial Ombudsman Service.

Earning money from your home

Your home doesn't have to be a drain on your finances. If you need some spare cash or a regular source of income, there are various ways in which you could make money from your home.

Here are some ideas to consider:

- *Rent a room scheme*: this is the government's incentive that allows owner-occupiers and tenants to receive tax-free rental income if furnished accommodation is provided in the main – or only – home. The maximum amount you can earn is £7,500 per year. If you live in a suitable area, you could find a commuting lodger who only wants the room on week nights – see websites such as www.mondaytofriday.com or www.airbnb.co.uk. Whilst this could give you additional income you do, however, need to balance this with the possibility of a certain loss of privacy and assess how you can manage any risk to you and your property.

- *£1,000 tax-free property allowance*: you can also earn £1,000 from letting out your home and not pay any tax via the HMRC property allowance. If you own a property jointly with others, you are each allowed the £1,000 allowance. For more information see www.gov.uk and search 'tax free allowances on property and trading income'.

- *Rent out your drive*: some areas of the United Kingdom are chronically short of available parking for people going to work or travelling from a nearby airport. There are many evolving websites in this area (try www.justpark.com).

- *Your home in lights*: it is possible to rent out your home as a film or TV set, particularly if it is quirky or charming. You can list your home via an online agency such as Film Locations (www.filmlocations.co.uk), or Amazing Space (www.amazingspace.co.uk), although agencies will take a fee if your home is used.

- *Host students*: offer your home as a base for a foreign language or exchange student. This pays typically £100 per week. Contact your local language schools, colleges and universities to see if they offer a pairing service for would-be lodgers and hosts.

- *Holiday lets*: if you own a second home, renting it out for holiday lets can be profitable and quite tax efficient as long as certain conditions are met. To qualify for the best tax reliefs the property must be available for at least 210 days during the tax year and actually be let for at least 105 days. For more information visit www.gov.uk and go to 'furnished holiday lettings'.

Finally, make money from clearing your clutter and surplus possessions that could be converted into cash. Obvious outlets are eBay and the local car-boot sale; www.preloved.co.uk is another popular marketplace website.

Benefits and taxes

Housing benefit

More than 250,000 pensioners who are tenants could get their rent reduced by claiming housing benefit (which will be replaced by universal credit in due course) and some could be missing out on an average of more than £60 per week. The biggest reductions are for those on pension credit. If you have less than £16,000 in savings you may be able to get this financial help from your local council. For advice contact your local authority or Citizens Advice Bureau. The amount of benefit you receive depends on several factors: the number of people in the household, your eligible rent, your capital or savings, your income and your 'applicable amount' (which is the amount the government considers you need for basic living expenses). If you think you may be eligible, contact your council for an application form or apply online. For further information see www.gov.uk and go to 'housing benefit'.

Council Tax

This is based on the value of the property you live in and also consists of a personal element. Most domestic properties are liable for Council Tax, including rented property, mobile homes and houseboats. The value of the property is assessed according to a banding system. Not everyone pays Council Tax. The bill, which is sent out in April each year, is normally sent to the resident owner or to the tenant. The valuation of each property assumes that two adults are resident. The charge remains the same if there are more adults. However, if there is a single adult only living in the property, the bill is reduced by 25 per cent. For further information see www.gov.uk and go to 'Council Tax'.

Exemptions from Council Tax include:

- Property that has been unoccupied and unfurnished for less than six months.
- The home of a deceased person; the exemption lasts until six months after the grant of probate.
- A home that is empty because the occupier is absent in order to care for someone else.
- The home of a person who is or would be exempted from Council Tax because of moving to a residential home, hospital care or similar.

- Empty properties in need of major repairs or undergoing structural alteration can be exempt for an initial period of six months, but this can be extended for a further six months. After 12 months, the standard 50 (or possibly full 100) per cent charge for empty properties will apply.
- Granny flats that are part of another private domestic dwelling may be exempt, but this depends on access and other conditions. To check, contact your local council's 'Valuation Office'.

Disputes

If you are responsible for paying the Council Tax on a property that you feel has been wrongly banded, you have six months to appeal and can request that the valuation be reconsidered. If you have grounds for appeal, you should take up the matter with the Valuation Office. If the matter is not resolved, you can then appeal to an independent valuation tribunal. For advice and further information, contact your local Citizens Advice Bureau.

Council Tax reduction

Since council tax benefit was done away with in 2013 the scheme has now moved from national coverage to a series of local schemes. The amount you get depends on your income, savings, personal circumstances, who else lives in your home (in particular whether they would be counted as 'non-dependants') and your net Council Tax bill (after any deductions that apply to your home). For further information see Citizens Advice at www. citizensadvice.org.uk and go to 'Council Tax reduction'.

Inspired? Remember to fill in your plan for a good retirement at the end of the book.

CHAPTER TWELVE

Personal relationships

You don't develop courage by being happy in your relationships every day.
You develop it by surviving difficult times and challenging adversity.

EPICURUS

Personal relationships and health go hand in hand and feature as must-read parts of the 'live better' section of this book. But do good relations promote good health (this is covered in Chapter 13) or is it the other way around? Logic says that if you get your personal relationships right, much positivity will flow from them, which should improve your overall health. Personal relationships within the family can make life much easier and more enjoyable but they can also make life more difficult if they become fractured.

Having good personal relationships also provides you with a group around you for emotional support, advice, different viewpoints that challenge you, shoulders to cry on and folk with whom to share daft jokes, social occasions and transport. Don't forget the importance of having people around you who will take you down a peg or two if you sometimes tend to get beyond yourself.

More fundamentally it will be a rare person who is happy every day, as there will always be difficult times and challenging situations so it is just as much about how you survive them – as Epicurus said 2,300 years ago. His basic philosophy was about living a self-sufficient life surrounded by friends and, without getting too heavy about it, he made a good point when he said

'You don't develop courage by being happy in your relationships every day. You develop it by surviving difficult times and challenging adversity.'

This chapter at a glance

This is the shortest chapter but one of the most important in this book. If your personal relationships are maintained and improved you will be happier:

- Personal relationships: retirement brings big changes to the dynamics of your personal relationships. If your life was your work and your friends were at work, the changes will be bigger than you could have realized.

- Adjust to this new life balance with your partner and try not to get under each other's feet.

- We offer reminders about those other people who matter most to you – children, grandchildren, parents, other close relatives and good friends.

- We offer pointers to the new friends who will emerge from your new social groups in retirement – and remember good friends tend to stick around during the highs and lows of life.

Personal relationships

Reaching retirement age is something many people look forward to, but it is a major lifestyle change. According to Relate, 91 per cent of people aged over 50 in the UK said that a close personal relationship is as important as good health and financial security. This emphasizes the fact that as we grow older we find that strong and healthy personal relationships count for even more. This covers the spectrum from former work colleagues to your partner, your children, your parents and other friendship groups. It may come as a big surprise but your retirement brings a change in these dynamics and this means that some may change, some may be lost and some new ones will be found. With some warning and preparation there should not be too many bumps along the way, but adjusting will take a little time.

Work

The chances are that most people will have spent a great deal of their time in a working environment where they will have established a whole series of relationships. Those will include working colleagues, fellow professionals, customers and suppliers; some of those colleagues may well have become close friends. Once you retire, those contacts and relationships will become much less significant in your life.

While individual circumstances can vary, the general advice on retirement is that you should not seek to return to your old working environment. You may initially be tempted to drop in to see how things are going and to have a quick chat with old friends, but generally it is not a great idea to do so. Things can change very quickly, as can personnel, and life moves on. Whatever your previous role may have been and however important it was you will now be seen as an outsider. People in work will want to get on with the job in hand and will have little time for chit-chat – just think how you may have reacted when you were actually working. So unless you have agreed some very specific role with your old organization it is probably best to stay away right from the very start. That is not to say that you should not stay in contact with people with whom you were particularly friendly. But do so on the basis of a network outside the actual working environment.

Partner

The other major change will be with those nearest and dearest to you and you may have seen some relationships fracture after the age of 60. If you are a couple you will now spend much more time together, and indeed this is something that you both may have been looking forward to. But you may need a little time to adjust to this new life balance and you need to be careful not to get under each other's feet. You may just need to give each other a bit of personal space. In that respect you both might take a quick look over the leisure and holidays chapter of this book (Chapter 15), which provides ideas, thoughts and prompts on activities that could keep you challenged and occupied. Also, if only one partner has retired you may need to sit down and work out how responsibility for undertaking all those everyday but necessary tasks might have to be readjusted.

These very personal relationships will be a key factor in how happy your retirement years are likely to be. So grab some time out and a cup of tea and sit down as a couple, talk through how best to work through what will be a new relationship, and be prepared to accept that it may take a little time to adjust to your new situation. But generally you should find that things eventually do fall fairly neatly into place. Should the need arise, the following organizations can offer help and advice:

Marriage Care: www.marriagecare.org.uk

The Spark (Scotland): www.thespark.org.uk

Relate: www.relate.org.uk and in Northern Ireland www.relateni.org

Children

You may also find that you have more time to devote to those wider family relationships. Your children may have moved on to start developing their own families, but it is likely they will continue to value whatever support you can give them. This may involve the occasional – or in some cases regular – babysitting duties. This can be a great bonus to both parties: you establish a closer bond with your grandchildren and your own children get a bit more freedom at an important stage of their own life. Also, if they are finding it difficult to get a foot on the property market, and you now find yourself with some available capital, you may want to discuss the possibility of giving or loaning them a helping hand to get started. But a word of warning: you should not impose yourself, your ideas of how things should be done or how to spend a gift – 'give and let go' could be a useful phrase here. As in all things, a sensible balance is needed and don't forget that you need to retain your own freedoms to do as you wish, within reason. After all, you have worked hard for what you have now got and are entitled to enjoy it.

Parents

At the other end of the age spectrum your own or your partner's parents may now be getting to the stage where they may need some support or even just a little more of your time. Again, you need to tread carefully to avoid imposing your solutions on their problems and to ensure that they don't become overly dependent on you.

Sandwich generation

Those in their fifties and sixties are the 'sandwich generation' where dual pressures may influence the relationships. This could be caused by 'boomerang' kids who return home after university/college whereas, in previous generations, they tended to find their own independence at an earlier age. House prices and rent prices (especially in London and the south-east of England and other property 'hot spots') make the opportunity of living a few more years with parents an attractive one. The same may apply if you have vulnerable or elderly parents who have needs and potentially need care. Chapter 2 sets the scene on the sandwich generation but the dual pressure just points to needing more care on how these special relationships work.

Friends

You will probably already have a wide circle of social friendships and that is unlikely to change on retirement. Indeed, it is important to retain and even develop those links now that you have more time to do so. You should also take every opportunity to develop new acquaintanceships as you start to get involved with all of those activities you never had time to pursue during your working life. With more time there will be more opportunities to join new groups – and remember, as shown in Chapter 15 (Leisure), if there is not a group around then take the lead and form one (hints and tips are provided in Chapter 15).

So the general message is that every person and relationship is individual and will differ slightly from another. Usually things boil down to compromise and learning to work things out. An active social life, combined with building on those personal and family relationships, is a sure-fire way to enhance your retirement years and live better. Fractured relationships, on the other hand, usually have the opposite effect.

Some people may stay as friends and some may come and go but the true friends tend to stick around through the highs and lows of life; sharing these events and getting through them is all part and parcel of your personal relationship 'network' – and as a species we can be a resilient bunch!

Useful help

The book *Men are From Mars, Women are From Venus* by John Gray styles itself as the 'definitive guide to relationships'. Some parts of it are fairly obvious but it does help underline the point that we are all different and some compromise is needed for a better overall outcome.

Inspired? Remember to fill in your plan for a good retirement at the end of the book.

CHAPTER THIRTEEN

Health

It is health that is the real wealth and not pieces of gold and silver.
MAHATMA GANDHI

The media is full of information about important advances in medical research, breakthroughs in diagnosis or treatments for serious illnesses. Whilst that may be good news, the media at times has a tendency to exaggerate so it is probably wise not to take as gospel everything you may read or hear. It is, however, a fact that clinical trials and other medical advances are helping to find cures for diseases that would previously have been life impairing or fatal. It is heartening to know that all these new discoveries have the power to improve our health and mean that we are likely to live significantly longer than previous generations.

Despite this, remaining healthy after the age of 50 is, it seems, to some extent in our own hands. The recipe at first glance is fairly easy. A prescription of a better and healthier diet, not smoking, reducing alcohol intake, staying mentally active and keeping fit seems to be sensible. It would be easy if it was as simple as that. The human species is outstanding in its ability to waste hundreds of pounds on advice books that are not started or never finished. The same applies to fitness or diet programmes that end up a temporary activity. We have all probably been there at some point. The bottom line is simple. It really is down to you. To help you get underway this chapter provides information and tips that might just make you that bit healthier – and if you live better you will be happier.

This chapter at a glance

This chapter might just add a few more enjoyable years to your life. Surely that's worth the purchase price in itself! But here's the problem: as we age it gets harder to change our habits. However, if we do as we have always done, we will get what we have always got. So, take a deep breath, read on, and strengthen your willpower to make an impact. You will find in this chapter:

- The truth about obesity. Some help in recognizing the issue and action to take.
- Keep fit. Exercise is one of the greatest benefits to good health, so fight the urge to fall into a sedentary lifestyle in retirement. This chapter shows you some options and choices, but then it is over to you and that willpower thing. Go on, you can change old habits.
- You are what you eat. Is this true of you? Be honest! There is a section on fitness and diet, as well as suggestions on how to eat more healthily. Don't avoid the issue. It is worth repeating here that action could add years to your life.
- Have you had a recent health screening check? If not, when new to retirement this may well give you some peace of mind. There are also sections on the NHS and advice about going into hospital.
- Finally, this chapter gives information on some common health issues and where to go for more help.

Health

The big picture – the truth about obesity

The NHS is clear in its advice: being obese puts you at raised risk of health problems such as heart disease, stroke and type 2 diabetes. Losing weight will bring significant health improvements.

Do you know about the 'string test'? It's brilliantly simple, costs nothing and takes one minute – and it will help you know where you stand. It was promoted on the BBC programme *The Truth About Obesity* screened on 26 April 2018. On the programme, Professor Steve Bloom, the Head of Division for Diabetes, Endocrinology and Metabolism at Imperial College London, said:

If you manage to lose weight your cancer risk goes down to half, your diabetes disappears, you live longer, Alzheimer's disease is less of a risk and, of course, the long-term effects in the human race of not having this tsunami of obesity is amazing. People will live longer, they will be healthier, they will be more effective.

Here is how the string test works. Get a piece of string and measure your height with it and cut it off at your precise height level. Fold the string in half and now measure it around the widest part of your stomach. The two ends should touch – if you are left with a gap between the ends of the folded string you need to work on reducing the gap.

Keeping fit

Well, this sounds simple and – you've guessed it – it is something easy that most of us can do. Staying physically active improves our health and quality of life, and can help us live longer. Among the advantages of keeping active are a reduced risk of developing a life-threatening disease, a better chance of avoiding obesity, maintaining or reaching a healthy weight, improved sleep and increased daytime energy, feeling happier, and keeping your brain sharp. The more physically active you are, the longer you are likely to remain independent. Exercise makes you stronger, boosts confidence and increases your sense of wellbeing. It is best to start slowly and build up gradually. Experts recommend 30 minutes of moderate exercise per day about five times a week and it can be something as simple as a brisk walk. It's easy to boost your physical activity by incorporating some of the following into your everyday life:

- avoid lifts and escalators – take the stairs instead;
- cycle/walk rather than drive;
- take up walking/rambling (get a dog?).

We look at this more in Chapter 15 (Leisure).

Top tip

If you do need to increase your activity levels get a step-counter app on your phone or one of those wrist devices you can wear that counts your steps. There is no hiding place or scope for little white lies. It's simple – get your activity and steps up. Aim to eventually get up to **10,000** steps a day and the impact could be amazing. Check your plan out with your doctor/ health professional.

Organized activities

There are lots of ways of staying fit and in most local areas there are loads of classes to help you do it; some may even be free, or cut-price, at your sports or community centre or local park. Find out what is available in your area. There are all sorts of activities, including boxercise, Pilates, table tennis, circuit training, swimming, running, cycling, walking groups and even bowling, where your competitive streak can be let loose again. Getting fit as part of a group adds a social aspect and is probably more motivating, but if you want to get started on your own try Fitness Blender, which offers more than 400 free workout videos, ranging from high-intensity interval training to yoga (www.fitnessblender.com).

Healthy eating

We need fewer calories in our fifties and sixties than we did in our thirties. Eating a balanced diet and not overeating is important. There are a huge number of special diets and the media are forever commenting on what we should and should not eat. Treat that with caution and just stick to a sensible balanced diet. To get the best from your diet, follow these suggestions:

- eat at least five portions of fruit and vegetables per day;
- cut back on bread;
- drink plenty of water and reduce or cut out fizzy, sugary drinks;
- eat more fish;
- drink less alcohol;
- limit your salt intake.

Say 'no' to unhealthy food. If you have a tendency to overindulge and lack willpower try to avoid having tempting treats in your kitchen such as cake, crisps and biscuits.

Portion control is key. Cut down on the amount you eat, and make sure each meal contains a variety of protein, carbs and vegetables – colourful contents on the plate are usually healthier.

Top tip

- Buy smaller plates – size is everything here (supersize plates usually lead to supersize portions).
- Get a blender and try making smoothies.

- It's all about willpower – if you struggle with this then the self-support diet groups (we all know who they are) will help you for a fee. It's all about a new lifestyle for a lasting impact.

How to keep healthy in the heat

In the very hot weather there are certain groups of people who are at risk: the very young, the elderly and the seriously ill, as heat can make heart and breathing problems worse. As long as we take sensible precautions, most of us can safely enjoy hot weather. The main risks posed by a heatwave are dehydration, heat exhaustion and heatstroke. The NHS tips (www.nhs.uk – go to 'summer health') include:

- close windows and pull down blinds when it is hot outside;
- stay inside during the hottest time of the day;
- take cool baths or showers;
- drink cold drinks regularly, and avoid coffee and alcohol;
- wear loose, cool clothing and take a sun hat when outdoors;
- keep an eye on friends, relatives and neighbours who may be less able to look after themselves.

Food safety

One disadvantage of age is that we become more vulnerable to bugs and germs from incorrectly prepared food. As our immune system weakens, it is harder to fight off bacteria and serious illness. Once a food-borne illness is contracted, the infections can be difficult to treat. Many such illnesses have virus-like symptoms, which could lead to dehydration if not properly treated. The good news is there are some simple, sensible precautions that can help. The NHS advice here includes:

- *Cleaning*: wash your hands with soap and warm water before you start preparing any food, after touching raw food and after touching the bin or a pet. If you are ill with stomach problems, *do not* handle food.
- *Cooking*: cooking food thoroughly – particularly chicken and most types of seafood – is important in order to kill any harmful bacteria that might be present. If you reheat food, ensure that it is steaming hot all the way through. Don't reheat food more than once.

- *Chilling*: some foods must be kept at the right temperature to stop harmful bacteria from growing and multiplying. Your fridge should be set to 0–5°C (32–41°F). Cooked leftovers should be cooled quickly and then put in the fridge or freezer.

- *Cross-contamination*: raw meat needs to be kept in sealable containers at the bottom of the fridge to stop it from dripping on to other foods. If you have chopped or placed raw food on chopping boards or used knives and other utensils on it, these need to be fully cleaned afterwards. Don't wash raw meat or poultry – it is not necessary to do so because all harmful bacteria will be killed in the cooking process and washing it could spread, through splashing, harmful bacteria around your sink and kitchen.

Drink (alcohol)

There is so much reported about overindulgence with alcohol that this topic may seem too obvious to mention. The more you drink, the greater the risk to your health. The NHS suggested limit is 14 units per week; a pint of beer and a 175ml glass of wine count as two units each. For people who suspect they may have a drinking problem, the first point of contact should be their GP. There are organizations to help those in need of support, such as:

Al-Anon Family Groups UK & Eire: www.al-anonuk.org.uk

Alcohol Concern: www.alcoholconcern.org.uk

Alcoholics Anonymous: www.alcoholics-anonymous.org.uk

Top tip

If you drink every day and feel you don't want to give up, you could try the 5:2 method – having two 'dry' days a week (Monday and Tuesday maybe) when you don't drink alcohol.

Smoking

The only advice to give is that you simply should not smoke – and if you still do you should stop. There is a lot of help available for giving up the habit:

National Centre for Smoking Cessation and Training: www.ncsct.co.uk

Quit: www.quit.org.uk

Smokefree: quitnow.smokefree.nhs.uk

Smokeline (Scotland only): www.canstopsmoking.com

Stop Smoking UK: www.stopsmokinguk.org

Accident prevention

The prevention of accidents – particularly those likely to occur in the home – is something we should all be aware of and there is more advice in Chapter 16. Prevention of falls is something worth highlighting here. Did you know that one in three over-65s have a fall each year? Across the UK every year 1.2 million people end up in A&E after a fall, costing the NHS £1.6 billion. The Chartered Society of Physiotherapy uses a simple 'get up and go' test to assess the risk you may have of suffering a fall and injury (maybe a broken hip, or worse). This involves getting out of a chair, walking three metres and returning to the chair and sitting. If it takes longer than 15 seconds it is a sign to get more active and get stronger. They guide you on activities and precautions you can take to reduce the risk of falls. Find out more by visiting www.csp.org and going to 'get up and go'. The test should not be done alone. The Royal Society for the Prevention of Accidents also has some excellent safety advice: www.rospa.com, 'home safety'.

Should you be injured in an accident, whether in the street or elsewhere, consider whether you can claim compensation if there has been a genuine fault by another person or organization and you have suffered injury and/or financial loss. There is an abundance of assistance on this, ranging from 'no win no fee' solicitors to claims companies. Be clear on the terms and conditions of engaging such a firm and read the small print – if you don't understand the small print then change to a firm where it is understandable.

Aches, pains and other abnormalities

How can we recognize serious warning signs when things ache or are painful? These can vary hugely from person to person. For example, chest tightness or pain is the most common symptom of a heart attack in both men and women, yet some people will not experience chest pain at all.

Use the NHS 111 service for non-emergency calls. Trained advisers, supported by health-care professionals, will ask you questions to assess your symptoms and immediately direct you to the best medical care for you. NHS 111 is available 24 hours a day, 365 days a year and calls are free from landlines and mobile phones. For less urgent health needs, contact your GP or local pharmacist for advice. The following symptoms should always be investigated by a doctor:

- any pain that lasts more than a few days;
- lumps, however small;
- dizziness or fainting;
- chest pains, shortness of breath or palpitations;
- persistent cough or hoarseness;
- unusual bleeding from anywhere;
- frequent indigestion;
- unexplained weight loss.

> **Top tip**
>
> If in doubt, check it out. Talk with a family member and then to your doctor.

Health insurance

Health insurance or private medical insurance (PMI) allows you to avoid long queues for treatment, receive fast-track consultations, and pays for you to be treated privately in an NHS or private hospital. PMI is not essential and the cost of it can increase significantly as you get older. You therefore need to look carefully at the balance between cost and benefit depending on your own situation. If you have an accident or serious illness such as a heart attack or cancer then the NHS steps in and can be world class. But problems can arise from other conditions that may be debilitating but not life-threatening; the challenge may be in getting a timely intervention so that you are more comfortable and can get on with enjoying your retirement years. If you have disposable income and your finances are in order you may be able to buy in the help you need for extra peace of mind. Not every eventuality is covered by PMI, so it is important to check your policy details and review the cost and affordability from time to time. Take care before moving from one provider to another and find out if pre-existing conditions are covered – get this wrong and you could be in for a nasty surprise. The following are some of the best-known organizations that provide PMI cover:

Aviva: www.aviva.co.uk

AXA PPP Healthcare: www.axappphealthcare.co.uk

BUPA: www.bupa.co.uk

The Exeter: www.the-exeter.com

Vitality Health: www.pruhealth.co.uk

Saga: www.saga.co.uk

Simply Health: www.simplyhealth.co.uk

Private patients – without insurance cover

If you do not have private medical insurance but want to go into hospital in the UK as a private patient, there is nothing to stop you, provided your doctor is willing and you are able to pay the bills from your savings. Start the process by asking your doctor 'Can I get this done privately?' – and they will guide you from there.

Medical tourism

The term 'medical tourism' refers to travellers who have chosen to have medical/dental/surgical treatment abroad. Cosmetic surgery, dental procedures and cardiac surgery are the most common procedures that medical tourists undergo. Since the standards of medical treatments and available treatments vary widely across the world, anyone considering undertaking medical treatment abroad should carry out their own independent research. Further information and advice can be found here:

www.nhs.uk/NHSEngland/Healthcareabroad

Hospital health-care cash plans

A hospital health-care cash plan is an insurance policy that helps you pay for routine health-care treatment such as eye tests, dental treatment and physiotherapy. It is totally different to private medical insurance and can be a cheap way to pay for everyday health costs. You pay a monthly premium, depending on how much cover you want. When you receive the treatment you pay upfront, send the receipt to the insurer and it reimburses you, depending on the terms of your policy. More information is available from the British Health Care Association (www.bhca.org.uk).

Income protection, lump-sum critical illness benefit and some life insurance policies

Income protection insurance used to be known as permanent health insurance. It is a replacement-of-earnings policy for people who are still in work (employed or self-employed). Critical-illness benefit policies pay a lump sum on diagnosis of a critical illness (and some life policies may pay out on diagnosis of a terminal illness rather than awaiting death to make the payment – read the small print if you are unsure). Take advice from a financial adviser on the appropriateness of these policies and check that they are regulated by the Financial Conduct Authority (FCA). The FCA maintains a register of approved financial advisers. Find out more at www.fca.org and go to 'check the register'. In addition, help may be available through policies arranged by your work in the form of sick leave policies or stand-alone cover. If you are nearing retirement or have significant borrowings you may wish to revisit the adequacy of your cover from these sorts of products and check when they expire.

Health screening

Personalized health assessments are a wise investment because they give an overview of your current general health and aim to identify any future health risks. Private health screening, outside the NHS, can give people peace of mind that they are not suffering from a serious health problem. There are a number of health assessment options depending on your personal needs, covering key lifestyle and health risks. For more information see:

www.bmihealthcare.co.uk

www.bupa.co.uk

www.privatehealth.co.uk

National Health Service

Choosing a GP

If you need to choose a new GP for whatever reason it is a good idea to check how good they are. If you live in England or Wales you can do this quite easily via the Care Quality Commission (www.cqc.org.uk); at the top of their website toggle the drop-down box to doctors/GPs and then search by postcode.

Assessments ratings of 'outstanding', 'good', 'requires improvement' and 'inadequate' are provided for each of the following:

- treating people with respect and involving them in their care;
- providing care, treatment and support that meet people's needs;
- caring for people safely and protecting them from harm;
- staffing;
- quality and suitability of management.

Otherwise the usual best way to find a good GP is to ask for recommendations from trusted friends or, if you are new to an area, from your neighbours.

Changing your GP

Since January 2015 all GP practices in England have been free to register new patients who live outside their boundary area. These arrangements are voluntary; if the practice has no capacity at the time or feels that it is not clinically appropriate for you to be registered, it can refuse registration and explain its reasons for so doing. If you know of a doctor whose list you would like to be on, you can simply turn up at his or her surgery and ask to be registered. You do not need to give a reason for wanting to change, and you do not need to ask anyone's permission. A request will then be made to your current GP for your medical records to be transferred to the new GP surgery.

NHS 111 service

The NHS non-emergency number is 111. It is fast, easy and free. When you call 111 you will speak to an adviser, supported by health-care professionals, who will ask a number of questions to assess symptoms and direct you to the best medical care available. NHS 111 is available 24 hours a day, 365 days a year, and calls are free from landlines and mobile phones. See www.nhs.uk for further information.

Prescriptions

The current prescription charge is £8.60, but both men and women aged 60 and over are entitled to free NHS prescriptions. Certain other groups are also entitled to free prescriptions, including those on low incomes, and they are free in, for instance, Northern Ireland and Scotland. Find out more at www.nhs.uk and go to 'prescriptions'.

Top tip

If you are under 60 and pay for prescriptions, a 12-month prescription certificate costs £104 (as of summer 2018); if you need two items each month you can save over £100 (and over £300 if you have four items each month). You can do this online via the NHS website or your chemist can help you arrange it.

Going into hospital

Going into hospital can cause people a lot of anxiety. You may be admitted as an outpatient, a day patient (day case) or an inpatient. Many patients are unaware that they can ask their GP to refer them to a consultant at a different NHS trust or even, in certain cases, help make arrangements for them to be treated overseas. Before you can become a patient at another hospital your GP will need to agree to your being referred. Those likely to need help on leaving hospital should speak to the hospital social worker, who will help make any necessary arrangements. Help is sometimes available to assist patients with their travel costs to and from hospital. Remember to take your phone charger and headphones. If you go into hospital you will continue to receive your pension as normal.

Complaints

If you want to make a complaint about any aspect of NHS treatment you have received or been refused, go to the practice or the hospital concerned and ask for a copy of their complaints procedure. This is the same for GPs, opticians, dentists, hospitals and any care given in the NHS. Full details of how to do this can be found at www.nhs.uk – 'complaints'. You can take the matter to the Health Services Ombudsman should you be dissatisfied after an independent review has been carried out. For further details see:

Parliamentary and Health Service Ombudsman for England: www.ombudsman.org.uk

Public Services Ombudsman for Wales: www.ombudsman-wales.org.uk

Scottish Public Services Ombudsman: www.spso.org.uk

An alternative would be to get in touch with your local Patient Advice and Liaison Service (PALS) office in the event of a problem with the health service. Find out more at www.nhs.uk – 'Patient Advice and Liaison Service'.

Complementary and alternative medicine

Complementary and alternative medicines are treatments that fall outside mainstream health care. Although the terms 'complementary' and 'alternative' medicine are often used interchangeably, there are distinct differences between them. Complementary medicine is a treatment that is used alongside conventional medicine, whereas alternative medicine is a treatment used in place of conventional medicine. The best known of these practices are homoeopathy, reflexology, osteopathy, chiropractic, aromatherapy, herbal remedies and hypnosis. Information on the most popular forms can be found on the following websites:

Association of Reflexologists: www.aor.org.uk

British Acupuncture Council: www.acupuncture.org.uk

British Chiropractic Association: www.chiropractic-uk.co.uk

British Homoeopathic Association: www.britishhomeopathic.org

British Hypnotherapy Association: www.hypnotherapy-association.org

General Osteopathic Council: www.osteopathy.org.uk

Incorporated Society of Registered Naturopaths: naturecuresociety.co.uk

National Institute of Medical Herbalists: www.nimh.org.uk

Eyes

If you are a keen driver who needs to wear glasses when behind the wheel ensure that your current prescription is accurate. Some of the most common eye problems include difficulty reading, floaters, cataracts, glaucoma and macular degeneration. Some people on low incomes can get help with costs of eye tests, and people with mobility problems can request an eye test in their own home. People who are registered blind are entitled to a special tax allowance – for 2018/19 it is £2,390.

For more information on matters relating to sight, see:

Royal National Institute of Blind People (RNIB): www.rnib.org.uk

International Glaucoma Association: www.glaucoma-association.com

Feet

Many of us will develop some foot problems with age, simply as a result of wear and tear. Most common problems can be treated successfully by a chiropodist or podiatrist. You can find some good advice for 'fitter feet' on the Age UK website (www.ageuk.org.uk).

The professional association for registered chiropodists and podiatrists has a list of over 10,000 private practitioners: Society of Chiropodists and Podiatrists (www.scpod.org).

Hearing

Deafness is on the rise in the UK, with recent research showing that more than 800,000 people are severely or profoundly deaf, and one in six of us suffer from some form of hearing loss. Signs of hearing loss can be subtle and emerge slowly, so when changes occur to this sense, it is not immediately apparent to ourselves or to others. However, over time you may find social situations more stressful and this may affect you emotionally.

If you are concerned about hearing loss, early tests are advisable before deafness adversely affects relationships and your quality of life. Deafness can be socially isolating and 4 million people in the UK have undiagnosed hearing loss, according to the UK charity Action on Hearing Loss. Hearing aids are now so discreet as to be almost undetectable, and hearing-aid technology is advancing constantly. If you think you are losing your hearing, take a free hearing test. Your GP can then refer you, if necessary, for further tests and advice. Here are some of the specialist organizations that can help with hearing aids and other matters:

Action on Hearing Loss (formerly RNID): www.actiononhearingloss.org.uk

British Deaf Association: www.bda.org.uk

British Tinnitus Association: www.tinnitus.org.uk

Hearing Link: www.hearinglink.org

Sleep/insomnia

Experts suggest that most healthy adults require seven to nine hours of sleep every night, yet over one-third of the population suffers from insomnia or difficulty getting to sleep or staying asleep. But it is difficult to define what 'normal' sleep is, because everyone is different. Sleeping problems tend to increase with age, and women are more likely to be affected than men. Many things can help you get a good night's sleep, such as controlling the light and shutting out noise. Some tips to help you get a good night's sleep include: don't eat too close to your bedtime; avoid stimulants (alcohol, caffeine, TV and computer) if you have trouble getting to sleep; drink water before you go to bed and on waking; open the bedroom window to get fresh air; sleep when you are actually tired rather than at a particular time. Alternatively, should your bed or mattress have seen better days, why not consider investing in new ones, which could give you more comfort and aid better sleep? If you have difficulties sleeping then speak to your GP. There is some good advice to be found on the following websites: www.sleepcouncil.org.uk and www.nhs.uk – 'insomnia'.

Teeth

Should you experience any of the following, visit your dentist or hygienist for a check-up: inflammation of the gums, unpleasant taste in the mouth, bad breath, loose teeth or regular mouth infections. Dentistry is one of the treatments for which you have to pay under the NHS, unless you are on a very low income. This also applies to the hygienist, should you need to see one. Increasingly we are seeing private dental practices who operate dental insurance plans operated by firms such as Denplan (wwwdenplan.co.uk). To find a dentist in your area, search NHS Choices (www.nhs.uk).

Prevention is always better than cure. If you want free, independent and impartial advice on all aspects of oral health, and free literature on a wide range of topics, including patients' rights, finding a dentist and dental care for older people, see the British Dental Health Foundation (www.dentalhealth.org).

Depression, mental health and loneliness

Depression can occur when other health problems are diagnosed such as hearing loss and visual impairment. It can cover the spectrum of mental illness from undue anxiety to self-harm, psychosis and suicide. Outwardly it may be barely noticeable but behaviours that you may notice include: being withdrawn; getting upset quickly and sometimes without much apparent reason; not enjoying things as before; refusing opportunities to socialize; loss of appetite and/or weight loss; feeling irritable; sleeping badly. Sometimes people just need that offer of someone to talk to but they may also need encouragement to see their GP. Depression is not a sign of weakness and requires the right help and support. Fortunately, there is help at hand once we know what we are dealing with; some outstanding guidance and help can be obtained from these websites:

Sane: www.sane.org.uk, call 0300 304 7000

CALM – The Campaign Against Living Miserably: call 0800 585858

NHS: call 111

Mind: www.mind.org.uk

Samaritans: www.samaritans.org, call 116 123

Some common disorders

The rest of this chapter deals with common disorders such as back pain and heart disease.

Aphasia

Aphasia is an impairment of language, affecting the production or comprehension of speech and the ability to read or write. It occurs from an injury to the brain, most commonly from a stroke, particularly in older people. This condition affects a person's ability to *communicate*, but not their intelligence. The national charity that can help is the National Aphasia Association (www.aphasia.org).

Arthritis

There are about 200 different musculoskeletal conditions. Arthritis is a term used by doctors to describe inflammation within a joint, while rheumatism is a more general term that is used to describe aches and pains in or around the joints. The two most common forms are *osteoarthritis* and *rheumatoid arthritis*.

Osteoarthritis affects over 8 million people, and mostly affects adults over the age of 40. It is characterized by gradually worsening symptoms, including sore or stiff joints, stiffness after resting (which improves with movement), and pain that worsens after activity or towards the end of the day. The most commonly affected joints are hands, spine, knees and hips.

Rheumatoid arthritis affects more than 400,000 people and often starts around the age of 40 or 50. Women are three times more likely to be affected than men. It is caused by the body attacking its own tissues, producing symptoms that vary but often involve pain, fatigue, and warm, swollen, inflamed-looking joints. Although arthritis is often thought of as an older person's complaint, it accounts for the loss of an estimated 70 million working days per year in Britain. You don't have to put up with the pain of arthritis, as there are a number of organizations that can help:

Arthritis Action: www.arthritisaction.org.uk

Arthritis Care: www.arthritiscare.org.uk

Arthritis Research UK: www.arthritisresearchuk.org

Asthma

Asthma is a common long-term condition that can cause coughing, wheezing, chest tightness and breathlessness. The severity of these symptoms varies from person to person. Asthma can be controlled in most people most of the time, but occasionally asthma symptoms can get gradually or suddenly worse; this is known as an 'asthma attack'. Asthma is caused by inflammation of the small tubes, called bronchi, which carry air in and out of the lungs. Common asthma triggers include house dust mites, animal fur, pollen, cigarette smoke, exercise and viral infections. Asthma can develop at any age (for more information: www.asthma.org.uk).

Back pain

Back pain is a common problem that affects most people at some stage of their lives. It may be triggered by bad posture while sitting or standing, bending awkwardly or lifting incorrectly. In most cases back pain will improve within a few weeks or months, although some people experience long-term pain that keeps recurring. Regular exercise such as walking or swimming, or activities such as yoga or Pilates, are excellent ways of improving flexibility and strengthening back muscles (more information is available from www.backcare.org.uk).

Blood pressure

As we get older we need to watch our blood pressure. The higher our blood pressure becomes, the higher the risk of (at some stage) a heart attack or a stroke. Having high blood pressure (hypertension) is not usually something we feel or notice. The only way to find out the level of our blood pressure is to have it measured.

The good news is that if it is found that you do have high blood pressure, healthy lifestyle changes will help to bring it down. Recommendations for keeping blood pressure low include reducing salt intake, eating more fruit and vegetables, keeping to a healthy weight, reducing alcohol and keeping active. A lot of information and advice can be found on the website for Blood Pressure UK (www.bloodpressureuk.org).

Cancer

Cancer has a high profile today and the media reports frequently about new research and survival statistics. Nearly all of us are or have been affected by this disease either directly or indirectly. According to Cancer Research UK, cancer survival in the UK has doubled in the last 40 years. One in 30 people living in the UK either has cancer or is in remission. More men are surviving prostate and bowel cancer, and women with breast cancer have a better outlook than ever before. However, the UK still lags behind other European countries in terms of cancer survival. Cancer Research UK says that part of the problem is unhealthy lifestyles. It is estimated that about one-third of cancers are caused by smoking, diet, alcohol and obesity. Early diagnosis is paramount, so it goes without saying that anyone with a lump or swelling, or unexplained tiredness or weight loss, should have it investigated by their doctor. There are now over 300 cancer charities in existence, each researching or focusing on a particular variant of the disease. The main ones include:

Cancer Research Institute: www.cancerresearch.org

Macmillan Cancer Support: www.macmillan.org.uk

Marie Curie Cancer Care: www.mariecurie.org.uk

Chest and heart diseases

Keeping your heart healthy, whatever your age, is the most important thing you can do to help prevent and manage heart disease. The earlier sections on smoking, diet, drink and exercise list some of the most pertinent 'dos and don'ts' that can help. The British Heart Foundation plays a leading role in the fight against diseases of the heart and circulation (www.bhf.org.uk).

Constipation

There are some simple steps that can be taken to avoid constipation or to relieve it:

- drink plenty of water;
- include lots of fibre in your diet;
- eat little and often;
- chew food slowly and thoroughly;
- establish a routine (bodies are creatures of habit);
- keep a food diary (if you suspect a certain food is causing problems).

Visit your GP for treatment if the condition persists.

Diabetes

Diabetes is a common lifelong health condition where the amount of glucose in the blood is too high. Symptoms occur because some or all of the glucose stays in the blood, and is not being used as fuel for energy. There are two main types of diabetes: type 1 and type 2. In type 1 diabetes the signs and symptoms are very obvious and develop quickly over a few weeks. In type 2 diabetes the signs and symptoms are not so obvious, as the condition develops slowly, possibly over a number of years, and may only be picked up at a routine medical check-up. The main symptoms of diabetes are: feeling very thirsty; urinating more frequently than usual (especially at night); extreme tiredness; weight loss and loss of muscle bulk; cuts or wounds that heal slowly; blurred vision. To help people get a better understanding of their diabetes, Diabetes UK have produced a book, *100 Things I Wish I'd Known About Diabetes*, written by people living with diabetes for people living with diabetes and available as a free download. For further information see the Diabetes UK website (www.diabetes.org.uk).

Migraine

A migraine is usually a severe headache felt as a throbbing pain at the front or side of the head. Some people have other symptoms such as nausea, vomiting, and increased sensitivity to light and sound. Migraine is a chronic health condition that affects over 10 million people in the UK. Most of the time migraines are not a threat to your overall health but they can interfere considerably with your day-to-day quality of life. Migraines are more common in women but often become less severe and less frequent with age. The Migraine Trust funds research, provides evidence-based information, and campaigns for and supports people affected by migraine in the United Kingdom. For further information see their website (www.migrainetrust.org).

Osteoporosis and menopause problems

Osteoporosis is a disease that causes bone tissue to thin and become less dense. Maximum bone density and strength are achieved around the age of 30. From the age of 35 our bones begin to weaken gradually as most of us become less active. For women, bone loss is usually most rapid during the first few years after menopause, during which time women's levels of the hormone oestrogen naturally decrease. This can lead to osteoporosis, a condition in which bones become so fragile that they can break very easily. The most common injuries from falls affect the spine, hip and wrist. One in two women (and one in five men) suffers from osteoporosis.

Age UK has compiled a list of ways to boost bone health:

- Weight-bearing exercise is important to help keep your bones strong. Walking, tennis, aerobics and dancing strengthen your bones.
- Enjoy a balanced diet. Milk, cheese, yoghurt, baked beans, lentils and dried apricots are great sources of calcium.
- Taking a stroll in the summer sun (just 10 minutes will help) is a great way of absorbing vitamin D, which keeps bones healthy.
- Avoid smoking. Smokers lose bone density at a faster rate than non-smokers.
- Drink moderately.

The following websites may be useful:

National Osteoporosis Society: www.nos.org.uk

The British Menopause Society: www.thebms.org.uk

Women's Health Concern: www.womens-health-concern.org

Stroke

A stroke is a serious, life-threatening medical condition that happens when the blood supply to part of the brain is cut off. Strokes are a medical emergency and urgent treatment is essential because the sooner the person receives treatment for a stroke, the less damage is likely to occur. Every year over 150,000 people in England alone suffer a stroke. People over 65 are most at risk and it has recently been discovered that iron deficiency may lead to an increased risk of suffering a stroke. Prevention is similar to the steps you can take to avoid heart disease.

A stroke has a greater disability impact than any other medical condition. Most people experience a fast period of recovery just after a stroke, which is followed by a longer period of slower rehabilitation. If you come across someone who may be having a stroke, remember the word 'FAST'. This stands for face – arms – speech – time. Look out for:

- *Face*: if the person's face droops on one side or they cannot smile evenly.
- *Arms*: if the person cannot lift one or both arms and keep them up because of weakness or numbness.
- *Speech*: if speech becomes slurred or garbled, or if the person finds it difficult to talk.
- *Time*: if you see any of these symptoms and suspect a stroke, dial 999 immediately. A stroke is a medical emergency that requires immediate professional attention.

The Stroke Association is the only UK-wide charity solely concerned with combating stroke in people of all ages. Information is available via their website (www.stroke.org.uk).

Top tip

Whilst the short summaries on common health issues and suggested websites may be helpful the key message is that if you are worried don't depend on self-diagnosis – always make an appointment to see your GP. If you have not seen your doctor for years maybe that is another action point for your good retirement plan at the end of the book – go on, book that check-up.

Useful help

The NHS website is the go-to source for more information and explains medical conditions and provides advice.

Inspired? Remember to fill in your plan for a good retirement at the end of the book.

CHAPTER FOURTEEN

Volunteering

We make a living by what we get, but we make a life by what we give.
WINSTON CHURCHILL

This chapter is probably relevant to thinking about retirement planning, as the one vital ingredient for volunteering is time. Let's start by making the point that in looking forward to retirement we have in our mind's eye all those deck-chair images, thoughts of relaxation and 'chilling'. You have probably worked long and hard and deserve a rest – so you will want to enjoy your retirement. But there comes a point when there should be time available. While we all have our 'to do lists', remember Parkinson's law, which says 'work (ie activities) expands to fill the time available'. So be careful not to con yourself that you don't have any spare time. Try finding a cause, making the effort and seeing what volunteering roles there are and you might just surprise yourself. The one thing you will be doing is making a difference to someone or something that may not have been as lucky as you. The chances are that, quite simply, you have loads to offer and would be really valued and just don't realize it (yet).

This chapter at a glance

- How to find volunteering opportunities.
- Some examples of volunteering types of work.
- A detailed look at one organization that depends on volunteers who all make a difference: Citizens Advice.
- Why giving could be just the thing for you.

Volunteering – first steps

Lots of volunteering is inspired by friends and relatives who have taken the plunge or been touched by a cause. That's a good starting point so ask around and you could be introduced sooner than you think.

It's a two-way process so expect some form of interview or chat and find out the benefits of working with the organization, time expectations and flexibility. If it's not right don't waste each other's time and instead seek a different opportunity.

Maybe you have been inspired by dipping your toe in the water? Do some research about the issues that really are important to you, think about the skills that you bring and start your search.

Volunteering – finding opportunities

Finding opportunities is not as difficult as you may think. Community notice-boards, websites and the local library or doctor's surgery notice board were the old-fashioned ways but are still worthwhile. Then, as you would expect, there is the online noticeboard: www.do-it.org is a great starting point. A very tiny sample of current vacancies in one town in England includes: minibus driver to take eight elderly people to a lunch club; a branch trustee of an animal welfare charity; guide dog puppy walker/socializer; unit leader – Brownies; Samaritans listening volunteers; Garden Club member at a community garden; sports and arts volunteers for a youth club; helper to disabled horse riders – and over 200 other roles, so you are spoilt for choice, ideas and inspiration.

Regional-focused websites include:

Northern Ireland: www.volunteernow.co.uk

Scotland: www.volunteerscotland.net

Wales: www.volunteering-wales.net

England: www.ncvo.org.uk

Don't forget opportunities right on your doorstep – it may be at the local primary school helping with things like reading or they may need a governor, or perhaps it's just helping someone nearby who is struggling to tend their garden due to old age or a disability.

Why people become volunteers

The most frequently cited reasons why people volunteer include:

- it is their interest or passion;
- maintaining friendships, teamwork, status and a sense of belonging;
- wanting to 'make a difference' to other people's lives;
- enjoying using their skills in new and valuable ways;
- feeling better both physically and mentally;
- supporting local activities and neighbourhood organizations;
- being a committed member of social and charitable projects;
- actively participating in democratic institutions such as parish/community councils, boards of school governors, or neighbourhood watch;
- finding opportunities to help in education, sport, culture, leisure, conservation and the environment.

The type of volunteer work

There are so many types of work available to volunteers, depending on what you enjoy doing and what skills you have – you should be able to find something to suit. It is entirely dependent on you what you choose – the range is enormous, from the large international or national charities to much smaller organizations. Always play to your strengths; you should be able to find many opportunities in your local community to volunteer. Types of work could include:

- *Administrative*: any active group is likely to need administrative and financial help, from stuffing and labelling envelopes to organizing committees to keeping the finances in order. This may involve a day or so a week or occasional assistance at peak times. Many smaller charities are desperate for help from individuals with IT expertise and accountancy experience.
- *Committee work*: this can cover anything from very occasional help to a virtually full-time commitment as chair, treasurer or secretary. People with business skills or financial or legal backgrounds are likely to be especially valuable, and those whose skills include minute-taking are always in demand.

- *Direct work*: hands-on building and maintenance work, driving, delivering 'meals on wheels', counselling, visiting the housebound, working in a charity shop, gardening in a community garden, running arts classes or sports clubs, helping with a playgroup, respite care for carers. The list is endless and there are many interesting and useful jobs for those without special training.

- *Fundraising and marketing*: every voluntary organization needs money, and when donations are static or falling, more creativity and ingenuity are required to help bring in funds. Events are many and varied, but anyone with energy and experience of organizing fundraising events would be welcomed with open arms as a volunteer.

- *Overseas*: many more people in later life are now combining volunteering with travel. There are many in their fifties and sixties who are seizing this opportunity as they may have missed their 'gap year' when they were young. Further information on long-term voluntary work and working overseas will be found later in this chapter.

A case study in detail: Citizens Advice

There are, literally, thousands of opportunities in volunteering but picking one allows us to penetrate and explore the 'what they do, why and how a volunteer can help'. The case study is Citizens Advice but it could, quite literally, be any organization.

Have you ever had a problem or crisis in your life when you needed advice? Citizens Advice provides people with advice for all kinds of problems without judging them. The organization is powered by an army of volunteers who make a difference and benefit from all that volunteering brings. There is probably a role for you at your local Citizens Advice outlet.

But first some context. Citizens Advice provides a reliable and consistent service by sticking to a few key aims and principles:

- providing advice that people need for the problems they face;
- trying to improve the policies and practices that affect people's lives by showing the people who make the decisions what people's experiences are.

Citizens Advice is independent and provides free, confidential and impartial advice to everyone regardless of race, sex, disability, sexuality or nationality. It is the largest advice-giving network in the United Kingdom, with over 3,000 outlets (there should be one near you) and 20,000 volunteers. They help people deal with nearly 6 million problems every year by phone, e-mail and outreach sessions. The volunteers come from all walks of life and are committed to providing an independent advice service. The advice is based on four principles:

- *Independent*: they will always act in the interests of their clients, without influence from outside bodies.
- *Impartial*: they will not charge their clients or make assumptions about them. The service is open to everyone and they treat everyone equally.
- *Confidential*: they will not pass on anything a client tells them, or even the fact that they visited, without their permission.
- *Free*: no one has to pay for any part of the service they provide.

Putting these principles into action enables them to provide a vital service to millions of people each year. They, and therefore you, can help make a real practical difference to people with problems in your local community.

What do their volunteers do?

There are lots of different roles and a few are summarized below – there really is something for everyone:

- *Caseworkers/advisers*: an adviser will assist clients at drop-in sessions, appointments in the outlet, over the phone or at outreach sessions, explaining the choices and consequences that clients face. They may refer clients to other agencies. They need to be good at listening, work as a team, be open-minded, non-judgemental and enjoy helping people.
- *Administrators*: help ensure everything runs smoothly. There are many different roles that may match your skills and time availability. These can include developing administrative systems, helping to arrange events, receptionist activities such as greeting clients, and arranging appointments.
- *IT support coordinators*: support training and troubleshoot hardware and software problems, develop networks, design spreadsheets, databases and websites.
- *Campaigners*: train staff and volunteers, conduct research on local issues and manage media campaigning.

Each area is run autonomously as a separate charity. You should be able to make contact with the organization serving your area through the website or by making enquiries through local churches or libraries.

What training is available?

You will initially receive a briefing lasting about two hours, which will explain more about your local Citizens Advice and the potential opportunities that are available. At this session you will be with 6–10 other potential volunteers (although numbers can vary regionally) and have an opportunity to ask lots of questions. It is a very comfortable session without any obligation. Following this session, if you do wish to volunteer, you then undergo the initial stage of training, which lasts about eight weeks and takes about half a day per week. After that it is up to you what you want to give and how your new volunteering will progress. To find out more just check out www. citizensadvice.org.uk; in the volunteering section of the website you can search for opportunities by entering your postcode.

Top tip

So you want to volunteer and you have done some research, not found the right role and three months have passed since you retired. You are still fresh and your batteries have been recharged after a few nice holidays. Contact Citizens Advice, go on their volunteers' course and take it from there. You may just have found the perfect role for the next 20 years that is rewarding, flexible and leaves you with a glow (and as a bonus you will have a new social circle if that's what you would like). Is it time to add another action point to your good retirement plan at the back of the book? Remember, it's your guide.

Long-term and overseas volunteering

If you have a particular interest in overseas development it might be worth considering taking a 'gap year'. Volunteering overseas offers a large and ever-expanding wealth of opportunities. Depending on the organization you choose, projects vary in length from five weeks to up to two years. As long as you are in good health, many organizations welcome volunteers up to the age of 70 and some beyond that. This sort of work requires a different kind of commitment, but there is a wide range of opportunities. Some volunteering roles require specialist skills such as engineering or medicine, while others essentially need people with practical qualities, common sense and enthusiasm. Each organization has a minimum period of service. One of the better-known organizations involved in this area is Voluntary Service Overseas (www.vsointernational.org) but there are many others that you can check out on the web.

Volunteering overseas is a serious commitment and while extremely rewarding it can be demanding and, in some ways, it is like being back at work. You should not, therefore, take it on lightly and should also carefully check the reputation of the organization with which you are seeking to get involved – you don't want to get stranded in a strange country without ensuring there is adequate support available. General conditions can vary but generally travel is paid, plus a living allowance or salary that is based on local levels rather than on expatriate rates. Couples without dependant children are welcome, as long as both have the necessary skills. National Insurance contributions are provided, and a resettlement grant is paid on completion of the tour. In addition, for an overseas position you would expect to be examined and cleared by their medical team, have access to face-to-face and online training, receive prior security and cultural training, and be clear on your objectives. If any of these are missing you may need to start shopping around for another position as your health, welfare and safety should be the utmost concern for both you and the organization; if they are not, then something is not adding up. If you are up to the challenge, overseas volunteering can be immensely rewarding.

We make a life by what we give

If you have read this far the chances of you being interested are fairly good so it is time to remind you of Winston Churchill's famous quote headlining this chapter: 'We make a living by what we get, but we make a life by what we give.' As stated at the start of this chapter, the chances are that you probably don't appreciate the talents you have and how wonderful they could be to one of our thousands of voluntary organizations or folk who just need a hand. Have a go and the real chances are that the art of giving will help you live better and be happier.

Inspired? Remember to fill in your plan for a good retirement at the end of the book.

CHAPTER FIFTEEN

Leisure and holidays

Choice not chance determines your destiny.
ARISTOTLE

For many this may be the chapter they first turn to on opening this book. After all, it's what you have been working towards for decades and may be where your vision of perfection takes you. A time of endless leisure and holidays? Is that the vision? Well, it's each to their own but the big factors are what you have planned and aspire to and then what your financial planning allows. So this chapter is all about making the best of the time that is available to you. For some it may involve splashing out £30,000 on a 180-day round-the-world cruise with all food and drink included and you just sit back and take it all in. For others it may be developing the good life of allotments, home-grown food and devoting themselves to helping others less fortunate through volunteering. For others the early active years of retirement may involve bringing in some extra money through a part-time job or small business, trimming costs a bit and then enjoying a mix of regular holidays four or five times a year combined with some new interests. See how the chapters of this book come together! Get it right and you will live better and be happier in retirement, but remember we are all different and, just to repeat the point – it is 'each to their own'. Importantly this chapter is where the good stuff happens – leisure and holidays as this is 'my time' and 'payback time'.

So the question is: 'How do I achieve excellence in the leisure part of my retirement?' Well, as you may have picked up from other headline quotes in other chapters in this book, the Greek philosophers pop up now and again. It was Aristotle who said:

> Excellence is never an accident. It is always the result of high intention, sincere effort and intelligent execution; it represents the wise choice of many alternatives – choice, not chance, determines your destiny.

Putting this into 'happiness in retirement' speak this means planning the sort of retirement you want over the three phases of retirement, recognizing that the active years of retirement (as outlined in Chapter 1) are going to potentially involve more holidays and leisure activities. Some cost nothing and some cost a lot. So what do you aspire to? More holidays and perhaps even an overseas holiday home? Learning a new craft or skill? Reading all the books that have piled up by your bedside over the years? Taking up a new sport or leisure interest and getting a bit fitter? Cultivating the garden or an allotment and learning to grow more of your own food? Or is it volunteering to help those less fortunate than yourself? Spending more quality time with family and friends? Or is it now a chance to go and see all those bands you didn't see first-time around, now that reunion tours are proving lucrative for the bands and fun for the audiences?

It is, then, just a case of doing something to bridge any financial gap. The earlier you plan for this in life the more dramatic the impact you will make on the outcome. So get on with it and do something about it. This chapter is intended to get you thinking ahead about the sort of leisure and holiday activities you could tackle as you embark on your 'active retirement years'.

This chapter at a glance

- Keeping fit – some reminders of the easy starting points; then just keep going.
- Sporting activities, watching sport and forming your own club. Don't sit around waiting for someone else to do it – it's easy and our three-step model will help get things going.
- Entertainment and hobbies – try something different, you just never know what you might ignite. This includes how to access free 'big name' entertainment by getting hold of TV/radio audience tickets – we all like things that are quality and free (and those two words do not often go hand in hand).

- How to get started on writing that book you have had buzzing around your head and how to follow through on any study aspirations.
- Tips and pointers on holidays, cruises, short UK breaks and starting to tick off some more European city breaks (especially if you can buy a flight for £40 each way).
- In reading this chapter you might surprise yourself at finding a hidden talent that has lain dormant until now.
- Travel insurance and help if things go wrong on holiday – some essential tips. Don't leave home without them.

Keeping yourself fit

A good starting point is to look at ways of keeping yourself reasonably fit. The fairly basic rule is a simple one: the fitter you are, the better and longer your quality of life.

Walking and running

Walking costs nothing, doesn't require expensive equipment and is the best form of natural exercise. It keeps you healthy, prolongs your life and improves your mental health. There is walking (in the park), hiking (in the hills), rambling (across country), hill walking (in mountainous areas), fell walking (particularly in the Lake District and Yorkshire Dales – fell meaning high, uncultivated land) and scrambling (sometimes applied to mountain walking).

Some of the positive things walking can do for your health:

- help your heart and lungs work better;
- lower your blood pressure;
- keep your weight down;
- lighten your mood;
- maintain strong joints, muscles and bones.

Why not join a small group, which may even have a side benefit of introducing you to a new circle of friends. Get on to the web and see what might be available locally, or take a few soundings from friends and acquaintances. Failing that, try the Ramblers' Charity (www.ramblers.org.uk).

If you are more enthusiastic, try running as a hobby. You can do this indoors (at the gym) or outdoors – by yourself as a solo activity, with a group or by joining a club. Try the following websites for more information:

England Athletics: www.englandathletics.org

Run England: www.runengland.org

Association of Running Clubs: www.runningclubs.org.uk

You can also try your local area for park 'fun runs'.

Swimming

Britons used swimming as a means of staying fit for the constant warfare they were engaged in during the Dark Ages. Swimming is one of the best forms of exercise; it builds strength and endurance and is beneficial for your metabolism and the cardiovascular system. Swimming as a hobby, whether you are a beginner or a seasoned swimmer, is a great way to relax and get fit. For more information see British Swimming (www.britishswimming.org).

Sporting activities

The list of possibilities is virtually endless and you might as well give some a try; you never know – old dogs can learn new tricks! The UK's top six leisure sports are listed below; the list may just spark that 'oh, why not, I'll give it a try' moment!

Golf

Golf is seen by many as a social game, but it is also a way to get healthy and is an effective exercise programme. Golf can be a great addition to a vacation and provides the perfect opportunity to travel and experience different cultures and exotic scenery.

Tennis

The tennis court built at Hampton Court in 1625 survives to this day. According to the Tennis Industry Association, some of the reasons for the sport's popularity are that it is social, the whole family can participate, it is good for personal fitness and it can be played nearly all your life.

Boats and boating

Being out on the water can be really special and relaxing on the right day, although winds and rain can bring a different experience! Your nearest sailing club may be able to arrange a trial sail, or you could try a water-sports holiday. For further information, see New to Sailing (www.newtosailing.com).

Cycling

More than 2 million people across the country now cycle at least once a week. This is an all-time high, according to British Cycling, the sport's governing body in the UK. Whether you are a 'mamil' (middle-aged man in Lycra), or one of the growing number of female road bikers, you will be part of the third most popular recreational activity in the UK. Cycling is one of the easiest ways to fit exercise into your daily routine because it is a non-impact sport, so does not put strain on the joints. It saves you money, gets you fit and is good for the environment.

Fishing

Fishing gives you lots of time in the fresh air, enjoying beautiful countryside and scenery; it's relaxing, and you can do other things at the same time such as read, listen to music or just think. There are many varieties of the sport: fly fishing in local rivers and lakes, deep-sea fishing and much more. If you are new to it, check it out on the web and take a few local soundings.

Watching sport and forming your own club

The above suggestions are no more than an attempt to give you a flavour of things you might consider. If you spend a little time exploring websites, the possibilities are endless and of course you can always watch sport. There is of course excellent coverage of many sports on TV but it is really enjoyable to get out and watch live sport. There are many different opportunities – you can watch your local football, hockey or rugby team, and of course there are also the big international events and major golf tournaments, which all provide a good day out with a bunch of friends. Why not try watching something different like ice hockey, American football, basketball or snooker? The main thing is to get off the couch and get out and support your favourite team in person or even try something new. Transport and cost issues can be solved by forming your own 'club' – just follow these three easy rules:

1 Find three or four like-minded friends – that is all you need to get started.

2 Agree the briefest of 'rules' – going to events, enjoyment, friendship and sharing the cost.

3 Manage the money. The rules require everyone to chip in £50, which the 'treasurer' keeps. You then top it up after each event so that the pot always comes back to the number of members x £50. The 'secretary' identifies the event, date and cost, and people decide if they want to go or not. If you don't go then the £50 in the pot is rolled forward. Every group needs a 'chairperson' who makes the final decision if there is a split vote – then you get on with it. You will soon find that the group of four extends to six and then 10; at some point you will have to call it a day on new members as part of the fun is the friendship of a smallish group. Anything above 20 may lose the 'friendship' bonus that comes from these small groups. Otherwise, off you go – don't sit around waiting for someone else to organize it. And don't forget the Christmas party for the group!

Top tip

Don't wait for someone else – get your own club going. The sort of informal club mentioned above can apply to anything – sports followers, entertainment viewing, or even a club that follows both! Just get on with it; agree a few simple rules, have someone trustworthy to keep a tab on the money pot and off you go.

Entertainment

Approaching – and reaching – retirement means you will probably have in-creased opportunities to head off for a night's entertainment. You probably already do this but may have got into something of a routine so why not try something new?

Film

Look beyond your local mainstream cinemas. There are many local cinema groups so look around and see what is available in your area – this could also give you an opportunity to expand your local social contacts.

Theatre

Don't restrict yourself to the big professional events. Most towns and many relatively small villages have excellent local drama groups that are well worth supporting. Not only will you find the experience enjoyable but you will also be doing your bit in supporting an important aspect of the life of your local community. You might even have a go at getting involved yourself. You don't necessarily need to be a budding actor or actress – local theatrical groups need a variety of talents to keep them going, including electricians, set designers and builders, front-of-house staff, treasurers, etc. They will certainly find a use for you.

A bit of culture – opera, ballet, concerts and museums

Love, hate or don't know? Some of the gems of the UK are its museums and music concerts (from punk to a full orchestra). If you have never tried a ballet or a night at the opera then why not give it a go?

TV and radio audiences

Participating as members of studio audiences and making contributions to programmes can be entertaining and free. Tickets for very popular shows can be hard to obtain but you never know – and a new show could be the next big thing. The Applause Store (www.applausestore.com) and BBC Shows (www.bbc.co.uk/showsandtours/tickets) websites are worth checking out – maybe add yourself to their waiting lists.

Hobbies and other interests

If your working life was so busy that you never had time for anything else, now you can start thinking about what might be possible. There must be something that has grabbed your interest despite your busy working life –

now is the time to develop that interest. If you are literally starting from scratch then explore the options on one of the many websites available. For example, Wikipedia has compiled a great 'list of hobbies' page that lists literally hundreds of possibilities along with their usual click-through facility to reveal more. They range from acting to yoga – there is something to suit everyone. If something in particular takes your fancy then do a bit more specific exploring on the web and then locally. Don't be worried if you then find it is not for you, just move on to something else – you have time to get it right and find something that really sits with your time, skills, values and beliefs. Do that and you are on to a winner. Is this something to add to your plan for a good retirement at the end of the book – if none of the hobby examples below grab your attention? Remember, the seven selected below are just random examples and this book could literally have been filled with lists of hobbies so there is absolutely no limit on what you could do.

Gardening

Views differ on where to classify gardening – is it a hobby, a pastime or a necessity? Whatever view you may take, most of us do have gardens and either enjoy looking after them or are forced to do so. If you are already a keen gardener who really enjoys working and relaxing in the garden then keep the good work going and you will enjoy the fact that you now have the time and opportunity to do even more. If you are amongst the less enthusiastic, perhaps due to a busy working schedule, now may be the opportunity to devote a little more time to it. Don't regard it as a chore, and just concentrate on the simple things at first. A nice lawn is the centrepiece to many gardens, and the fact that you will now have the time to give it a weekly trim rather than a quick cut when time permits will work wonders for the appearance of your garden. You will soon find that a well-kept garden is a pleasure to you and to others, as you can develop it and make a real impact.

Jazz appreciation society

This is another randomly selected hobby just to illustrate the range and diversity of hobbies. This could be a group of enthusiasts who meet in a hall or bar to listen to recorded jazz. At each meeting a member presents an hour of their choice of jazz followed by members playing music from their own collections, based on a regular monthly theme. If there is not a club, or if you want to change the genre and form your own, then follow the tips in the 'watching sport' section above on how to form your own club.

Mentor

You could help young people in your area. There are many government-backed schemes and one is Mosaic, a national-charity mentoring network backed by the Prince's Trust (www.mosaicnetwork.co.uk).

Model railway clubs

Enthusiasts include Tom Hanks, Warren Buffett, Eric Clapton, Bruce Springsteen and Ringo Starr. Clubs provide a social scene and new members can benefit from the experience and wealth of knowledge, and good clubs always adapt to the needs of their members. All aboard for a new hobby?

Museum volunteer

From the Imperial War Museum to the Natural History Museum to local museums. The opportunities are abundant for paid and unpaid roles. Check out your favourite museums for opportunities – and if it follows one of your passions then even better.

Painting

Get those creative genes flowing onto canvas and try exploring skills that may have lain dormant since art classes in your school days. It is never too late to take up this hobby and find your preferred medium (watercolour, pastel or ink etc) and style. Local clubs can be found by an internet search or from your circle of friends, where someone will know someone and can introduce you. New member events are usually held throughout the year, welcoming novices into a friendly, creative environment.

Zookeeper

Zoos depend on volunteers and training will be provided. It keeps you fit and will be sociable as there can be lots of interacting with the public. Enquire at your local zoo.

Write that book?

Why not write that book you've had buzzing around in your head? You might discover a hidden talent and write a bestseller. If you are determined then just start at the beginning, with a fair idea of the ending, and take your readers on the journey. Your motto will be to write, read, rewrite (and repeat). It may end up being self-printed for family and friends or self-published for a wider audience. Or you may find yourself in the realms of working with a publisher, either with or without the help of an agent. As far as top tips go, you will find that lots of people have lots to say on the internet about writing. So we will leave you with just two suggestions. First, make writing a habit; it requires perseverance. Create a routine and write at the same time every day; if it just isn't working one day then go and do something else. Buy a guidebook to help steer you through the maze of options and opportunities – try the *Writers' and Artists' Yearbook 2019* (more at www.writersandartists.co.uk). Once you are established as a writer, and if you meet the criteria, the Society of Authors is the 'must join' organization (www.societyofauthors.org). In the meantime, a check online should find any local writers' group in your area, which is another good starting point.

More study?

You may well feel that during your working life you have done enough studying and attended enough courses – and consider you are more than due a break from all of that. However, when the pressure of being almost forced to do something disappears, you can study what takes your fancy, and of course you now have time to do so. You may enjoy holidaying abroad in a particular area but miss out on a lot because of language barriers – now is the time to try to pick up the basics; your computer and IT skills may be a bit rusty – again, you now have time to put that right. Try www.learndirect.com for IT courses and help. You might want to tune up your home-cooking skills. There is a wide range of part-time vocational-type courses available at local further education colleges and other institutes of learning throughout the country. Take a little time to find out what is available in your own area. Your local community will offer various social and learning activities, so visit your leisure centre, church, community centre or library to find out what is available. Libraries are an endangered species these days so pop in – you never know what or who you might spot, see or meet.

Also worth investigating is the University of the Third Age (U3A). This organization could almost be described as 'one size fits all' because it is committed to lifelong learning, can help combat loneliness with social inter-action, and offers a huge range of activities and courses, both cerebral and physical. There are plenty of U3A branches around the United Kingdom, so you should be able to find one near you. For more information, visit their website (www.u3a.org.uk).

Holidays

This may well be the part of retirement that you are really looking forward to. With all that time now available you might be thinking about a world cruise, more overseas visits to relatives and close friends, taking an expedi-tion to some remote corner of the world, visiting cities on your must-see list, or maybe just long, leisurely days somewhere in the sun. Retirement really does give you additional options. You are no longer stuck with set holiday dates, which has the additional bonus of allowing you to take advantage of last-minute offers and cheaper rates at off-peak times. Also, of course, you now have time to shop around for the best bargains. So get out there and start looking for your ideal holiday or adventure at the best price. If you are reasonably competent with computers and the internet you can do a great deal of your business in that way and it frequently represents good value for money. But don't ignore a tried-and-trusted travel agent, many of whom are very knowledgeable about locations and prices.

Below are a few examples to get your mind working on the endless opportunities.

Bus travel and coach and rail holidays

If you are 60 or over, or have a disability, you may be entitled to conces-sionary travel in London, Wales, Scotland and Northern Ireland. For the rest of England you receive this, generally, when you reach the female re-tirement age. The Senior Railcard can save one-third of the cost on stand-ard or first-class fares (www.senior-railcard.co.uk) and National Express offers a Senior Coachcard that entitles you to one-third off ticket prices (www.nationalexpress.com).

While we are on the subject of transport, it is worth drawing attention to the Campaign for Better Transport (www.bettertransport.org.uk), which campaigns for communities to have affordable transport that improves quality of life and protects the environment. One particularly endangered species is the rural bus service, which faces further drastic cuts by many local authorities. Buses are the favoured mode of transport for lots of older people, particularly those living in the country, where often it is their only means of getting from A to B if they are unable to drive. Buses support independent living, have a direct impact on social exclusion and play a huge part in ensuring people do not become isolated.

The possibilities are endless. Start exploring the internet to find out what is available – but shop around and don't sign up to the first option you come across. And of course take a look at what the travel agents are offering.

Cruising

The cruise market continues to break records with new and often larger ships constantly being launched. Of course, cruising does tend to be particularly attractive to the older generation. Don't, however, be put off by that as you will find a full cross-section of age ranges on most cruises – perhaps particularly in the main holiday season.

Cruising can take you to virtually anywhere in the world, with the real advantage that with a modern cruise ship your own first-class hotel travels along with you. You can simply relax in the sun of the Mediterranean or the Caribbean; explore a range of classic cities; get to know the Scandinavian countries or Alaska; explore the mysteries of the Far East; or visit Australia and New Zealand. The possibilities are endless, as can be seen from a quick browse of cruise brochures in any travel agents. Or get online and type in the names of a couple of cruise lines.

There are various reasons why so many people enjoy cruising: many operators have ships leaving from the UK, reducing air travel; seeing multiple destinations but unpacking only once; the wide choice, as cruise ships come in all shapes and sizes. Cruise vacations are easy to plan, they are social and there are activities and entertainments galore. If you want to take a closer look at the range on offer from cruise companies, and what their individual ships are like, get hold of a copy of the Berlitz book on cruising, which is regularly updated and provides a mine of valuable and dependable information on all aspects of cruising and cruise ships.

Cruising tips

- *Inside cabins* can be an absolute bargain for those on a budget but wanting exceptional itineraries. However, there is no natural light, which can play havoc with your body clock and they can be in poor locations (corridor, lift, engine or other noise) – but don't dismiss them as an option.

- *Buy early or buy late.* Experienced cruisers know the form. Buy early to get the best cabins in the best locations and deep discounts or hang on to the last minute to get a bargain on an underbooked cruise. Shopping around or staying with the same agent (loyalty bonuses and trusted knowledge) can both help with the price you pay. Try negotiations around the amount of on-board spend they will credit to your room as part of any 'deal'.

- *How much!* Many cruises make deep profits on the price of drinks and that final day when you settle up your bill can be sobering. Think about pre-paid drinks packages; some cruises offer these free as an inducement.

- *How much (part 2)!* Cruise lines also make deep profits from excursions. The bonus is that their ship probably will not leave port if your coach breaks down and you miss the scheduled departure time. On the other hand you can probably halve the cruise excursion price by going with a local alternative, and enterprising organizations have set up 'shore excursion' companies offering trips that mirror the cruise-company offering. A brief search on the internet will find these, but always check out the independent reviews.

- *Cruise from the UK or a European port?* We know our lovely UK weather but who has crossed the Atlantic or the Bay of Biscay when it has been rough? The passage to warmer, smoother seas may eat up four or five days of your precious holiday, so is it worth it? Or do you fly out and pick up a cruise from a Mediterranean port in the more challenging months outside the May-to-mid-September window?

- Some useful websites are www.whatsinport.com for overviews and hints and tips on what is in and around the port area, with maps and suggestions that may help if you don't want to go on excursions. Another useful website is www.cruisecritic.co.uk for port and ship overviews and user reviews.

Cargo ship cruises

Seeing the world by cargo ship doesn't offer the trappings of a conventional cruise, but being aboard a freight ship as a paying passenger is like being in another world. Many carry up to 12 non-crew members on routes from a week to months long. Securing a berth can be complicated, and periods in port tend to be brief, but life on board is uneventful – perfect for reading and writing. See the website for Cargo Ship Voyages (www.cargoshipvoyages.com).

River cruising

This type of cruising has some similarities to ocean cruising but there are differences. Riverboats are much smaller and tend to be more intimate, which some people prefer. Because of their size there tends to be less concentration on entertainment. They do, however, give an excellent opportunity to explore inland towns and cities. Frequently the mooring is very close to the city or town centre – just step off the boat and you are there.

Short breaks

The UK is a brilliant place packed with diversity and places of interest – that's why the world flocks here as a must-see destination. So as a quick reminder and a starter for 10 you could start planning those weekends:

- go monster spotting at Loch Ness;
- grab a laugh at Edinburgh's comedy festival;
- spot royalty at Buckingham Palace or Windsor Castle;
- shop in London (as it's better for shopping than New York, Paris or Milan);
- take in the pretty gardens and villages in the Cotswolds;
- see Caernarfon Castle;
- hit the lanes and seafront at Brighton;
- take in the rugby, shops and restaurants in Bath;
- have a titanic experience in Belfast;
- dine at a London roof garden and go to a concert in Hyde Park in the summer;
- stride the Giant's Causeway;
- tackle the Lake District;
- drive across Bwlch y Groes (Hell Fire Pass) in Wales;
- put a bet on at Newmarket racecourse;
- take a steam train to historic York;
- do all the famous museums in London.

The list is literally endless; just google 'what's on' in different areas and start your own list.

You may already have taken advantage of weekend breaks during your working life. A short trip of three or four days is an excellent way to explore somewhere new, and has become increasingly attractive due to relatively low-cost air fares. If you book early and can travel mid-Wednesday afternoon with only hand baggage, you can nab some of those £40 seats. Next best is to try starting your trip on a Sunday night – it is usually the cheapest time for hotel rates.

The list is endless and the budget airline websites carry decent overviews and tips. To get your list going try:

- Amsterdam – art, culture, wacky cafes and red lights.
- Barcelona – excellent flight connections make this a must-see city with its Olympic stadium, beach and Las Ramblas all combining very well. Gaudi's Sagrada Familia Cathedral will stop you in your tracks (oh, and there is that football team as well).
- Belfast – according to the *New York Times* 'an eye-watering experience in the best possible way'.
- Any island in the Canaries – for a long weekend and some proper winter sun.
- The walled City of Dubrovnik – nearly every roof was replaced following the shelling it endured less than three decades ago, but the city is standing tall again.
- Milan – where old and new fuse together to create a special weekend steeped with fashion and food delights.
- Paris – a proud and beautiful city that never ceases to amaze.
- Prague – exceptional value and perhaps one of the most beautiful places you will visit.
- Rome – culturally outstanding, if a little expensive.
- Venice – enchanting.
- Reykjavik – highlights include the Northern Lights and National Parks. Timing can mean lots of daylight or darkness and the cost of living when out there can seem expensive.

Top tip

Plan and plan. Some city festivals are truly stunning and world class, leaving an indelible memory. Try La Mercè in Barcelona in September to see what we mean. Prices may go up so plan and book your flights and hotel early and enjoy!

Activity holidays

Holidays that involve your hobby can be a double bonus. Rambling, golf, sport, war tours, history club tours, motor racing, art, reading, painting, yoga retreats – the list is endless. Check with your local contacts and look online – the internet is a great way to explore what is available.

Holidays for people with disabilities

Affordable, accessible and enjoyable holidays for the disabled are many and varied. Airlines, hotels and resorts are providing people with disabilities or mobility issues the opportunities to travel, enjoy holidays and see the world. Specially designed self-catering units are more plentiful and of a higher standard. Also, an increasing number of trains and coaches are installing accessible loos. An elderly or disabled person seeking a holiday must explain clearly what their care needs are, not only in terms of getting to and from, but also with regard to accommodation requirements. Some people take companions/carers with them. There is a great deal of information available on the internet, so do take time to research carefully. Organizations that can help you include:

Age UK: www.ageuk.org.uk

Able Community Care: www.uk-care.com

Accessible Travel: www.accessibletravel.co.uk

Disabled Holidays: www.disabledholidays.com

Disabled Access Holidays: www.disabledaccessholidays.com

Hotels and Airbnb

Airbnb (www.airbnb.co.uk) has come into everyday use over recent years and helps you find homes and rooms in holiday hotspots for much less than hotel-room rates. The quality can be amazing but remember the incidence of scam accommodation and, therefore, revisit the tips in Chapter 8. For security pay by credit card on amounts above £100. Otherwise check for a history or reviews (both quantity and quality over a few years).

Big hotel groups have loyalty programmes that can stack up and beat price-comparison-website prices; the 'loyalty' also helps ensure you don't end up with the nightmare room (above the kitchen, no sea view, beside the lift etc).

Holidays on your own

When it comes to travelling there are many single people who want to see the world but are daunted by the prospect. Many people travel solo; some may be single, others not. There are companies specializing in singles holidays, tour holidays, exploring holidays and relaxing escape holidays – try www.tui.co.uk and 'holidays for solo travellers' and www.friendshiptravel.com for an idea of the offering. Singles holidays should help improve safety, security and the certainty of help and support when needed. There is advice for single travellers on the Age UK website – visit www.ageuk.org.uk and go to 'Tips for single travellers' (including tips on breaking the ice, making time for yourself and staying safe).

3G holidays

Increasingly popular, this is a trip consisting of at least three generations. New research reveals that having multiple generations holidaying together has a positive impact, enabling families to spend quality time together on holiday that they otherwise would not. Other reasons for taking such a trip can vary, from a special occasion to helping with holiday expenses. Whatever your taste, you can always find a great location for a multi-generational holiday. *Mature Times* offers some top tips for 3G holidays:

- *Plan the money beforehand*: who pays for what, whether you have a kitty system, or prefer taking turns – a conversation beforehand avoids misunderstandings later.
- *Work out the babysitting*: discuss what you are prepared to do, how many evenings, whether you want a day off alone; plan it before you leave.
- *Cooking, shopping, chores*: it helps to agree what works best for all. Make sure everyone is involved, from the youngest to the oldest, and stick to the routine.
- *Respect others' privacy*: whether that is bedtimes, bathroom usage, visiting each other's rooms; not everyone is the same, so discuss before you leave where the boundaries are and what preferences others have.

Home-swapping holidays

With everything now available at the press of a button thanks to the internet, house swapping with someone on the other side of the world is easy and is becoming increasingly popular. It saves money on accommodation, and the bonus for those who dare to do this is the experience of living life as a local, not a tourist. Holiday-swap internet sites are on the increase, but do pay attention to the rules and conditions: some are more stringent than others. Whether you want to restrict yourself to the UK or Europe, or go global, most home-swapping sites require payment of an annual subscription. If this idea appeals, talk to your insurance company first in case they place restrictions or exclusions on either your home contents or buildings cover, and then have a look at some broker sites and check out the frequently asked questions about 'problems and damage' (who is responsible for what). Some broker sites are:

- Exchange Holiday Homes: www.exchangeholidayhomes.com
- Home Exchange: www.homeexchange.com
- Love Home Swap: www.lovehomeswap.com

Travel insurance

As we age we are far more likely to have a pre-existing medical condition that needs to be declared and covered on our travel insurance. The main reason the cost of travel insurance increases for older people is that we are more likely than younger travellers to claim for health problems whilst on holiday. Medical claims are much more expensive than most other types of claim. Travel insurance is an essential safety net should anything go wrong and it is not worth taking the risk of travelling uninsured. As you get older, insurance does become more expensive and you will probably have to shop around to get the cover you need. Don't just go for the cheapest option either; it could be false economy.

Some tips on buying holiday insurance

- If you are travelling solely to Europe, *don't rely on your European Health Insurance Card for protection*; it won't cover everything.
- Adequate *personal liability cover is essential*; a minimum of around £1 million is advisable.
- For safety, *medical expenses cover* should be around £2 million.
- Your policy should have appropriate *cancellation and curtailment cover* in case you fall ill or cut your holiday short – read the small print for limitations and exclusions.

- *Don't leave arranging cover until just before you depart*, in case anything happens between booking and departure.
- If you are planning a few breaks over the next year, it could be more cost effective to buy *annual worldwide cover*. Take a look at some of the comparison websites.
- *If you have a packaged (paid-for) bank account, check if it includes travel insurance*. Some bank accounts include a family travel policy, or winter sports cover.

A cost-effective idea may be to extend any existing medical insurance you have to cover you while abroad. Then take out a separate policy (without medical insurance) to cover you for the rest of your travel needs.

The basic advice is that it can be a complex field and you do need to shop around to get the cover that suits you at the best price.

Things can go wrong

For complaints and assistance when things go wrong, and for the framing of a complaint, see Chapter 7.

Plane delays and missed connections can ruin a holiday but if you are armed with information about your rights you might just save the day. Concise, well-written guides are hard to find but we like the Consumer Council for Northern Ireland's 'Plane Facts'. Download and print a copy and stick it in your baggage just in case. Visit www.consumercouncil.org.uk and go to 'plane facts'.

Your rights and translating those rights when travelling abroad in Europe can be difficult if your knowledge of the host-country language is non-existent or rusty. Help is now at hand by downloading the app 'EEC-Net: Travel' for free. It provides a range of common problems you may encounter when travelling and the usual phrase that you would ask in English – at a press of a button the phrase is translated, with then further help prompted by yes/no buttons. And it works!

Top tip

Download, print and store 'Plane Facts' in your baggage and download the 'EEC-Net: Travel' app on your phone. Details of both are above.

Compensation for lost baggage and cancelled or overbooked flights

There is plenty of protection and we won't take up space here with the details of how to complain, your rights, appeals and the amounts you can expect – just download, print and keep 'Plane Facts' as mentioned above.

Some final tips

- *Safety.* If in doubt, trust your instincts on foreign travel where there is or is perceived to be an increased security threat – and leave it out this year. For more official information check the Foreign Office's latest advice at www.gov.uk and go to 'foreign travel advice' where there is detailed country-specific information and advice.

- *Most important – for everyone – when organizing travel, is to always pay by credit card* (if you have paid more than £100, credit cards give increased protection if things go wrong or a contract is broken). More information on these rights (known as 'Section 75 rights') can be found in Chapter 4, which also explains that a second-best route is to use a debit card because of the protection known as 'charge back'. Never transfer funds from bank account to bank account as this route offers no protection.

- *Always check the small print of your insurance.* Going for the cheapest option can come back to haunt you under the 'what you pay is what you get' rule of life.

- *Make sure that your carrier/travel company is ATOL (Air Travel Organizer's Licence) registered if your purchase involves a flight and a hotel.* Every company that sells holidays with flights is required to hold an ATOL licence in case it goes bust. This means you will be looked after if you are overseas and not left stranded, and you will get your money back if the holiday is cancelled. There is also the Association of British Travel Agents (ABTA), which deals with rail, cruise and self-drive holidays. Check your holiday provider is either ABTA or ATOL protected and, if not, find out why and consider whether you need to book elsewhere to ensure you are protected on your holidays. Note that ABTA has an arbitration scheme (£1,500 limit per person) for breaches of contract, which can be cheaper and more efficient than going to court. ABTA also has a mediation service for disputes about personal injury and sickness (with a limit of £10,000 per booking) (see www.abta.com).

- *Pack any regular medicines you require.* Even familiar branded products can be difficult to obtain in some countries. In addition, take a mini first-aid kit with you. If you are going to any developing country, consult your doctor as to what pills (and any special precautions) you should take.

- *An overdose of sun can be painful.* Take it easy, wear a hat and apply plenty of protective lotion.

- *Be careful of the water you drink.* If the local water has a reputation for being dodgy then take care, and watch out for ice, salads and any fruit that you do not peel yourself.

- *Get any inoculations or vaccinations well in advance of your departure date.*

- *When flying, wear loose clothes and above all comfortable shoes, as feet and ankles tend to swell in the air.* To avoid risk of deep vein thrombosis, which can be fatal, medical advice is to do foot exercises and walk around the plane from time to time. For long-haul travel wear compression stockings, drink lots of water and, another tip, unless advised otherwise by your doctor, take a mini aspirin before flying.

Inspired? Remember to fill in your plan for a good retirement at the end of the book.

PART FOUR

End-of-Life Planning and Care

CHAPTER SIXTEEN

Taking care of elderly parents and relatives

Ageing is an extraordinary process, whereby you become the person that you always should have been.

DAVID BOWIE

The increasing life expectancy and associated cost of caring for the elderly is placing pressure on our welfare system. The issue also creates pressure within the family unit as challenges emerge from the responsibilities and risks that looking after a house brings. The first phase of retirement, the active years of retirement as discussed in Chapter 1, have passed and your relative may have then enjoyed a further decade or more in the second phase of retirement, the passive retirement years when they just took things a bit easier but managed to deal with the house and garden. The third phase of retirement may be approaching your relative when home maintenance issues and costs start to run away with themselves and perhaps even raise questions of safety and welfare. The garden may get to be too difficult to cope with. There may also be medical factors that are making things not as easy as they used to be. Their being alone in a house, however cherished, may also bring pressures of loneliness and depression. Of course it may not get to be that way but there could be an alternative, which is the decision about moving into a care environment. This chapter is the first of two chapters in Part Four (End-of-life planning and care). In these two chapters we recognize that your relatives cannot always keep going as they once did and they may have to compromise their independence to find a safer environment.

This chapter at a glance

- Maintaining independence for as long as possible and the ways in which quality of life can be preserved, via help from local authority services, health-care professionals and specialist services.
- Home repairs and adaptations, so that your loved ones can remain safely in their own home, retaining their dignity and independence.
- Accommodation, housing options and costs.
- Voluntary organizations that can help.
- Practical help and information on benefits and allowances and how to obtain financial assistance, if eligible.

Maintaining independence

There is no question about it, being able to remain independent for as long as possible, and living in our own home, is hugely important as we get older. The challenge is the cost, safety and convenience of the home as the years roll by. The cost is relatively straightforward if you face the facts – are the maintenance costs of the house and garden, insurance and Council Tax too high? On top of that, is there the time and ability to maintain both the house and garden? Perhaps more importantly, it is a simple fact that decent suitable housing underpins health and wellbeing, particularly in later life. The English Housing Survey found over 1 million homes occupied by those over 55 where there is significant risk to health (such as excess cold, or injury from falling on poorly designed steps). These findings emphasize the importance of 'future-proofing' your home as you grow older so you can live safely and independently for as long as possible.

Another issue is the question of the balance between independence and loneliness. The Campaign to End Loneliness estimates that nearly 2.5 million people over the age of 60 would not know where to go for help if they were feeling lonely. According to Age UK more than 2 million people in England over the age of 75 live alone. More worrying is the statistic that over 1 million older people say they can go for over a month without speaking to a friend, neighbour or family member. Loneliness can, and does, affect health and wellbeing. The time may come when a care home or nursing home becomes necessary to counter safety and loneliness risks.

Local authority services

Local authorities have a responsibility to help elderly people and provide services that vulnerable people and those with disabilities may need.

After an initial discussion with your GP, who may be able to assist with some local knowledge, hints and tips, you then need to approach your adult social services department, explaining you need to arrange a 'care assessment'. Find your local council at www.gov.uk – go to 'find your local council'. They will be able to advise you about what is needed and how to obtain the required help. Your relatives should be assigned a social worker who will be able to make the necessary arrangements or advise you on how to do this. Some of the services available include:

- practical help in the home, with the support of a home help;
- adaptations to the home, such as a ramp for a wheelchair;
- provision of day centres, clubs and similar;
- blue badge scheme for cars driven or used by people with a disability;
- advice about other transport services or concessions that may be available locally;
- assistance with preparing meals, bathing and washing, getting in and out of bed and cleaning.

There is a range of support personnel that you may encounter and they include:

- *Occupational therapists* have a wide knowledge of disability and can assist individuals via training, exercise or access to aids, equipment or adaptations to the home.
- *Health visitors* are nurses with a broad knowledge of health matters and specialized facilities that may be required.
- *District nurses* are fully qualified nurses who will visit a patient in the home, change dressings, attend to other routine nursing matters, monitor progress and help with the arrangements if more specialized care is required.
- *Physiotherapists* use exercise and massage to help improve mobility and strengthen muscles. They are normally available at both hospitals and health centres.
- *Medical social workers* (MSWs) should be consulted if patients have any problems on leaving hospital. MSWs can advise on coping with a

disablement, as well as such practical matters as transport, aftercare and other immediate arrangements. They work in hospitals, and an appointment should be made before the patient is discharged.

Following the assessment a care plan will be agreed and written out for you. Most councils charge you for care costs they provide at home; this remains an item high on the political agenda and costs are subject to both change and limits. Amounts, limits and caps vary depending on where you live. If you are over 65 you might be able to claim Attendance Allowance and if under 65 a Personal Independent Payment (see below). Age UK advises:

> Most local councils charge for the services at home they provide. Some place an upper weekly limit on the amount you have to pay. Before charging you for services, your local council must work out how much you can afford to pay and this amount should leave you with a reasonable level of income. Check your local council's website for their charging information.

Follow this advice and check back for updates at www.ageuk.org – go to 'finding help at home'.

Council Tax

There may be deductions available to you in the amount of Council Tax you have to pay (or in Northern Ireland the equivalent rates scheme). Typically these can include: 25 per cent reduction if living alone; if the property is empty as the resident is in a care home; disability deductions, including for severe mental impairments such as dementia. Contact your local council and enquire about help.

Help with home repair and adaptations

Disabled Facilities Grant

Some grants may be available from your local council to help a disabled person with changes that need to be made to their home. Such adaptations include widening doors and installing ramps, improving access to rooms and facilities by installing stairlifts or a downstairs bathroom, a suitable heating system, and adjustment of heating or lighting controls. The grants are means tested and therefore your relative may need to pay towards the cost of the work. If eligible, the applicant could receive up to £30,000 in England, £25,000 in Northern Ireland and £36,000 in Wales. Disabled Facilities Grants are not available in Scotland – instead see www.gov.scot and go to 'equipment and adaptions'.

Home-improvement agencies and handyperson service providers

These are local organizations dedicated to helping older people with disabilities live in safety and dignity in their own homes. There are currently 200 home-improvement agencies in England covering over 80 per cent of local authorities. Locally they may be known as 'Care and Repair' or 'Staying Put' agencies. The following websites will give you all the information you need:

Foundations: www.foundations.uk.com

Care and Repair Cymru: www.careandrepair.org.uk

Care and Repair England: www.careandrepair-england.org.uk

Care and Repair Scotland: www.careandrepairscotland.co.uk

Equivalents in Northern Ireland include www.radiushousing.org

Age UK: www.ageuk.org.uk (Age UK stairlifts, chairs and easy bathing come under the Age UK mobility range and are provided by Handicare).

Alarm systems

Personal alarms

Personal alarms provide security for vulnerable elderly people as they know that help can be summoned quickly in the event of an emergency. It gives an elderly person independence and their family peace of mind. Some alarm systems allow people living in their own homes to be linked to a central control, or to have a telephone link, enabling personal contact to be made. Others simply signal that something is wrong. Sometimes a relative or friend who has been nominated will be alerted. For more information on what is available see:

Callsafe: www.callsafe.org

Care Harmony Solutions: www.careharmony.co.uk

Age UK also has its own system that you can buy; go to www.ageuk – 'personal alarms'.

Community alarms

Community alarms are also known as Lifeline, Careline, telecare or emergency-monitoring services. They operate 24 hours a day, 365 days a year, giving elderly and vulnerable people the freedom to live life independently, knowing that assistance can be obtained when needed. They work via a special alarm unit connected to the telephone line, or can be activated via a pendant that is worn around the neck or on a wristband.

Emergency access

How can someone gain access in an emergency or if worried and you are not around with a set of keys? An alternative is a KeySafe system, which can be fitted to an external wall or inside a garage etc, which allows access via a code system. In the event of an emergency you can direct someone to locate the key and gain access.

Special accommodation for the elderly

The time to start looking for appropriate accommodation for elderly parents or relatives is before they need it. A lot of research will have to be done, and there will be a better (and happier) outcome for all concerned if this process is not rushed. The earlier you make an assessment of their needs, the more choices and control you all will have.

At first glance, the loss of some level of independence can be overwhelming for many older people and thoughts may turn to feelings of shame, fear and confusion. But with your help and increased knowledge you may be able to tilt these initial feelings towards the opportunities and choices that may come with the change, such as increased safety, companionship, new views, closer proximity to a town's amenities and more. Brainstorm with family and trusted friends, and involve their medical team. Often the older person may listen more readily to their doctor or an impartial third party.

A good place to find information about options and funding is FirstStop Advice, an independent, impartial and free service provided by the national charity Elderly Accommodation Counsel (www.firststopcareadvice.org. uk). This service is for older people, their families and carers. It aims to get elderly people the help and care they need to live independently and comfortably for as long as possible. You will also find first-rate independent help from the Carers Trust (www.carers.org). You are not alone and are treading a well-worn path, so start improving your knowledge and options on one of the most vital pieces of support you will provide in your lifetime.

Housing options

The following is a very brief overview of the different types of housing for elderly people.

Living with family

This might at first seem the simplest option, but will the elderly relative have friends and social amenities after moving in? What would happen if the family relationship broke down? Talk with the rest of the family and others who have done this (local networks at www.carers.org should be able to help place 'issues' on your list of things to think about). Sit down with your solicitor and consider any financial or legal implications that could arise before selling the person's home and building expensive annexes or extensions.

Sheltered or retirement housing

If your elderly relatives are able to buy or rent a retirement property from their own private means, the choice is entirely theirs. Prices and types of property vary enormously, from small flats to luxurious homes on sites with every amenity. The majority of properties are sold on a long lease (typically 125 years). It is advisable to check that the management company is a member of the Association of Retirement Housing Managers and therefore bound by its Code of Practice. There is usually a minimum age for residents of 60 or sometimes 55.

Some points to consider when assessing this option could include:

- Do they allow pets?
- Location and proximity to local amenities.
- Guest suites that can be rented (cost?) for families and friends visiting.
- Camera entry and 24-hour call system for added peace of mind.
- The availability of a homeowners' lounge for relaxing with other homeowners in a 'neutral' environment, which can also be used for events.
- Is there a house manager who takes care of the day-to-day running of the site and any organized activities? How accessible are they?
- Is there a complaints book – can you take a look at it?
- The quality of the communal gardens.
- If the property is rented what is the percentage cap on annual rental increases? 'Stealth' increases above the rate of inflation can seem very unfair once you are settled in. Ascertain the increases over the last three years.
- Most importantly, what is the annual service charge for amenities and shared costs (and what has it been over the last three years)?

Home care or care at home

This is where the elderly person remains in their home and receives support during the day and/or at night. The time may come when elderly people are no longer able to cope with running their homes and caring for themselves without a bit of assistance. There are various options, some more expensive than others. If approaching agencies, it is well worth asking friends and neighbours for personal recommendations, as this can give a lot of peace of mind. Some of the agencies listed overleaf specialize in providing temporary help, rather than permanent staff. Others can offer a flexible service and nursing care, if appropriate. Fees are normally paid by private funding but, depending on individual circumstances, public financial assistance may be available.

There are some things to bear in mind when hiring a carer:

- Should you organize home care for your elderly relative, you or your relative actually become an employer, which brings obligations around administering a payroll and, potentially, a pension for the carer. Search 'payroll help' for local help on this or ask around for recommendations. Another alternative is to try it yourself by downloading HMRC's basic payroll tool (www.gov.uk – go to 'basic payroll tool'). If you employ the carer, undertake a DBS check. Criminal Records Bureau (CRB) checks are now called Disclosure and Barring Service (DBS) checks. Help is available with these at www.gov.uk – go to 'DBS checks'.

- Elderly people organizing care themselves also have the responsibility for checking eligibility to work in the UK and conducting a DBS check.

- Carers need clear guidelines as to documentation, medication, care plans and dietary guidance.

- There must be a contingency plan should the chosen carer fall ill or be unable to work for other reasons.

Fees are around £15 per hour and you have the advantage of being in familiar surroundings. Visit www.thenationalcareline.org and www.carers.org for more information.

Housing with care

This is a newer form of specialist housing, sometimes referred to as extra care housing. Properties can be rented, owned or occasionally part-owned/part-rented. They are fully self-contained homes, usually with one or two bedrooms. To find some options just google 'housing with care' and your region.

Care homes

Deciding whether a care home is right for an elderly relative is a difficult decision that sometimes has to be made in a hurry. All care homes in England are registered and inspected by the Care Quality Commission (CQC) and must display their CQC rating ('outstanding', 'good', 'requires improvement' or 'inadequate') throughout the home and on their website (see www.cqc.org.uk).

In Wales, the inspectorate is called the Care Standards Inspectorate for Wales: www.cssiw.org.uk

In Scotland it is called the Care Inspectorate: www.careinspectorate.com

In Northern Ireland it is the Regulation and Quality Improvement Authority: www.rqia.org.uk

---

Top tip

The oversight organizations listed above provide thorough independent information and reports on each care home in the UK. You simply cannot do your relative any justice if you do not access, compare and review the information they have for the areas being considered for your relative.

The next step is to start visiting some care homes – possibly by yourself at first – and just doing a drive past to get a feel for a possible 'shortlist' from a longer list established from a review of the above websites and, of course, the care home's own website if they have one. Then download the Age UK care home checklist and start your visits (www.ageuk.org – 'finding a care home'). There are lots of invaluable hints and tips; use the checklist together with a few of our own tips:

- Overall, recognize that often it comes down to fees, and generally speaking rooms with a view and high-quality services and amenities all come with a cost – the better the standard, the higher the price.
- Recognize that all of your relative's belongings will probably need to fit into one room.
- Look at any entertainment schedule and pop along to see it for yourself.
- Check if there is free internet access.

- Ask about special situations such as dementia – what is their approach for both those who have it and those who do not?

- Ask to see sample menus and, better still, ask to pop in to see the kitchens whilst mealtimes are in progress. Visit two or three times and reconsider this point; the quality of food reveals a lot.

- Ask about visiting times – are there restricted hours?

- Is contents insurance included in the fee?

- Ask about links to a hospital and any assigned doctor.

- Ask how personal care is addressed and at what cost – typically this is hairstyling and care of fingernails and toenails.

- Ask if you can bring your pet in to visit your relative.

- Trust your instincts about your overall feelings about the home and how it may be suitable for your relative.

There are two main types of care homes: residential and nursing homes:

- *Residential homes* can range from small in size with a few beds, to large-scale facilities. They offer care and support throughout the day and night. Staff are on hand to help with personal care. Rates vary but fees can be around £30,000 to £40,000 per annum.

- *Nursing homes* offer the same type of care as residential homes but with the addition of 24-hour medical care from a qualified nurse. Rates vary but fees can be around £40,000 to £50,000 per annum.

Care-home costs and help

There are currently over 500,000 older people living in residential and nursing homes in the UK. Care homes vary in cost, and fees rise depending on how complex the needs are of the elderly person.

The funding aspect is complex and can be subject to political pressure and change. Funding may be available for part or all of the nursing/medical care element of any fees. There are then fees for the 'accommodation aspect'; currently (summer 2018), if your savings and capital come to less than £14,250 you will not have to use any of this money towards care-home fees. If you have savings and capital worth between £14,250 and £23,250 the council will contribute towards your care-home fees, but you will also have to pay towards them at a rate of £1 per week for every £250 in savings and capital you have between £14,250 and £23,250. If you have savings and capital worth over £23,250 you will have to pay all your care-home accommodation fees – this is called 'self-funding'. Your home counts towards 'capital' although, in some situations, your home may not be taken into account in the test. For instance, currently (summer 2018) it may not be counted if your home is still occupied by your partner; a relative who is aged over 60; a child of yours aged under 18; or a relative who is disabled.

If you give your home away to a child or relative in an attempt to exclude it from the test on income and capital limits it may count as a deliberate 'deprivation of assets'. This is the technical term used by councils and it means that you still pay the same level of care fees as if you still owned the home.

Top tip

Take care if an organization seems to be promising to shelter your home and finances from the grasps of the local authority with schemes and arrangements involving trusts and tax planning to remove your home from your ownership in order to avoid care-home fees being paid by you. There are suggested questions and checks in Chapter 6 in the section on Inheritance Tax.

Other assistance

In addition to the services provided by statutory health and social services for elderly people living at home there are a number of voluntary organizations that can offer help, including:

- lunch clubs and day centres;
- holidays and short-term placements;
- aids such as wheelchairs;
- transport;
- odd jobs and decorating;
- gardening;
- good neighbour schemes;
- prescription collection;
- advice and information;
- family support schemes.

You will be able to find out more via your local Citizens Advice Bureau (www.citizensadvice.org.uk) but some of the key agencies are:

Age UK: www.ageuk.org.uk

Age Scotland: www.ageuk.org.uk/scotland

Age Cymru: www.ageuk.org.uk/cymru

Age NI: www.ageuk.org.uk/northern-ireland

Care Information Scotland: www.careinfoscotland.scot

Centre for Individual Living, Northern Ireland: www.cilbelfast.org

Contact the Elderly: www.contact-the-elderly.org

Disability Wales: www.disabilitywales.org

Getting around

When mobility becomes an issue, quality of life is quickly diminished. For help with getting around, the facilities run by the organizations we have mentioned may be of assistance. Otherwise, look at these websites:

Driving Mobility: www.drivingmobility.org.uk

Motability: www.motability.co.uk

Older drivers

According to the AA there is no safe or unsafe age for a driver, as everyone ages differently. But older people are frailer and more likely to suffer serious injury in accidents. It is up to the individual to inform the DVLA of any medical conditions that may affect their driving. Your relative's GP should be approached to help indicate when this becomes necessary.

Driving licence renewal at 70 is now compulsory. All drivers aged 70 and over will have to reapply for their licence every three years. There is no test or medical, but a medical declaration is mandatory. Find out more at www.gov.uk – 'renew driving licence at 70'.

And another idea

When it comes to forward planning, many older people shrink from discussing their wishes with loved ones. But if their preferences are not known to their nearest and dearest, it may be difficult when the time comes to do what is in their best interests. A helpful booklet available from Age UK is their *LifeBook*. This is a practical tool designed to help older people work through all the things they need, or wish, to put in order. The *LifeBook* will not only help an older person be more organized but it could also be invaluable to a family member or friend if they need to locate important information in an emergency. It is free and available from Age UK; see www.ageuk.org.uk – go to 'Lifebook'.

Emergency care for pets

Older people love their pets, as they give companionship, fun and can be stimulating too if they require regular outdoor exercise. When an elderly relative becomes ill, incapacitated, hospitalized or dies, leaving a beloved pet, this can cause problems for relatives. To ensure the pet continues to receive care should something unexpected happen, the following organizations may be able to help:

Blue Cross: www.bluecross.org.uk

Cats Protection: www.cats.org.uk

Dogs Trust: www.dogstrust.org.uk

Practical help for carers

The UK has 6.5 million carers and while your elderly relative is reasonably active and independent – visiting friends, able to do his or her own shopping, enjoying hobbies and socializing – the strains of caring for them may be light. However, when this is not the case, far more intensive care may be required. Make sure you find out what help is available and how to obtain it.

Top tip

Download, review and follow through on the advice and information in the free guide 'Looking after someone: information and support for carers', available from www.carersuk.org.

Holiday breaks for carers

Various schemes enable those with an elderly relative to go on holiday alone or simply enjoy a respite from caring. Some local authorities run fostering schemes, along similar lines to child fostering. There may be a charge, or the service may be run on a voluntary basis (or be paid for by the local authority). Some voluntary organizations arrange holidays for older people in order to give relatives a break. Different charities take responsibility according to the area where you live. Citizens Advice or your local social services department should know whom you can approach.

Another possible solution is a short-stay home, which is residential accommodation variously run by local authorities, voluntary organizations or private individuals, catering specifically for elderly people. If, as opposed to general care, proper medical attention is necessary, you should consult your relative's GP. Many hospitals and nursing homes offer short-stay care arrangements as a means of relieving relatives. The doctor should be able to help organize this for you.

Benefits and allowances

Should you have responsibility for the care of an elderly person, there are benefits and allowances available to help financially. The best place to look is on the government website, which has the latest and widest range of online public information. This is the gateway for government advice. There is a section for carers, covering support services and assessments, carers' rights, working and caring, Carer's Allowance and much more. For full information see www.gov.uk – 'disabled people'.

There is other help to be found on the NHS website: see www.nhs.uk and go to 'social care and support guide'.

Entitlements for carers

Carer's Allowance

This is currently (summer 2018) £64.60 a week, paid to anyone who is caring for someone more than 35 hours per week. It is subject to certain conditions; see www.gov.uk and go to 'Carer's Allowance'.

Entitlements for elderly or disabled people

Attendance Allowance

This is an allowance paid to people aged 65 and over to help with personal care if they are physically or mentally disabled. It is paid at two different rates and how much the elderly person receives is calculated on the level of care needed because of their frailty or disability. See www.gov.uk and go to 'Attendance Allowance'.

Personal Independence Payment

This payment helps with some of the costs caused by long-term ill health or a disability. It has replaced the Disability Living Allowance for eligible people aged between 16 and 64. It is made up of two parts: a daily living component and a mobility component. There are two rates, standard and enhanced. See www.gov.uk and go to 'PIP'.

Cold Weather Payment

If your elderly relative is in receipt of certain benefits, he/she may be eligible for a Cold Weather Payment. These are made when the local temperature is either recorded as, or forecast to be, an average of zero degrees Celsius or below, over seven consecutive days. The amount paid is £25 for each seven-day period of very cold weather between 1 November and 31 March. Those eligible should receive it without having to claim: see www.gov.uk and go to 'Cold Weather Payment'.

Winter Fuel Payment

If you were born before 5 August 1953 you could get a special tax-free payment of between £100 and £300 to help pay heating bills. See www.gov.uk – 'Winter Fuel Payment'.

Free off-peak bus travel

An older person's bus pass is available to people once they reach retirement age. Disabled people can also travel free on any bus service in the country. For full information on how to obtain a bus pass in England, Scotland, Wales and Northern Ireland, see: www.gov.uk and go to 'apply for an older person's bus pass'.

Free TV licence

Once your elderly relative reaches 75, he/she is entitled to a free TV licence. This licence covers the individual and anyone else who lives with them. It is important to apply for this whilst the person is 74 as it is not something that will be sent to them automatically. See www.tvlicensing.co.uk for further information.

Financial assistance

In cases of hardship, there are charities that give financial assistance to elderly people. For many people one of the main barriers to getting help is knowing which of the many thousands of charities to approach. There are free services that help older people in genuine financial need. When seeking financial assistance, have patience and be prepared to do a lot of research. Two helpful organizations are Charity Search (www.charitysearch.org.uk) and Turn2Us (www.turn2us.org.uk).

Some special problems

Elderly people can suffer from special problems that cause great distress. Families do not necessarily talk about these and they may be unaware of what services are available. Practical help and sometimes financial assistance may be obtainable, so it is worth doing some research and talking with your relative's GP if there is risk of any of the following:

Falls

One in three people over the age of 65 have a fall each year. Across the UK every year 1.2 million people end up in A&E after a fall, costing the NHS £1.6 billion. Bone density slowly decreases as part of the ageing process but falls can be prevented if the correct action is taken. The Chartered Society of Physiotherapists has published a guide called 'Get up and go', which provides exercises to improve strength and balance and tips on how to fall-proof your home.

Hypothermia

Living in a cold home significantly increases the risk of death during the winter months. Approximately 24,000 more people die in England and

Wales between December and March than at other times. Damp is another danger to health. In cold weather the risk of hypothermia is greater; those most at risk are people with dementia, who may not be able to recognize the symptoms of hypothermia or recognize when they are cold.

Incontinence

More than 3.2 million people over 65 in the UK suffer from urinary incontinence, and 6.5 million people of all ages are affected by some form of bowel problem. Many do not talk about this or seek help because of embarrassment and they often think nothing can be done. Bladder and bowel problems can often be cured, or at least alleviated, by proper treatment.

Malnutrition

Malnutrition and malnourishment are common occurrences in the elderly. The digestive tract is important to our health and elderly people should be aware of how to eat and drink to get the most out of their digestion. People who have difficulty in moving about may not bother to go into the kitchen to get a meal or a drink. Malnourishment leads to hypothermia and dehydration. Drinking enough fluids is as important as eating properly.

Dementia

The most common type of dementia is Alzheimer's disease, and dementia is the illness most feared by people over the age of 55, who are understandably concerned about losing their memory and identity.

The Alzheimer's Society suggests the following simple 'lifestyle tweaks' to help reduce the risk of the disease:

- *Get active.* There is evidence that regular exercise will prevent dementia more than any other measure.
- *Eat Mediterranean style.* Pile on the veg, fruit, fish, olive oil and nuts.
- *Keep up with the check-ups.* Diabetes and high blood pressure increase the risk of dementia.

Should your elderly relative have been diagnosed with dementia there are some treatments available that can delay progression of some forms of the disease. Clinical signs are characterized by progressive cognitive degeneration, a decline in the ability to carry out common daily tasks, and behavioural changes.

The Alzheimer's Society has masses of information and advice for carers – see Alzheimer's Scotland (www.alzscot.org) and Alzheimer's Society (www. alzheimers.org.uk).

Lasting power of attorney

If there is a risk of your relative losing mental capacity, review the matter with your GP and solicitor and consider implementing a lasting power of attorney (more information in Chapter 17). In the long run, this may save significant costs and ease the stress on those administering the financial affairs of your relative.

Useful help

The cost of care is an area subject to considerable pressure and potential change. Quality advice and updates can be found at www.citizensadvice. org.uk, www.ageuk.org.uk (go to 'paying for permanent residential care'), www.independentage.org (go to 'paying care-home fees' to download their latest factsheet) and 'How to fund your long-term care – a beginner's guide' (at www.moneyadviceservice.org.uk). Support is available for carers at both the national level and their local groups (via www.carers.org).

Inspired? Remember to fill in your plan for a good retirement at the end of the book.

CHAPTER SEVENTEEN

Wills and final plans

The fear of death follows from the fear of life.
A man who lives fully is prepared to die at any time.
MARK TWAIN

Preparing for the end of life is something few of us are comfortable thinking or talking about, whether it is our own life or that of a loved one. This is particularly so while we (or they) are happy, healthy and enjoying a good quality of life.

This chapter sits within the 'no one is immortal' part of retirement planning – making your wishes known and getting your affairs in order well ahead is neither gloomy nor unhealthy: quite the reverse. It is prudent, sensible and unselfish. Being prepared will also allow more quality time with loved ones as you know things are 'sorted'. It is helpful and will relieve family and care givers lots of strain and stress. Conversations will differ depending on when and with whom such things are being discussed, and if you think you will find it hard to raise the issue just use this book and your own plan for a good retirement to prompt discussions. Please be assured, tough discussions and decisions are often not so difficult once the subject is broached.

This chapter at a glance

- The mess of intestacy and how it could all be so much easier with a few hours of time and some modest costs.

- Wills. Why these are a 'must do', how to go about getting one together with costs and help on 'deeds of variation', which can assist with wills that may have overlooked an event or fact.

- Executors. More important than the best man or chief bridesmaid at a wedding. Now the friendship and trust really count for something.

- Powers of attorney. Enduring powers of attorney, financial and property lasting powers of attorney, and what about a health and welfare lasting power of attorney? Confused already? We will take away the confusion and, armed with this knowledge, our relatives and executors will forever be grateful – powers of attorney are the magic wand of life planning and may be even more important than a will. You must know this stuff.

- Only two things are certain – death and taxes, as was highlighted in the quote headlined in Chapter 6 (Tax). Do you remember who said it? We give you another reminder on Inheritance Tax (IHT), what it is, how you can plan for it and when to tread carefully.

- Help with end-of-life care, dealing with a death, state benefits and some vital support for you – the organizations who care and can help. We provide the signposts.

- Funeral planning is another important factor. You probably already know whether you want to be buried or cremated, but where do you want your funeral to be held and what type of funeral?

Laws of intestacy

If you die without leaving a will your finances are dealt with under the rules of intestacy. The rules differ slightly between England and Wales, Scotland and Northern Ireland but that should not detract from our key message. An intestacy is basically a great big mess that will take time, money and effort to sort out and even then things will not follow a smooth path. Rules set by the government (the laws of intestacy) will determine who inherits the deceased person's estate (possessions, property and money). There is no guarantee that the deceased person's wishes will be carried out or that their estate will go to those they intended. Promises made will count for nothing and may only cause confusion and perhaps upset. Only married or civil partners (actually married at the time of death) and close relatives can inherit under the rules of intestacy. An unmarried partner and stepchildren have no automatic rights. Possessions, including the home, may have to be sold to split the proceeds between the heirs – and if there are no relatives the Crown gets the lot.

All is not bleak, as usually a close relative will have the legal right to step in, prove their position and relationship and seek to sort out the estate of the person who has died intestate. To administer someone's estate you apply to the deceased's local Probate Office for a 'Grant of Letters of Administration'. You can ask your solicitor to help you with applying for a grant or you can make a personal application. When you get the grant you become the 'administrator' of the estate. The grant provides proof to banks, building societies and other organizations that you have authority to access and distribute funds that were held in the deceased's name. If IHT is due on the estate, some or all of this must be paid before a grant will be issued.

Top tip

Intestacy is a mess so don't put your relatives through it. Make a will and use that as an opportunity to revisit your end-of-life plans and the other matters covered in this chapter. Remember the motto of this chapter: 'Tough discussions and decisions are often not so difficult once the subject is broached.'

Wills

A will is a legal document that sets out a person's final financial wishes. There are six main reasons why you should make a will if you have not done so already:

- The alternative is the mess of intestacy as above.
- It means your wishes are known with clarity (after all you will not be around to clarify things!).
- It helps avoid disputes between relatives. Some relatives may not agree and some may still seek to make a claim on your estate, but the fact that

you have clarified what you want goes a very long way to preventing disgruntled relatives disputing things.

- It can protect assets for future generations. If you are fortunate to have assets that can stay in the family and you wish these to be preserved for future generations the will can be directed to put certain assets or funds into a trust to help preserve them for the benefit of future generations. This may help prevent the next generation blowing the lot and can be useful in large and complex estates or family situations that appear chaotic.

- Inheritance Tax. If you leave your estate to your husband, wife or civil partner then no IHT is paid. Anything left to a charity is also exempt from IHT. Armed with some of the information on gifts from Chapter 3 (Tax) you will also see how you could be more tax efficient with more knowledge and advice.

- Clarify the funeral that you would like and provide for the costs of the funeral and any after event (catering and venue hire) to be paid from your estate. This allows you to specify what you would like and also anything that you do not want, and removes significant stresses from those left to make the arrangements.

Having a will becomes absolutely essential if you live with an unmarried partner, have divorced, remarried, or need to provide for someone with a disability. You can write your will yourself or with the assistance of do-it-yourself will-writing kits available online or from stationery shops. Both routes can be prone to error and misinterpretation and therefore advice and assistance really should be sought.

There are several different types of wills, amongst which are:

- a *single will* relates to an individual;
- *mirror (or joint) wills* are designed for couples who have the same wishes;
- a *property trust will* places the estate into trust for beneficiaries;
- a *discretionary trust will* allows trustees to decide what is best at the time of your death.

There is no 'one size fits all' answer to deciding which sort of will is best. Specialist advice is essential and researching your circumstances (personal and financial) will reveal what kind of will is right for you. Your will should be stored carefully where the relevant people can find it and needs to be formally witnessed and signed to make it legally valid. If at any time you wish to update your will, this must be done officially, by means of a 'codicil'.

If your circumstances change (divorce, death of a loved one, or new family members) you should review the position and decide if a new will is necessary.

Keep with your papers at home a list of your 'assets'. Where is the treasure buried? By keeping this information up to date you can save your executors hours of work wasted on wild goose chases. Ultimately, those you wish to benefit will get more if your paperwork is accurate.

Banks

Some banks offer a will-writing service. Make sure that you can choose your own executor or understand in advance the bank's charges for acting as executor, as fees can be relatively expensive if banks undertake the executor service.

Professional will-writing specialists

A will-writing service can be cheaper than using a solicitor, and more reliable than a DIY will. A will-writing service could be a good choice if you understand the basics of how wills work, you wish to pay less than a solicitor would charge, and your estate is not complex. Before you instruct a will-writing service make sure they have professional indemnity insurance, because if they get it wrong there may not be anyone to sue.

Solicitors

The best solution is usually through an appropriately qualified solicitor who will ensure your will is interpreted the way you want and may tease out tricky issues that you may not have anticipated. If you do not have a solicitor, ask friends for a recommendation, or ask Citizens Advice. You should budget for around £200 to £500 plus VAT for this help – more if you have very complex financial affairs.

What to include and terminology

Your will should explain the main assets you own (your 'estate') and indicate your debts (what you owe). This is not an exhaustive list but it will be helpful to detail any homes, significant assets, investments, savings and life policies, their location and the main debts owed (usually mortgages, loans and a listing of credit cards). Jointly owned property should be clarified and remember 'joint tenants' will see your share automatically passing to the other joint tenant(s) on death and 'tenants in common' means you can leave your share to someone else. 'Executors' are the vital people who make sure your will happens as you intended – more on them below.

'Beneficiaries' are the people you name to receive something in your will; remember to give their full names and precise relationship to you to make sure they are correctly identified. 'Legacies' is the name for gifts you make to beneficiaries. A 'residual beneficiary' is the person or charity that receives the remainder of your estate once specific gifts have been paid out.

'A letter of wishes' can often accompany a will as an annex and can be helpful in avoiding cluttering up a will with a long list of people who are to be given specific assets. It can be useful for clarifying desired funeral arrangements and some health matters (such as do not resuscitate, organ-donation wishes, etc) but it is not a legally binding document. Particularly where you have created a discretionary trust in your will, a letter of wishes can flesh out the bones of a dry legal document. Typically, where young parents are worried about their children becoming orphans, they wish to say how they would like their children to be educated. A marmite question is often whether you want the trustees to pay for private education out of a trust fund.

Top tip

Ask for a quotation for completing the will and the costs of any anticipated extras (for instance lasting powers of attorney – see below). If using a solicitor, check that they are a member of the Law Society's Wills and Inheritance Quality Scheme and that anyone else entrusted to write your will is a member of the Society of Trust and Estate Practitioners (STEP); this gives you some added protection on the quality, accuracy and potential tax efficiency of your will and associated arrangements.

Deeds of variation

A deed of variation can be used to change a will up to two years after the date of death where all those affected by the alteration agree to the change. Typically it is used to redirect the stated benefit in a will from, say, a child to, say, a grandchild to keep down the IHT potential on the child's estate; specialist advice should be obtained from a solicitor on this potentially useful tool. The effect of the deed of variation is to rewrite the will as if the deceased person had made the new and altered instructions in their will.

Executors

An executor is the person you appoint in your will to be responsible for handling your estate and making sure your wishes are carried out after you die. Think of a best man or chief bridesmaid at a wedding, only this time it is 10 times more important, so choose wisely. It is usual to appoint more than one executor and they should be over 18, so perhaps it could be your husband, wife or civil partner and a child, brother or sister. This could take some of the pressure off your husband, wife or civil partner in the initial period when emotions and loss are so significant.

Bear in mind that a complex estate can involve the executor in a significant amount of work and possibly stress. If the estate is complex and the will includes trusts, appointing a professional executor to act with lay executors is worth considering.

The main duties of the executor are:

1 Registering the death at the Register Office (find your local one at www.gov.uk) and locating the final will. You will need to take the medical certificate signed by a doctor when you register the death. Once you register the death you will get a Certificate for Burial or Cremation (the 'green form') and a Certificate of Registration of Death. Think about how many copies of the death certificate you will need.

2 Arranging the funeral. The costs will usually be payable from the deceased's estate. Check on funeral wishes in any will or 'letter of wishes' or in any funeral plan (perhaps left with an undertaker) and with close family on the preparations. Notices may need to be placed in newspapers and social media informing people of funeral arrangements and any donation wishes (or the fact that donations should not be made). Emotions will be high and time is short, making this a difficult time, and so funeral specifications provided in the will can prove a blessing.

3 Valuing the estate. Gather in and ensure you have control of everything the deceased owned and also establish everything they owed. Obtain valuations from a professional valuer of expensive items and any residential property.

4 Apply for probate, which gives the legal right to deal with someone's estate (for instance to sell their house), complete the relevant IHT form and pay any tax due. The process varies between England and Wales, Scotland and Northern Ireland; the specifics can be found at www.gov.uk (go to 'probate').

Top tip

The 'Tell Us Once' service lets you report a death to most government departments; the local register office will tell you how to use this service when you register a death. Go to www.gov.uk – 'Tell Us Once'.

The executors are also responsible for making sure the right amount of IHT, Capital Gains Tax or Income Tax gets paid. It is important to choose your executors with care, since the job involves a lot of work and responsibility. The person must be over 18, and it would be wise and courteous to ensure that your chosen executor is happy to take on the role. Even if someone is appointed in the will, they have no obligation to take on the role. Choosing a professional and impartial executor will incur charges, so bear this in mind if you appoint your solicitor, your accountant or your bank. If you ask a friend or family member who is not benefiting directly from the will it would be customary and nice to leave a legacy (gift) specified in your will for them.

The following steps, if taken, will make your executor's job easier:

- List where important documents such as wills, bank accounts and share certificates are stored.
- Get valuations of expensive assets (anything individually worth over £2,000).
- Appoint more than one executor to share the workload.
- Ensure your will is up to date and safely stored.
- Be specific with your bequests – especially for items of sentimental value.

Mike and Tom Bottomley of Ewart Price Solicitors have a combined 40 years' practice in advising families on their wills and share their top five tips for a successful will:

1 Think carefully about what you own (your assets); are there any unusual things about them that you need to consider?

2 Whom do you wish to benefit? People might have expectations, for example close family members. If you are not benefiting them, why not? Seek advice about whether a disappointed individual might have a claim against the estate.

3 Meet with a solicitor and instruct him or her to draft a will for you.

4 Carefully check the draft, and ask for an explanation about anything you do not understand. There is no point signing a document you do not understand.

5 Leave the original will with the solicitor and keep a copy. You can register the will with Certainty, the National Will Register officially recognized in the UK, who will be able to say from their database who has the will (www.nationalwillregister.co.uk).

Lasting power of attorney

Dementia can develop slowly or suddenly, especially following a stroke or an accident, and the emotional turmoil will be substantial. There are one or two very simple procedures that can and should be done to ease the situation. The first is to set up a lasting power of attorney (LPA); some solicitors consider this to be just as important as making a will. This has to be done before losing mental capacity, otherwise it is invalid. Before doing anything it would be wise to discuss the options with family or someone you trust to see what they think and whether they can help. To find out more about mental capacity and making decisions use www.gov.uk and go to 'make decisions for someone'.

An LPA gives someone you trust the legal authority to make decisions on your behalf and therefore you retain control through that person, known as the attorney. The attorney could be a husband, wife or civil partner, a son or daughter, a brother or sister, nephew or niece or just someone you trust. The person allowing the LPA to be drawn up is known as the donor. There are two types of LPA: one for *property and financial affairs* and another for *personal welfare*. It is safest to have both types. A health and welfare LPA allows others to make decisions about the donor's day-to-day care, where they live, who they should have contact with and, if desired, their choice for end-of-life care. The property and financial affairs LPA covers paying bills, collecting benefits, selling property and investing money. Without an LPA the only way a person can take charge of another person's finances is via the Court of Protection, which is a lengthy, costly and stressful process.

Once you have made your LPA it is very advisable to register this immediately with the Office of the Public Guardian. This process takes at least two months, so if things deteriorate quickly an unregistered power is not valid.

The right time to draw up an LPA is while the individual is in full command of his or her faculties, so that potential situations that would require decision making can be properly discussed and the donor's wishes made clear. If you are considering setting up an LPA for yourself or an elderly relative it is important to consult both the relevant GP and the family solicitor as well as members of the family. When making an LPA make sure the attorneys can be relied upon to always and 100 per cent place your best interests at heart. LPAs were introduced in October 2007, replacing the old system of Enduring Powers of Attorney (EPA). An EPA created before October 2007 remains valid.

The personal welfare LPA could save endless amounts of angst amongst family and friends when dementia and then the end of life occurs. According to Compassion in Dying:

> Seventy per cent of us want little or no medical intervention at the end of life; 53 per cent believe family can make health-care decisions on behalf of a loved one; and only 4 per cent of us have made our treatment wishes known in an Advance Decision.

Being prepared will also allow more quality time with loved ones, particularly when those precious final months, weeks or days come. It will also relieve lots of strain and stress so consider incorporating the following in either your LPA or in a 'letter of wishes' appended to your will; your solicitor will be able to guide you on the best route:

- your end-of-life care plan;
- where you wish to be cared for;
- advance decision to refuse treatment (do not resuscitate (DNR) form);
- organ and tissue donation;
- planning your funeral.

The NHS website gives general advice on end-of-life planning at www.nhs.uk (go to 'end-of-life care') and there is also quality information available from Age UK (www.ageuk.org.uk).

Solicitor Mike Bottomley highlights some of the pitfalls and potential costs of not having powers of attorney in place in a YouTube video that is definitely worth watching. Simply go to www.youtube.com and search for Michael Bottomley and 'lasting power of attorney'. The eight-minute clip is enlightening and if you are short of time there is a condensed two-minute version.

Inheritance Tax

Some people think that what happens to their estate after they have died doesn't matter as they will not be there to worry about it. For others, the prospect of IHT will not arise because the value of their assets is not high enough. Remember that more information is set out in Chapter 6 (Tax) and, therefore, this chapter is more about capturing the 'headlines'. The IHT threshold (the level at which you will need to pay tax) is set at £325,000 and is currently frozen at this rate until 2020/21. The threshold amount for married couples and civil partners is twice this as they can transfer the unused element of their IHT-free allowance to their spouse or civil partner when they die, giving an attractive effective threshold of £650,000. The £650,000 can, in turn, be stretched to £1 million with the Main Residence Nil Rate Band where the main residence is being left to lineal descendants. The value of estates over and above this sum is taxed at 40 per cent. For others, this tax at 40 per cent above £325,000 of assets could be a problem. To help avoid some issues, make sure there is a valid will and a list of assets and their current value. Make sure that any life insurance policies are written into trust; hopefully, the fact that they are 'in trust' should keep the value when paid out on death outside of the estate, meaning that no 40 per cent IHT is payable if you exceed the estate limits (your solicitor should ask and follow up on this point – if they don't, you should ask for their help in reviewing it). Consider making any substantial gifts in good time, and the earlier the better if you are sitting on substantial wealth. If you survive three to seven years after the gift it could save thousands of pounds in the future, and if you survive for more than seven years it could save significant amounts of IHT. Remember, IHT is a tax on capital, so if you have income in excess of expenditure you can give all that away if you arrange matters properly and, if under 75, certain pension funds can be structured to bypass your estate and any IHT. Some of the issues are complex so 'if in doubt check it out' with the help of professional advice.

> **Top tip**
>
> Review your life policies and check if it would be beneficial to have them written in trust so that they fall outside of your estate for IHT purposes – this is a fairly straightforward task. Consider gifting excess wealth away sooner rather than later, given the seven-year rule and the income in excess of expenditure rule. However, there is no such thing as a magic wand that makes significant IHT disappear on your home if you continue to live in it or guarantees local authorities will not chase down assets such as homes that are deliberately given away. Tread carefully if someone offers you a magic wand for a large fee – and ask the questions set out in Chapter 6.

Provision for dependant adult children

A particular concern for parents with a physically or mentally dependant son or daughter is what plans they can make to ensure his or her care continues when they are no longer in a position to manage. This is a complex area and there are no easy answers. Each case varies according to the severity of the disability or illness, the range of helpful voluntary or statutory facilities locally, and the extent to which they, as parents, can provide for their child's financial security in the long term. While social services may be able to advise, parents thinking ahead might do better to consult a specialist organization experienced in helping carers in this situation in order to explore the possible options available to them. Useful organizations are Carers UK (www.carersuk.org) and Carers Trust (www.carers.org).

Parents concerned about financial matters such as setting up a discretionary trust or making alternative provision in their will should consult a solicitor.

Money and other worries – and how to minimize them

It is quite usual for people to disregard forward planning until some important lifestyle change occurs, such as the death of a parent or sibling, or the birth of a first child. It is only then that they get a mortality jolt, and start thinking, 'Is it me next?' and other 'what ifs'. Anyone with a family should consider – and review from time to time – their life insurance and mortgage protection. Most banks and building societies urge homeowners to take out mortgage protection schemes. If you die, the loan is paid off automatically and the family home will not be repossessed. Banks also offer insurance to cover any personal or other loans. This could help a family to avoid being left with debts.

End-of-life care and support

End-of-life care includes palliative care, which means you have an illness or condition that cannot be cured, and is all about making you as comfortable as possible and managing your pain and other distressing symptoms. It may last a few days, months or years; if you are being cared for in your home your GP has overall responsibility for your care and will be supported by community nurses and therapists. The NHS states:

> End-of-life care should help you to live as well as possible until you die, and to die with dignity. The people providing your care should ask you about your wishes and preferences, and take these into account as they work with you to plan your care. They should also support your family, carers or other people who are important to you. You have the right to express your wishes about where you would like to receive care and where you want to die. You can receive end-of-life care at home or in care homes, hospices or hospitals, depending on your needs and preferences. People who are approaching the end of life are entitled to high-quality care, wherever they are being cared for.

Find out what to expect from end-of-life care at www.nhs.uk and go to 'what end-of-life care involves'.

The cancer charity Macmillan provides the most important of reminders, which we endorse:

> When you are reaching the end of your life, it doesn't mean that you have less need for love, companionship, friendship and fun. For many people, partners, family and friends become even more important and are a vital source of support and reassurance.

> **Top tip**
>
> Those caring for others at the end of life need just as much support and perhaps one of the best short and helpful resource guides available is the free booklet *End of Life: A guide*, available from www.mariecurie.org.uk

Funeral

The main issues around funerals are the emotions on the day, the ceremony itself and then the cost and understanding the options and pricing of associated elements of the funeral. This is where the executors step in; if they are armed with directions from those early discussions things can and will run smoothly, leaving fond memories and giving as good a send-off as could be hoped for. Having said that, there is little in terms of words, preparation and help that can truly prepare us for the feelings we can experience when saying farewell to a mother, father, brother, sister, child, relative or great friend.

The service itself will be remembered for the people coming together and remembering their relative or friend, and the flow and order of the service can be constructed to your wishes. Directions left by you may assist the executor, or if all is unclear your close relatives' views and wishes will inform this. For some it will be a religious service interspersed with readings and hymns; for others it may be a humanist service interspersed with poems and tributes. The choice is yours, and your executor may have to put their foot down on your behalf if eyebrows are raised in seeking to follow through on your wishes, unless they really get the impression you are crossing a red line or may cause some unnecessary upset. In terms of the tributes, some words will be right for the service and others for the informal gathering afterwards – generally folk know what is right or wrong in each environment and equally other folk are usually around to help the executor guide things with a quiet word and some encouragement where appropriate. In reality the service itself will flow with the help of the funeral director and it will go all the better if everyone knows what they want to say; the executor should encourage people to write up their tribute in a script beforehand. About 5–10 minutes should be fine as a tribute. As a guide, 100 words equates to one minute and the usual service is about half an hour; be guided by your funeral director on going below or beyond this. There are caring and helpful websites to assist with choices around hearse, coffins and music – maybe try www.thegoodfuneralguide.co.uk to get started and speak with trusted family and friends and your funeral director.

The executor can pay for the funeral by presenting the deceased's bank with the invoice (not an estimate); as long as there are sufficient funds this will be paid ahead of probate.

The information and tips within this chapter can help remove the unknowns and potential worry you may have about funeral costs. The Royal London National Funeral Costs Index Report 2017 provides some 'average' benchmarks:

- Direct cremation is offered by some companies and includes the collection of the deceased, a simple coffin, and no viewing or ceremony beforehand. You then request the ashes, collect them and hold a ceremony at a time and place of your choosing: £1,600.

- Cremation using a funeral director includes collection and care of the deceased, a basic coffin, hearse and managing a simple service: £3,311.

- Burial using a funeral director includes collection and care of the deceased, a basic coffin, hearse and managing a simple service: £4,257.

Check what costs are included and also the cost of any extras. Burial fees are usually included in a funeral director's costs and can vary enormously across the UK (this covers the cost of leasing the plot and digging and then filling the grave). Other costs may include the type of coffin beyond the basic coffin or shroud, a headstone, catering, flowers, venue hire, funeral notice, obituary notice, order of service sheets and death certificate copies. Do shop around between at least two funeral providers as there are big differences in what funeral directors charge for the headline cost and then extras. Legally, you don't have to use a coffin and a shroud is a suitable and affordable alternative; the crematorium or cemetery can advise you on what personal items you can place with the body if using a shroud.

Dealing with a death

If someone dies at home, you should first *call the family doctor and nearest relative* immediately. If the death was expected the doctor will give you a medical certificate showing the cause of death. If the person dies in hospital, the medical certificate and formal notice will be issued by the hospital. If someone *dies unexpectedly*, or the family doctor has not seen the person within 14 days of death (28 days in Northern Ireland), *the death is reported to the coroner.* They may call for a post-mortem or inquest. In these circumstances the funeral may need to be delayed. Thereafter the executor undertakes their role and responsibility, assisted by their solicitor if one has been appointed. Although loved ones left behind are initially in a position they never wanted, they will find that their executor, close friends and their solicitor will help them through the early weeks, resolving things like bills and bank accounts in the deceased's name. You will find a way through this difficult time in terms of the administration issues that arise.

Top tip

The Age UK booklet *When Someone Dies: A step-by-step guide to what to do* is all you need and is full of practical information. It is available to print off as a pdf for yourself or an elderly relative: www.ageuk.org.uk.

Receiving direct mail bearing the name of the deceased is often painful and unnecessary. To avoid this, contact The Bereavement Register, www.thebereavementregister.org.uk, who will be able to assist.

Funeral plans – is there a better way?

Funeral plans offer to cover the cost of a funeral for a fixed lump sum or series of instalments. The basic idea is that there is less pressure on loved ones. Pre-paid funeral plans can be bought in two main ways: from a funeral-plan provider or from a local funeral director. Payment is flexible, and most providers allow a one-off payment in advance or the option to pay in instalments over 12 to 120 months. But are they good value for money after commission is paid out to the sales team and for any administration? What are the alternatives?

Before you take out a funeral plan check:

- What costs are covered and what are not covered? What costs are guaranteed? Check things like burial plot, headstones and wreaths.
- What commission is paid out of your payments?
- Do your instalments earn interest?
- What happens if they go out of business in the future, ie what guarantee do you have and from whom?

Then look at the alternatives:

- Make specific provision in your will for funeral costs to be paid from your estate.
- Open up a savings account at a bank, earn interest and get the UK financial services safety net.

For more information on funeral plans see the following websites:

Age UK: www.ageuk.org.uk

Co-operative Funeral Care: www.co-operativefuneralcare.co.uk

Fair Funerals: wwwfairfuneralscampaign.org.uk

State benefits and tax

Bereavement Support Payments are paid if your husband, wife or civil partner died when under State Pension age and in situations where they either paid National Insurance contributions for at least 25 weeks or died because of an accident at work or a disease caused by work. If you have children under 20 in full-time education you get a first payment of £3,500 and a monthly payment of £350 for 18 months. If not, the payments are reduced to £2,500 and £100 respectively. The payment will not affect your other benefits and is not taxed; it replaces the previous bereavement allowance, widowed parents allowance and Bereavement Payment.

War Pensions: if your late spouse or civil partner served in the armed forces, you may be entitled to help. Contact the Service Personnel and Veterans Agency for more information (www.veterans-uk.info).

State and private pensions

You may get a payment from your husband/wife/civil partner's workplace or private pension and you will need to contact the pension scheme to find out. It may be helpful to check this out and leave a note of what entitlement your partner or dependants would continue to receive if you were to die.

Once a widowed person reaches state retirement age, he or she should receive a State Pension in the normal way. A widow or widower may be able to use the late spouse's National Insurance contributions to boost the amount he or she receives; more information is available at www.gov.uk – go to 'State Pension'. If you are unsure of your position or have difficulties, ask Citizens Advice, which will at least be able to help you work out the sums and inform you of your rights (www.citizensadvice.org.uk).

Organizations that can help with bereavement

People deal with bereavement in various ways. For some, money problems seem to dominate everything and Turn2us can help with money concerns, grants and benefits (www.turn2us.org.uk). In addition there is an abundance of quality information at Age UK (www.ageuk.org.uk).

For others, the hardest thing to bear is the loneliness of an empty house. For older people who have been part of a couple for decades, widowhood creates a great gulf where for a while there is no real sense of purpose. Talking to other people who know the difficulties from their own experience can be a tremendous help. The following organizations provide an advisory and support service:

- Cruse Bereavement Care: www.cruse.org.uk or phone 0808 8081677;
- Care for the Family and their specialist bereavement support: www. careforthefamily.org.uk (go to 'bereavement support' or phone 02920 810800);
- Samaritans: www.samaritans.org. With Samaritans remember their motto: 'Whatever you're going through, call us free any time, from any phone on 116 123.'

Many professional and other groups offer a range of services for widows and widowers associated with them. These include the Civil Service Retirement Fellowship (www.csrf.org.uk) and the War Widows Association of Great Britain (www.warwidows.org.uk).

Many local Age UK groups offer a counselling service. Trade unions are often particularly supportive, as are Rotary Clubs, all the armed forces organizations and most benevolent societies.

Experiencing the loss of someone close through death is an inevitable part of life, but that does not make it any easier when we experience it, even when the death was expected. This can be even more difficult if circumstances mean that practical changes have to be made, such as moving house. Adjusting to life without the person takes time, usually more than we realize.

Top tip

With the help of family, friends and the organizations listed above you will never be alone.

Inspired? Remember to fill in your plan for a good retirement at the end of the book.

YOUR PLAN FOR A GOOD RETIREMENT

Things to start doing or planning

	Page number	Issue	Priority (high/medium/low)
1			
2			
3			
4			
5			
6			
7			
8			
9			
10			
11			
12			
13			
14			
15			
16			
17			
18			
19			
20			

Things to follow up

	Page number	Issue	Website or source of help
1			
2			
3			
4			
5			
6			
7			
8			
9			
10			
11			
12			
13			
14			
15			
16			
17			
18			
19			
20			

INDEX